BANGOR

Light of the World

BANGOR

Light of the World

IAN ADAMSON

COLOURPOINT

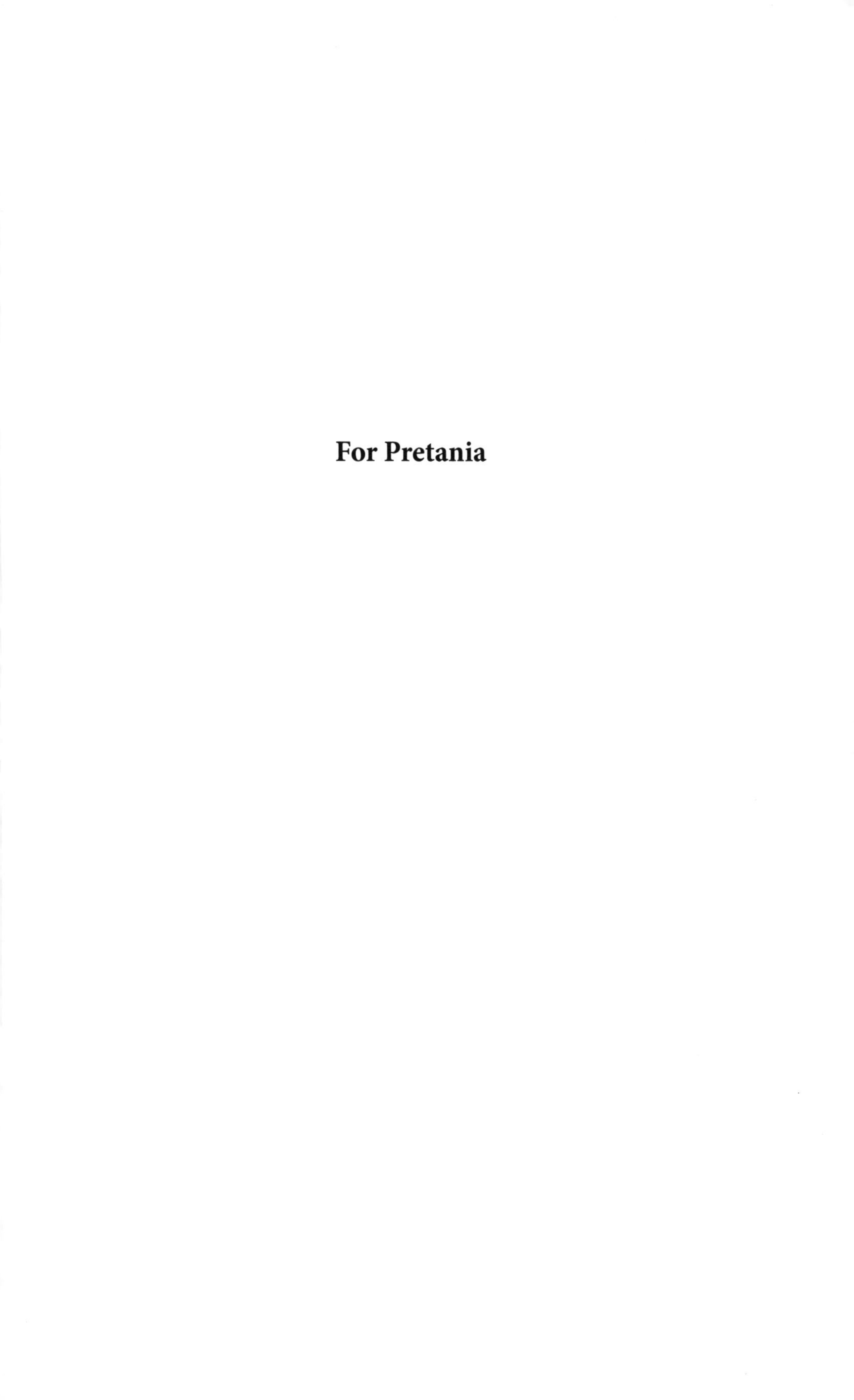

For Pretania

First published 1979 by
Pretani Press

Third edition published 2015 by
Colourpoint Books
an imprint of Colourpoint Creative Ltd

Colourpoint House, Jubilee Business Park
21 Jubilee Road, Newtownards, BT23 4YH
Tel: 028 9182 6339
Fax: 028 9182 1900
E-mail: sales@colourpoint.co.uk
Web: www.colourpoint.co.uk

Third Edition
First Impression

A catalogue record for this book is available from the British Library.

Designed by April Sky Design, Newtownards
Tel: 028 9182 7195
Web: www.aprilsky.co.uk

Printed by GPS Colour Graphics Ltd, Belfast

ISBN 978-1-78073-093-6

Contents

Acknowledgements

THERE ARE MANY people I would like to thank in the making of this book, though the opinions expressed in it are entirely my own.

I am grateful to the North Down Arts Committee for its financial assistance; to the Friends of Bangor Abbey; to Mary O'Fee and her son James; to the Bangor Historical Society; to Canon Hamilton Leckey and the Abbey Church, Bangor; to Kenneth Webb, Chris Hill and Mark Hamilton; to Ian Wilson of the Heritage Centre, Bangor; to the poet John Hewitt; to Dr Matthew T Mellon; to Dr Ian and Katherine Brick of Atlantic Bridges, Nashville, Tennessee; to Rev Dr Ian Paisley, the Lord Bannside PC, Baroness Eileen Paisley and family; to Andy and Agnes Tyrie and family, and the directors and members of the Ullans Academy of which I am President and he is Patron; to Robert and Mark Williamson and the members of the Dalaradia organisation, of which I am Patron; to Jim Wilson; to Jackie McDonald; to Dee Stitt; to Professors René Fréchet and Wesley Hutchinson of the Sorbonne and their families; to Georges Blanchard of Châtelaillon, la Rochelle, and Le Musée du Désert, France; to Professors Michael Grant, JC Beckett and Ronnie Buchanan, Dr ATQ Stewart and Dr Ivan Herbison of the Queen's University, Belfast; to Professors Alison Henry and Paul Arthur of the University of Ulster; to David and Linda Campbell and family; to the directors and staff of the Somme Association, of which I was founding secretary and a former chairman; and to Brian and Jennifer Craig and family for advice on the death and resurrection of Jesus.

Thanks are also due to Adam Smith; to David McFerran; to Robin Hall; to Bertha and Alison McGimpsey; to Anne Johnston; to Jim Driscoll of Bangor Grammar School for his translations from Latin into English; to Keteryna Rudnytzky, Maria Zmurkewycz, Dr Peter Kluk and Christine Perfecky for their translations from Ukrainian into English, which were coordinated by Maria Kasian of the Ukrainian American Education and Cultural Centre, Philadelphia, Pennsylvania, USA; to James Dennison of the Bible Society for the Biblical Translations; to Monsignor Michael Fedorovich; to Reverend Brian Smeaton; to Michael Hall; to Tom Huggins; to Joan Blair, Vera Govan, Maureen McMullan and Jill Thompson for their care and patience in typing the script; to the Linen Hall Library and Central Library, Belfast; to the Ambrosian Library, Milan; to Marsh's Library, St Patrick's Cathedral and the Chester Beatty Library, Dublin, where I learned much about the great

Moslem medical polymaths Avicenna, Averroës and the Golden Age of Islam; to the Royal Irish Academy, Dublin; to Minister Jimmy Deenihan TD, the first minister for the Diaspora; to John Kennedy; to John Green and George McCullough of the Glasnevin Trust. Thanks are also due to my friends W Paul Loane of the Ulster-American Heritage Society and former chairman Violet Bowler, Jackie Hewitt, Fred Proctor, Ann Brown, the management committee, staff and employees of Farset Youth and Community Development Ltd, Belfast, and to all those who have helped our young people to follow in the steps of Columbanus throughout Europe.

On 18 July 1978 "le Docteur Ian Adamson s'est fait inscrire comme Membre de l'Association Medicale International de Lourdes" for services to the disabled children of the Parish of Falls in Belfast. In 1979 I first published in Bangor this book on Bangor, where I was born and went to school. I entitled it *Bangor, Light of the World* because of the reference in the Hymn to St Patrick in the seventh century Bangor Antiphonary, which was itself derived from a saying by Jesus, (Matthew 5: 14) which I heard during my visit to Lourdes as doctor to that group of disabled children from the Falls Road. The foreword was a beautiful one, written by my friend Reverend Brian Smeaton formerly of St George's Church, Belfast. The Parish of St George is a diverse, inclusive and vibrant community in Belfast city centre, who worship according to the best 'High Church' traditions of the Church of Ireland and the Anglican community, with excellent choral music and formal liturgy.

To the Indian people of North America 'Light' is their 'First Brother'. So it was that I travelled as a medical student among the Lakota (Sioux) and later, as a doctor, learned a little of their language, traditions and natural-world philosophy from the Spiritual Elders, so that I myself was later considered by some as a Wisdom Keeper also. But to me this has essentially meant that by learning their language more thoroughly by means of a Course in Conversational Lakota, bought for me by my sister Isabel Sloan Kerr Beegle in America, I could more fully understand their concept of a First Cause. My failure had lain, not with the idea itself, but with the inadequacy of the English language to express it. Wisdom Keepers all share the idea that the four-legged and winged nations, the creeping and crawling ones, the plant and tree nations, and those that dwell among the stars, are descended from and are part of a Great Holy Mystery (Wakan Tanka). All things are part of an incomprehensible totality which always was and always will be.

I republished this book in 1987 with a foreword by my friend Tomás Cardinal Ó Fiaich, which he wrote on St Patrick's Day that year. He presented the book to the Pope and it was placed in the Vatican Library. In August 1988, while Chairman of the Farset organisation, I initiated a meeting with Tomás Cardinal Ó Fiaich at the Bangor Heritage Centre, when a video recording of the Cardinal speaking about Columbanus took place. We then met Archbishop Robin Eames of Armagh, then Primate of the Church of Ireland, on Friday 2 September 1988 to tell him of our proposal to make a video, which was to be entitled *The Steps of Columbanus*. He too agreed to support it by participating in the video, giving a talk on Comgall. This was subsequently done under the auspices of Canon Hamilton Leckey at Bangor Abbey.

On Monday, 5 September 1988 I took Jackie Hewitt from the Farset Youth Project to follow part of the route Columbanus had taken. We stayed the following night at the home of Raymond Laurent, one of my closest Parisian friends. We travelled on to Auxerre, where both Columbanus and Patrick studied, and arrived in Lausanne where we had dinner with Pierre Dubois, Professor of European Studies at the University of Geneva. We then crossed the Alps via the St Gothard Pass, on the same route as Columbanus, going on to Milan and eventually to Bobbio where the saint rests.

In September 1989, I travelled with the young people of the Farset audio-visual project with Bahman Jamshid Nehad, an Iranian Project Supervisor, as our co-ordinator and Henry Mohammed as our cameraman. We visited Rheims, Luxeuil, the Rhine, St Gallen, Bregenz and Bobbio. The script was written by Michael Hall and Barney McCaughey acted as narrator. The initial video presentation was presented to Tomás Cardinal Ó Fiaich along with the Arts Council of Northern Ireland and the Cultural Traditions Group of the Community Relations Council, of which I was a member, early in 1990.

And in 1990 also I founded the Somme Association out of the Farset Youth Project, following a Press Conference held in Belfast City Hall under the auspices of Rhonda Paisley, then Lady Mayoress of Belfast, and her father Rev Dr Ian Paisley, MP, MEP, who, along with Eileen, now Baroness Paisley, have been among my closest friends. But my longest childhood friends from Conlig, Edmund and Kathleen Irvine, the parents of young Edmund (ie Eddie Irvine, formerly the Formula 1 racing driver) and Sonia, have also always been most supportive. They have visited the tomb of Columbanus at Bobbio. Later they called to see the Bangor Antiphonary in the Ambrosian Library in Milan.

On 13 January 1992 Professor René Fréchet of the Sorbonne wrote to me to ask for permission to translate my book, *The Ulster People*, into French and have it published by his University Press. He had spoken to his colleague, Paul Brennan, later to become Professor of Irish Studies at the Sorbonne, who had agreed to do so. Sadly, Fréchet's tragic death on 24 April of that year obviated the possibility of that proposed translation and publication. It was during this time that I began to become more involved in the promotion of Ulster-Scots with my founding chairmanship of the Ulster-Scots Language Society and the establishment of an Ulster-Scots Academy. Although Fréchet had not lived to see these projects develop, I would like to think that my vision for Ulster-Scots, as an integral part of an inclusive culture that stretches across the sectarian divide, would have met with his interest and approval.

In 1992, therefore, the year of Fréchet's death, I published, under my imprint, Pretani Press, the three-volume *Folk Poets of Ulster* series, thus initiating the modern Ulster-Scots revival in Northern Ireland. I had also suggested the new name 'Ullans' for the Ulster-Scots Academy which I proposed in June 1992, and formally established in Northern Ireland following a meeting in Vancouver, British Columbia, Canada, between Professor Robert Gregg and myself on Thursday, 23 July that year. The Ullans Academy was to be based on the Frisian Academy of Sciences in the Netherlands, which I had visited in 1978, and again in 1980, with a group of community activists from Northern Ireland, including Andy Tyrie and Glen Barr. The essential characteristic of the Frisian Academy was its division into three departments: Linguistics and Literature, History and Culture, and Social Sciences. This tripartite division was to become our model.

The new Ullans Academy was intended to fulfil a need for the regulation and standardisation of the language for modern usage. These standards were to have been initiated on behalf of the Ulster-Scots community, Protestant and Roman Catholic, nationalist and unionist, and would be academically sound. What we didn't need was the development of an artificial dialect which excluded and alienated traditional speakers. It seemed clear to me that it was fundamentally important to establish a standard version of the language, with agreed spelling, while at the same time maintaining the rich culture of local variants.

Therefore in 1995, I published for the Ulster-Scots Language Society, a regional dictionary by James Fenton, *The Hamely Tongue: A Personal Record of Ulster-Scots in County Antrim*, under the imprint of the Ulster-Scots Academic Press, from my premises in 17 Main Street, Conlig, County Down. This was the most important record yet produced of current Ulster-Scots speech and is now, under the imprint of the Ullans Press, in its third edition. It was distributed by my friend David Adamson. Then in November 2014, the Ullans Academy published *The Pentateuch* and *The Books of Wisdom of The Old Testament* by Gavin Falconer and Ross Arthur, the first complete translation into Plain Scots.

Like the Frisian Academy on which it was based, the Ulster-Scots or Ullans Academy's research was intended to extend beyond language and literature to historical, cultural and philosophical themes such as the life and works of Francis Hutcheson and CS Lewis, but also, as far as the present volume is concerned, to studies of the history of Ulidia in general, especially Dalriada, Dalaradia, Dal Fiatach, Galloway and Carrick, not forgetting Ellan Vannin, the Isle of Man, and Ulidia's successors, the Earldom of Ulster and Upper and Lower Clandeboye. We also looked at the commemoration of the great saints of Ireland, including Patrick, Comgall, Columbanus, Gall, Finnian (Uinnian), Columba and Molua.

Commemoration events by the Ullans Academy were first organised in March 2005 with the inaugural St Patrick's Breakfast, followed by a Feast of Columbanus in November, based on the Farset 'Steps of Columbanus' project of the mid-eighties. These events have been addressed by prominent speakers from across the whole community. The Rev Dr Ian RK Paisley, the Lord Bannside, accompanied by Eileen, Baroness Paisley, and President Mary McAleese, accompanied by her husband Martin, spoke together in the Park Avenue Hotel, East Belfast on Tuesday, 23 November 2010.

Prince Richard, His Royal Highness The Duke of Gloucester, attended our annual celebration of the life of Columbanus at the Clarion Hotel, Carrickfergus, County Antrim on 23 November 2011. Prince Richard's son is styled by his father's subsidiary title, Earl of Ulster. I accompanied Prince Richard throughout the engagement. HRH met over one hundred and fifty guests attending the 'Feast of Columbanus' lunch. Dr Ruairí Ó Bléine welcomed the guests in Ulster Gaelic, as I did later in Ullans. The Rt Hon and Rev the Lord Bannside PC gave a speech on Columbanus. The Master of Ceremonies, Sammy Douglas MLA, then invited HRH to speak.

The 2013 Feast of Columbanus event in Belfast City Hall was addressed by Rev Dr Ian RK Paisley, the Lord Bannside and by President Michael D Higgins, accompanied by his wife Sabina. Speaking at this event the President said:

> "I would like to thank very particularly the Ullans Academy and Dr Ian Adamson for inviting me to join you here today. Columbanus, in founding monasteries throughout Europe, did much more than just create high and abstract institutions. He created living communities where shared values and a sense of solidarity could and did lead to great engagement and vibrancy. He was a man of strong and complex character, independent thought, unafraid to ask the hard questions, even if it meant

> challenging those in positions of authority. Had he sought to withdraw or act alone, or had he meekly bowed to the received wisdom of the day, I doubt we would be recalling his name with such relevance well over a millennium later. His story tells us of both the power of leadership and of community. A strong and flourishing communal life gives staying power and enables values and ideals to pass through the generations. It is for this reason that support for a healthy, vibrant and engaged civil society in Northern Ireland is so important in cementing the progress the peace process has made to date."

This year of 2015 is particularly significant in that it is the 1400th anniversary of Columbanus' death in Bobbio. As he is the Patron Saint of Bikers, this will be commemorated by a Biker's event on 22 November under the auspices of Eddie Irvine at his magnificent Sports Centre in Bangor, Co Down, near where the great saint left to re-evangelise Europe on the decline and fall of the Roman Empire. Pretani Associates appreciate the help for this historic event given by Thomas Fegan, Assistant Chief Constable Drew Harris of the Police Service of Northern Ireland, Jim Shannon MP, Ken Perry, Robert Williamson of Dalaradia, Davy McAlonan of Dal Fiatach, John Laverty of the Ullans Academy and Pete Bleakley and Alan Morton of Visionworks.

In his message of support for it of 9 October, 2015, from His Excellency Michael D Higgins, Uachtarán na hÉireann, President of Ireland said:

> "St Columbanus is, of course the much loved patron saint of bikers throughout the world; an accolade that reflects his love of travel and great spirit of adventure and discovery. He was a man who looked past the perceived barriers and inevitabilities by which we so often live our lives in order to discover what was beyond those horizons, what was possible, what could be better. In many ways he was a man ahead of his time; a visionary who spoke and dreamt of a united Europe in which we could live and work together in peace. Many centuries after his death he continues to be an inspiring figure who we, in Ireland, are very proud to claim as one of our own."

And of Malachy, our second Columbanus, we have a reminder of his influence in the beautiful St Malachy's Church in Belfast, which was to have been the Cathedral Church of Down and Connor until funds were diverted to the destitute following the Great Famine. A Belfast City Council colleague brought me to see the plaque there to soldiers of the First World War and my friends Dennis and Maria Maloney have helped the church considerably. I have also been particularly fond of St Malachy's College, of which I was the school doctor for many years, where the memory of the great saint, the first Irish one to have been canonised by a Pope, lives on.

Finally, sincere thanks are due to all of my family, friends, associates, and indeed opponents, for their support, criticism and encouragement. I would also like to thank the publishers Malcolm and Wesley Johnston of Colourpoint Creative Limited and Jacky Hawkes. But I am especially grateful to my friend and colleague in Pretani Associates Helen Brooker, her husband David, and my wonderful wife Kerry, without whom we could not have even attempted to bring the twin volumes *The Cruthin* and *Bangor Light of the World* back into the public domain, or even attempted to do all we have done to promote Common Identity in recent years.

Dr Ian Adamson OBE
St Columbanus Day
21 November 2015

Foreword to the First Edition

The Wise Men from the East come to Bethlehem to see the sign of the baby Jesus. In so doing they become part of the sign themselves. They do not remain long, but give their gifts and go quickly back to their own place. For them the birth is an important element in what is a key to the Eastern Way – the wholeness or oneness of life.

Nearer to Bethlehem, the coming of the Christ as the sign of "all things earthly and heavenly gathered into one" was continually expected. The declaration of the forerunner, John the Baptist, comes from the long preparation in mind and body and spirit of the people of the Lord. The preparation of John the Baptist, like that of the Wise Men, involves the proper organisation of the daily acts of living so that as much time as possible can be concentrated upon the mystery of life itself. Out of this finely tuned understanding springs the *Laus Perennis* as practised at Bangor Mor.

When my friend Ian Adamson asked me to write a forward to his appreciation of the Rule of Bangor, I was aware of the depth of spirit which is part of his own expression of life. Therefore it is no surprise to me, in reading the manuscript, to see how lovingly and carefully he follows the subtle trails along which others have travelled in search of the reality of life. In his own capacity as a person devoted to healing, especially among children, the sensitivity he uses is all the more significant.

From out of that cauldron of living experience, the Middle East, in the opposite direction from the place of the Wise Men, the experience flows right to these hardly known islands at the western end of the European continent. And in a way which is mysterious to us as inhabitants of the twentieth-century world, conditioned by fast transport and instant talking machines, the Word came via the sea routes to these islands, and from there back to Central Europe. Students from all over Europe made Bangor Mor into a living centre of the Light.

At a time when people are so much taken up with the pain and pleasure of living, Ian Adamson is doing us great service in making the appreciation of how other generations saw beyond their pride and desire. There is much inspiration for the present in these pages. No matter what direction we are coming from we are all part of the sign. Here in Northern Ireland we have so many opportunities to express oneness. I am sure that the spirit and knowledge of this record will help us all.

In the pages following there is an emphasis upon the singlemindedness of Columbanus who followed his intuition against the whole political, religious and rational thought of the day. When it is realised just what Columbanus was up against, as a kind of local Saint Paul, the view often expressed that he, like other early saints, was a harsh, almost brutal, figure can be tempered to a certain degree. However, it should not be so difficult for us to understand, living as we do in a space which seems to be equally traumatic and brutal as any other period in this island's history.

The history of these islands is an amazing spectrum of darkness and light, feuds and love affairs, law and order, and 'blow' and order. And history tends to follow the current tide of power. So in Ireland history has long been presented in terms of the rapid Christianisation of paganism and also as a duel between Protestant Christianity and Roman Catholic Christianity. Nationalism feeds off its own versions of specially tailored myths, subtly emphasising something here and just as subtly playing down something elsewhere.

In another book, Ian Adamson has written at length about the Cruthin in order to develop an aspect of the history of this island of which I was previously unaware, as I am sure many others were also. His thesis is that the people in Ulster are not simply the descendants of a forced Plantation from the mainland after the Flight of the O'Neills and O'Donnells at the beginning of the seventeenth century. Long before that a native culture – part of the whole cultural tradition of this island but distinctive in terms of the Cruthin connection and also mostly untouched by the Anglo-Norman invasion – flourished in the North. The evidence of the native Ulster tradition remains plainly in the historical consciousness, but of course it is less emphasised on account of the nature of political power in the island. It has been squeezed between the Gaelic and English traditions and because of the pressure the reaction has been violent.

In this labour of love about Columbanus Ian Adamson has tried to develop one of the many strands of the native Ulster tradition. His aim is to show the Ulster people that they are not 'johnny-come-latelies' who suddenly appeared in the seventeenth century. Certainly there was a Plantation and without doubt the latter religious factionalism of the seventeenth century all over Europe created deep divisions which were, and still are, exploited. But, all that notwithstanding, the people of Ulster can stand with the same dignity as Cuchulain or Columbanus. This is their heritage.

Now is the time to widen the perspective beyond the religious divide. People do not change their minds; rather their horizons are widened. We begin to comprehend that what we thought was the whole of reality is but a small part, and that a representation. Nobody can lay claim to own reality, just as nobody can legitimately claim that there is only one view of history. So often, both politically and academically, history is presented as one of the pillars of the status quo. This is a contradiction in terms. History is nothing if it is not primarily a record of human relationships and of the vast network of variation in the manner of its evolution. Columbanus ventured into a Europe which held unknown dangers for the Irish Pict. He took with him a hard-headedness and a soft-heartedness – it was Martin Luther King who spoke of the "soft-headed and hard-hearted people" – which carried him through Europe. An Ulster trait, this hardness on the outside.

I am reminded of the Keats poem, "On first looking into Chapman's Homer". Here we are being invited to look at something which must be new and exciting. Because there is courage here; the courage which decided to explore an avenue which politics and learning had almost forgotten – at first just because it is there, but later with the comprehension that here lies a key to a new door in the development of relationships in Ulster itself and throughout these islands. The people have a proud and honourable, though bloody, tradition which can be traced to the idol stones of Killadeas and the remains of Dromena. Columbanus is part of that tradition as he is part of the tradition which developed the Christian capacity to take over the previous religious practices and places for its own use. It is dishonourable in the extreme to brand our pre-Christian forebears as any less than full human beings. It is a sad feature of our history that we can so condemn and divide with scant evidence and knowledge the lives and living of the early people, even more so when we ourselves have learned so little with our interdenominational disputes. Sometimes I feel much more at peace in an ancient, windswept, so-called pagan place than in the bland hypocrisy of some modern-day pharisaism. We have no right to condemn. How can we be smug and complacent?

And just as narrow is the way in which politics has ground out a history which sets our teeth on edge. The evil is the way in which we are taught to survive at the expense of others. The conclusion to that way is destruction for all – no winners or losers. So all the more welcome is the labour and courage of Ian Adamson which have the capacity to widen the horizons. Can we grasp this opportunity to look beyond our history to the present day? The way requires us to comprehend that reality is what is. We cannot just take what we ourselves desire and call that greediness reality. We have got to face the wholeness. This is what Columbanus had to do. He had the training and dedication developed and formed in Bangor and the nerve to challenge Europe. This is where we are at today. We need to challenge Europe with new ideas; to create opportunities for a wider vision. Is it not necessary?

We need new structures. The old ones do not allow for negotiation. We need tolls for negotiation and communication. We need to learn. Experience is the teacher. We need the steel and vision of Columbanus uprooting himself and travelling in dangerous ways. This is part of the experience. Nobody in Ulster should be dismissive or afraid to express what it is we are. I stand with Ian Adamson in this: it is our heritage now. We are part of it and we need the freedom to express it.

This is a re-statement of the Gospel of our time. We must enter with joy into the present and by grace we will see there the blessedness of the eternal present encompassing past and future. Blessedness is the recognition of perfection. Freedom is the comprehension that there is no choice; if we imagine we have choices then we are divided and diverted from the wholeness and unity of the universe.

I hope more people will come to comprehend the consciousness of Ulster, sharpened as it now is. I hope that a new vision will permeate the sullenness and apathy which affects us all. I do not believe the labours of Ian Adamson will remain unblessed. The blessing is ours who recognise in ourselves the wholeness that we seek.

Brian Smeaton
1979

Brian Smeaton is a Church of Ireland clergyman formerly attached to St George's Church, Belfast. Through his writings and broadcasting he is well known throughout the island of Ireland and further afield.

Foreword to the Second Edition

BANGOR IS ONE of a small group of Irish placenames which are well known to scholars in many European countries. Students of hagiography meet it in the lives of Columbanus and Gall. Students of the Irish annals meet it in connection with the so-called 'Ulster Chronicle'. Students of the twelfth century reform of the Irish Church encounter it in Saint Bernard's *Life of St Malachy*. Students of Irish hymnology, liturgy and palaeography are constantly referred to the *Antiphonary of Bangor* as one of the prime sources in all these areas.

It was a splendid idea on the part of Dr Ian Adamson to bring out a book centred on the Antiphonary in 1979. The great edition of the Antiphonary by Warren was issued in two volumes by the Henry Bradshaw Society as long ago as 1893. They provide a page by page facsimile for the scholar, but they are too bulky, too costly, too learned and too inaccessible for the ordinary reader. Dr Adamson's work reproduces the thirty-six folios (seventy-one pages, as one side of a folio is blank) of the original manuscript in a smaller scale facsimile, provides a transcript of the Latin text in beautiful calligraphy, supplies an English translation of some of the canticles, hymns, collects and prayers, and most important of all, places the manuscript in its Judaeo-Christian background within the cultural history of Bangor monastery.

Now that a new edition of Dr Adamson's work is shortly to be published, I deem it a high honour to be invited to write this foreword for it. Dr Adamson is already well known for *The Cruthin* (1974), an original and challenging contribution on the early history of the North of Ireland, and *The Battle of Moira* (1980), an edition of Ferguson's epic poem, Congal. In all his writings he has shown a special interest in the Pictish people of the North. Bangor was founded near their most important kingdom, Dal nAraidhe, and Comgall, its founder, was a member of their ruling aristocracy. Dr Adamson therefore writes of Bangor with new insights and with freshness, breadth of vision and unspoiled enthusiasm.

Twenty years ago I paid my first visit to Bobbio in Northern Italy where the manuscript of the Antiphonary of Bangor was lovingly preserved for many centuries. I then proceeded to Milan in order to see the manuscript itself in its present home in the Ambrosian Library. Imagine my frustration when I discovered that although the Library had reopened after the summer vacation, the manuscript room would not reopen for visitors until the following week.

As my return ticket did not allow me to stay over, I pleaded with the Library authorities and pulled out all the stops… came all the way from near Bangor… would only take a minute… was a professor of history… .but all to no avail. Every time a member of the staff passed in or out of the room I could see that there were manuscripts on show in the glass cases within… but I did not see the manuscript of the Antiphonary for another three years.

Lest the same fate should befall others I hope that Ian Adamson's new edition of *Bangor Light of the World* will have a wide circulation. It covers many themes which will be a revelation to most of us: The Perennial Praise in the Jewish Temple and its movement west with Martin of Tours, the Divine Office in Early Ireland and the Rule of St Columbanus, St Mahee of Nendrum and St Malachy of Armagh. It also provides that most unusual thing at the present time – a book about the religious history of Ulster, of which both Protestant and Catholic, both Nationalist and Unionist, can be equally proud. **Tolle, lege.**

Tomás Cardinal Ó Fiaich
Archbishop of Armagh
Ard Mhacha
Lá Fhéile Pádraig,
17 Márta 1987

1
The Family of Bangor

MANY CENTURIES AGO, in the days of the Cambro-Normans, there existed a tradition in Ireland which was already an ancient one. It was said that when St Patrick and his companions came one day to a certain valley in the north of County Down, suddenly "they beheld the valley filled with a heavenly light and with a multitude of the host of heaven they heard, as chanted forth from the voice of angels, the psalmody of the celestial choir." This place so enthralled those holy men that they called it 'Vallis Angelorum', the Valley of the Angels.

In the process of time there was built in this valley a holy place called Bangor, in which was celebrated a praise to God such as the world had seldom seen or heard. Such was the veneration in which it was held that St Bernard of Clairvaux wrote of it in the twelfth century:

> "A place it was, truly sacred, the nursery of saints who brought forth fruit most abundantly to the Glory of God, insomuch that one of the sons of that holy congregation, Molua by name, is alone reputed to have been the founder of a hundred monasteries: which I mention for this reason, that the reader may, from this single instance, form a conception of the number to which the community amounted. In short, so widely had its branches extended through Ireland and Scotland that these times appear to have been especially foreshadowed in the verses of David:
>
> 'Thou visitest the earth and waterest it; thou greatly enrichest it; the river of God is full of water; thou preparest them corn when thou hast so provided for it. Thou waterest the ridges thereof abundantly; thou makest it soft with showers; thou blessest the springing thereof.' *[Psalm 65: 9–10]*
>
> Nor was it only into the countries I have mentioned but even into distant lands that crowds of saints, like an inundation, poured. One of whom, St Columbanus, penetrating into these our regions of France, built the monastery of Luxeuil and there became a great multitude. So great do they say it was that the solemnisation of divine offices was kept up by companies, who relieved each other in succession so that not for one moment, day or night, was there an intermission of their devotions.

Although there is now nothing remaining of the buildings in which this celebrated perennial praise was sung, a precious and golden fragment of its ancient liturgy remains. This is contained in a manuscript called the Bangor Antiphonary which is preserved in the Ambrosian Library of Milan in Italy. The Perennial Praise or *Laus Perennis* was based on the Temple Praise in Jerusalem and the Community of Bangor were well versed in the scriptural basis of its authority. In this they were remarkably similar to those communities of the Jews known as Essenes and Therapeutae who sang a similar praise in Palestine and Egypt in earlier times. Because of it the Bangorians established what was for them a New Jerusalem in accord with the Revelation of St John the Divine, that disciple whom Jesus loved, to whom He entrusted his mother at the foot of the Cross and whose vision of the Apocalypse contained the final oracles of God.

This association is well illustrated by this extract from the Bangor Antiphonary, which is entitled 'Versicles of the Community of Bangor' and which has become better known as the 'Good Rule of Bangor'.

These verses contain the whole raison d'être of the Community or Family of Bangor. They were obviously inspired by John's Vision in Revelation, chapters 21 and 22, and the writings of Ezekiel in the Old Testament. Both speak of the eternal dwelling place of God, made not with hands but with 'living stones'. In other words John taught that those Jews and Gentiles who believed in Christ would build together a New Temple. As 1 Peter 2: 5 says: "You also as living stones are being built up as a spiritual house for a holy priesthood to offer up spiritual sacrifices acceptable to God through Jesus Christ."

Good Rule of Bangor

Straight and divine, holy, exact and constant,
exalted, just and admirable.

Blessed family of Bangor, founded on unerring faith,
adorned with salvation's hope, perfect in charity.

Ship never distressed though beaten by the waves:
fully prepared for nuptials, spouse for the sovereign Lord.

House full of delicious things and built upon a rock;
and no less the true vine brought out of Egypt's land.

Surely an enduring city, strong and unified,
worthy and glorious, set upon a hill.

Ark shaded by Cherubim, all overlaid by gold,
filled with sacred things and borne by four men.

A very Queen for Christ, clad in the light of the sun,
innocent yet wise, from every side invulnerable.

A truly regal hall with many jewels adorned,
of Christ's flock too the fold, and kept by the great God.

A fruitful virgin she and mother undefiled,
joyful and tremulous, submissive to God's word.

For whom, with the perfect, a happy life is destined,
prepared with God the Father to last to eternity.

Bangor Antiphonary (Bradshaw's translation)

Bangor was to be "an enduring city, set upon a hill" – a New Jerusalem. It was to be the Ark of the Covenant, a New Temple, "the true vine out of Egypt", a new Perennial Praise.

To fully understand the origins and history of Bangor we will therefore trace the whole course of the Temple worship both in Palestine and Egypt, centering first on Jesus of Nazareth who was the embodiment of that worship to his followers. We will then follow the story of the Bangor Community itself, for they it was who brought the Light of the Word of their Lord into the darkness of a barbarian Europe. The lands and peoples among whom they sang their perennial song, thus continuing "the psalmody of the celestial choir", constituted much of the then known world. It is a story of fortitude and courage perhaps unequalled in the history of mankind. The influence Bangor generated remains strong in Europe today and may be traced as far afield as Russia, the Ukraine and Bulgaria. Indeed, though many may not realise it, it is the very basis of modern Western civilisation itself.

On 13 March 1960 the literary-educational section of the prestigious South American daily newspaper *La Prensa*, published in Buenos Aires, Argentina, printed an article by Carlos Lussich about Irish monks founding monasteries and churches throughout Europe as far as Kiev. The interest in South America to this article was so great that it was reprinted in *El Plata* of Montevideo, Uruguay and in the English Language daily newspaper *The Southern Cross* of Buenos Aires. There were certainly Irish missionaries active in Poland about the tenth to twelfth centuries, and an Irish monastery was set up in Kiev about 1200 but the monks had to retire to Regensburg about 1260 owing to

Mongol invasion. Lussich believed that the celebrated Petcherskoi monastery in Kiev actually had its beginnings in the seventh century, ie at the time of the Irish expansion in Europe. The Ukranian writer George Tys-Krochmaluk comments:

> "In the sixth and seventh centuries Ireland was the centre of culture at that time and the school of all then known sciences. For two centuries youth from various corners of the world – Europe and Asia – journeyed to Irish universities to study philosophy and mathematics in the Greek language. Perhaps even some Antae (early Ukranians) found their way into this world famous educational centre. Here I am venturing into the realm of imagination, but why couldn't it be possible that these Antae students interested the Irish missionaries in their native land?
>
> In my opinion, it would be good if this matter were taken up by our Church historians, especially those who live in Europe and have access to the archives and libraries of Galacian history. It would be beneficial to ascertain if there exist any facts on the activities of the Irish monks in Ukraine in those monasteries and libraries founded by Irish monks. I have in mind here St Gall in Switzerland, Bobbio in Italy, where in 615 died mission initiator Columbanus, and others.
>
> This question carries a special importance for us, because if scholarly research can confirm the information regarding monasteries and churches in seventh century Kiev, we would be able to push back the beginnings of our history far into the preceding century and span the area between the Antae and the princedom of Rus."

As a result of this interest my book on Bangor was well received throughout the Ukrainian community in North and South America, and I liaised with them when I published the second edition of my work in 1987. I was therefore invited by Monsignor Michael Fedorovich of the Ukrainian Catholic Cathedral of the Immaculate Conception in Philadelphia to be the Guest of Honour at the Ukrainian Millennium celebration in Philadelphia in 1988. I took part in the Pontifical Divine Liturgy celebrating the Millennium of the Baptism of Rus'- Ukraine on 22 May 1988 in the Cathedral, which is a particularly beautiful one, constructed in 1966 to reflect authentic Byzantine architecture in the same style as the Hagia Sofia in Constantinople, which I have visited several times over the years.

2

The Legend of Altus the Centurion

THE FOCAL POINT in world history for the Family of Bangor was a low hill, just outside the city of Jerusalem, in approximately 30 AD, in the early days of the Roman Empire. This hill was popularly known as Golgotha, which is to say, 'The place of the skull' but many now call it Calvary. Here was crucified Jesus of Nazareth, 'the King of the Jews'. According to the Gospel of Mark:

> "And they gave Him to drink wine mingled with myrrh, but He received it not. And when they had crucified Him, they parted His garments, casting lots upon them, what every man should take.
>
> And it was the third hour, and they crucified Him. And the superscription of His accusation was written over, THE KING OF THE JEWS.
>
> And when the sixth hour was come, there was darkness over the whole land until the ninth hour. And at the ninth hour Jesus cried with a loud voice, saying, Eloi, Eloi, lama sabachthani? Which is, being interpreted, My God, My God, why hast thou forsaken me?
>
> And some of them that stood by, when they heard it said, Behold, He calleth Elias. And one ran and filled a sponge full of vinegar, and put it on a reed, and gave Him to drink, saying, Let alone; let us see whether Elias will come to take Him down.
>
> And Jesus cried with a loud voice and gave up the ghost. And the veil of the temple was rent in twain from the top to the bottom.
>
> And when the centurion, which stood over against Him, saw that He so cried out, and gave up the ghost, he said Truly this man was the Son of God." *(Mark 15: 23–26, 33–39)*

The traditions of Ireland say that the centurion who spoke thus at our Lord's Crucifixion was named Altus, and that this same Altus was an Ulster Warrior in the service of Rome. It would appear from the Gospels that few of the disciples were at hand when Jesus died, for fear that they might be betrayed by their accents. Since, like Jesus, they spoke Aramaic, most of the Galileans had fled from the city. But tradition says that Altus was so impressed with what he had seen that he became a follower of the man he had just crucified and returned to Ireland to preach the Gospel. Since crucifixion was so dishonourable a death that it was reserved, according to Roman custom at that time, for those who were not citizens of Rome, this change in Altus was profound.

For Altus ('the tall one') had risen from the ranks of the barbarian. He had become a man under the authority of the Roman State, and his dedication to his calling could only have been absolute. His conversion, in the face of the desertion of the Galileans, was even more poignant, since Jesus's indictment by the Sanhedrin was considered by Pontius Pilate not serious enough for the death penalty, and since his actual death was of so little significance to the Roman State that the great Roman historian Tacitus wrote in his *Annals* that during the reign of Tiberius there was little to disrupt the harmony of Roman rule. Strangely enough, Jesus had already found in "a certain centurion" faith such as he had not found previously, "no, not in Israel." (Luke 7: 9)

The rending from top to bottom of the veil of the Temple of the Lord in Jerusalem was of great significance for the world, not least for the Jews themselves. Altus could see that. For the Temple was for them the symbol of God's presence on earth. At the time of Jesus the Temple appears to have excited the admiration of His disciples for they had exclaimed, "Master, see what manner of stones and what buildings are here" (Mark 13: 1). But, amid all its splendour and magnificence, the Messiah sealed the doom of the Temple. For in reply to the excited exclamations of His disciples, Jesus had declared that the generations of those existing at that time would not pass away before the great building would be reduced to a mass of smouldering ruins.

Like all wandering soldiers, Altus must have asked of its history. The Children of Israel recognise two successive Temples at Jerusalem. The first, which is usually known as Solomon's Temple, was built on Mount Moriah in 967 BC, being selected by Jesus's ancestor, David, as the most suitable and commanding site on which to build a city of peace, set on a hill, and a Temple of the Lord as a home for the Holy Ark of the Covenant. It would appear to have been a most magnificent structure, built on the model of the Tabernacle which Moses erected in the desert, according to the commandment of God. King David projected this in the formation of a fixed place for the worship of God and made preparations with the Phoenicians for the provision of materials and workmen for its construction.

3
The Temple of the Lord

THE PHOENICIANS WERE a mercantile nation, akin to the Jews, whose commercial greatness was established on trade with Tarshish, the west of Europe, and its Atlantic seaboard, including the British Isles. Even before David's time relations between Jews and Phoenicians had been generally friendly – it would appear from Judges 5: 17 and Genesis 49: 13 and 20 that the Tribes of Asher, Zebulun and Dan acknowledged at least some dependence on the Phoenician city of Sidon and had in return a share in its commerce. Josephus, the great Jewish historian, has fortunately preserved for us extracts from two Hellenistic historians, Dius and Menander of Ephesus, which supply us with a synopsis of the history of the Golden Age of that other great Phoenician city of Tyre.

Thus we learn that Hiram I, son of Abibal, reigned from 980 to 946 BC, and was the great friend of, first, David and then Solomon, kings of the Jews. The two peoples grew close under the kings. It is certain that Hiram built David's palace (2 Samuel 5: 11) and supplied Solomon with cedar and fir trees from Lebanon as well as workmen to complete the Temple. He received in exchange large annual payments of oil and wine. The Phoenicians appear in Irish tradition as the African seafarers, the noble Carthaginians, who gave Ireland its name Herne or Ierne, the 'uttermost habitation'.

The Temple, like the Tabernacle, consisted in the main building of two parts: the Holy Place and the Holy of Holies. This structure was surrounded on each side, except the entrance, by three storeys of small rooms, which would have reached to about half the height of the body of the Temple, while the east end, or court, was a great portico. Around the whole building were an inner and an outer court, the inner being called the Court of the Priests, and the outer being used to store the articles used in the Temple's services. Beautiful though the whole building undoubtedly was, its main function was the continual Praise of God.

According to the scriptures some kind of devotional worship was maintained in the Temple both by day and by night, for we read that singers, as well as the priestly Levites, had their lodging in the house, because "they were employed in that work day and night" (1 Chronicles 9: 33). There is also a reference to the Perennial Praise of the Temple in Isaiah 30: 29, "Your song will then sound as in the night when a feast is celebrated." It must have been an inspiring sight to see the watches of white-robed priests greeting one another at the changing of the watch, saying, "Bless ye the Lord, all ye his servants which stand by night in the house of the Lord," and the retiring person would give the appropriate response. The psalmist sang, "Blessed are they that dwell in Thy house, they will be still praising Thee." The continual reciting of the Law was for them a direct commandment of God in that he said to Joshua, "This Book of the Law shall not depart out of thy mouth, but thou shalt meditate therein day and night."

Because of Solomon's idolatry, God is said to have taken the ten northernmost tribes of Israel and given them to Jeroboam. Solomon determined to kill Jeroboam and he fled to the protection of Shishak, King of Egypt (945–924 BC), who had started the 22nd or Libyan Dynasty. Solomon died about 931 BC. Dissension continued between Solomon's son, Rehoboam (of Judah), and Jeroboam (of the Northern Kingdom of Israel). By the fifth year of Rehoboam's reign, only thirty years had elapsed since the building of the Temple when Judah was invaded by Shishak (Shoshenq I) of Egypt. Shishak, supported by a large army of Lubrim (Libyans), Sukkim, and Kushites (Ethiopians), accepted the surrender of Jerusalem and plundered the Temple. The vessels and furnishings he removed are depicted in minute detail on a wall of the temple of Karnak in Egypt.

After this period the Temple was subject to frequent profanation and pillage before being finally and utterly destroyed by the Chaldeans under Nebuchadnezzar in the year 597 BC, when the Jews were first carried in captivity into Babylon. More were taken into captivity in 587 BC. During the period of seventy years' captivity, the Temple on Mount Moriah was left a heap of ruins, but on their return from Babylon under Cyrus the Great of Persia, who acceded to the throne of Babylon in 538 BC, the Jews set themselves under Zerubbabel to build a Second Temple, and they rededicated it some twenty-three years later in 516 BC, although they had not the sustenance to restore it to its former greatness. It is certain, however, that the full rites of the Temple Praise were restored and that continual praise to God was reinstated according to the Law.

4

Hasidim – The Pious Ones

In the year 332 BC the Near East fell to the all-conquering Greek, Alexander the Great. In that year also Alexander founded a Greek city on the island of Pharos in Egypt. This city, named Alexandria after its founder, was destined to become a great seat of learning. On Alexander's death Palestine and Egypt both had an ample share of the troubles arising out of the partition of his inheritance.

On the conquest of Syria by the Seleucidae the second Temple was profaned by Antiochus Epiphanes, who commanded that the Jewish priests discontinue their daily sacrifices and ordered that a temple to the Greek god Zeus be erected on the Altar of Burnt Offering. This abomination lasted for the space of three years when the Jewish hero, Judas Maccabaeus, the 'Hammer' in Aramaic, recovered the independence of his country and restored the purity of the Temple Worship as ordained by God, although never again did the Jews consider it contained the real presence of the Lord.

When the newly purified Temple had been rededicated by the Maccabean family in 165 BC, there had naturally been much rejoicing among the Children of Israel, so that the event is celebrated to this day (Hanukkah: Hebrew ה·ָכֻנֲח). At the same time a group of the Jewish people led by a section of the priesthood saw the Maccabean victories as but a palliation of a deeper sickness, which such success in battle could do little to heal. To this section of the Jewish population the persecutions of Antiochus were merely a just and merited punishment ordained by God for the continuing neglect of His Law and the breaking of that holy Covenant made so long before with Moses.

The basic requirement, they felt, which was asked by God of his people, was not the elimination of foreign domination by the Maccabees but the formation of a holy Israel ruled by a theocratic hierarchy. Many such people had fled to the desert before 168 BC, dying of starvation in the wilderness rather than submitting to the abomination of the defilement of the Temple. The Maccabees had persuaded many to return, abandoning their principles in the meantime, in order to rid Jerusalem of the Greeks, but others remained obdurate and true to the Law, earning the name of 'pious ones' or Hasidim. Out of this group developed two sects – the Essenes and the Pharisees.

The doubts in the minds of the Hasidim were soon enough justified by events. The Maccabeans, called Hasmoneans, were rewarded by the people with the High Priesthood of Israel, but, high as their ideals might have been, the High Priesthood of Israel was a divine office ordained by God, which should have been accorded to one who had satisfied strict criteria of race and purity before he could assume the spiritual and temporal leadership of the Jewish people. In the days of the despised Antiochus, the pious Onias III had been banished and the office given to the highest bidder. It was even worse that the Hasmoneans should assume the position of priest kings.

When the most unpopular of them, Alexander Janneus, actually offered the holy sacrifice at the Temple altar, the people hurled abuse at him and his reply was a dreadful massacre of the faithful by his mercenary troops. Such were the events that precipitated a teacher among the Hasidim to gather several priests around him out of the holy city of Jerusalem and flee to the desert. There they began their exile from the impurity and wickedness around them and awaited the Kingdom of God. The community they formed became known as the Community of Righteousness and, as Essenes, they formed with the Pharisees and Sadducees three of the main disciplines of the Jews in the time of Jesus.

In other parts of the old Greek Empire various communities of the dispersed Jewish people had become an effective part of the administration and were more open to Hellenising influences. The most important of these communities was in Egypt, so that in Alexandria was formed a distinct Canon law which culminated in the construction of a new Temple at Leontopolis in the Land of Onias, the only Jewish sanctuary outside Jerusalem where sacrifices could be made. These Alexandrian Jews were to have a profound influence on the philosophy of the early Christian fathers and the creation of what the Bangor Antiphonary calls the "true vine" which came out of Egypt. The most important of these communities was that of the Therapeutae, who were the Egyptian equivalent of the Essenes.

5
The Community of Righteousness

The word 'Essene' means 'healer' in Aramaic, which was the language spoken by Jesus, and 'Therapeutae' is the Greek equivalent. Medicine occupied a considerable part of their attention which seems to have been connected with inquiries into the hidden powers of nature. The sect arose in the country lying on the west side of the Dead Sea and much has been learned about their moral and religious philosophy from the Scroll of the Community at Qumran at its north-western edge. From this semi-monastic settlement at Qumran they spread over most parts of Palestine. Josephus says that there were many of them dwelling in every town and he mentions four different orders of them, all of which may be resolvable into two classes – practical and contemplative Essenes. The great theologian Pope Benedict XVI has linked Jesus with the Essenes, saying that He "celebrated Easter with his disciples probably according to the Qumran calendar, and thus at least the day before" mainstream observances at the time.

Before being fully united to the Essene society the initiate was, according to Josephus, "to first bind himself by solemn exhortations and professions to love and worship God, to do justice towards men, to wrong no creature willingly, nor to do it, though commanded; to declare himself an enemy of all wicked men, to join with all the lovers of right and equity, to keep faith with all men." He was likewise to declare if that ever he became advanced above his companions he would never abuse that power to the injury of his subjects or distinguish himself from his inferiors by any ornament of dress or apparel but that he would love and embrace the truth and bring false speakers to justice.

Josephus acknowledges that the Essenes sent gifts to the Temple and thus expressed their reverence for the original establishment, discharging in this manner the common duty of all Jews as it was their principle to fulfil every obligation which bound them. Yet they did not visit the Temple themselves for they maintained that only among the really sanctified members of their own sect was the truly spiritual temple where sacrifices could be offered with the proper consecration.

The Perennial Praise was carried out very strictly as shown in the Rule which follows:

> "Let the many keep awake in community a third of all the nights of the year in order to read aloud from the Book and to expound judgement and to sing blessings altogether."

One of the hymns which they sang has been recovered from their Scroll of Thanksgiving Psalms and is as follows:

> "I thank thee, O Lord,
> That thou has tied my Soul in the bundle of Life
> And fenced me about from all the snares of the pit.
> Ruthless men have sought my life
> Because I hold fast to thy covenant.
> But they are an empty crowd, a tribe of Baliol,
> Failing to see that in me is thy foothold,
> That Thou with Thy mercy will deliver my Soul
> Where my footsteps are of Thine ordering."

And so during the night, as two-thirds of the number of the Community of Righteousness slept in their tents and huts, the other one-third kept up their continual chant of readings, hymns and psalms. Therefore, in the Dead Sea Scrolls we have today selections from every Book of the Old Testament except Esther, as well as hymns and psalms, constituting the actual manuscripts of the *Laus Perennis* (Perpetual Prayer) according to the Old Dispensation. The Bangor Antiphonary is a remnant of the New.

The Qumran Community looked forward to the coming of a priestly Messiah or Christ who would be for them the supreme interpreter of the Law and who would usher in a new Kingdom of God which was essentially to be a holy institution devoted to God's service and the interpretation of His divine will. As well as this priestly Messiah there was to be a second Messiah who was to be a Prince of the line of David. This Davidic Messiah would be a warrior of God and the holy instrument by which God would restore his kingdom and protect that Community of the Poor who sought to know him. Both would be present at the Messianic feast at the End of Days when there would be an Apocalyptic war between the Sons of Light and the Sons of Darkness.

The Qumran Community lived for the day when the two Messiahs would lead them back to a new and purified Jerusalem and a detailed vision of the holy city and its Temple is contained in the fragmentary work which has been entitled, 'A Description of the Heavenly Jerusalem.' This was again doubtless inspired by the closing chapters of the Book of Ezekiel and so for the Community of Righteousness the strict discipline of their life was a rehearsal for those days when mankind would join the angels in the singing of the celestial choir.

6

The Temple of Herod

WHEN THE SECOND Temple had stood for 500 years, it began to show signs of structural decay. And so Herod, named the Great, in order to reconcile the Jews to his government under Rome, undertook to rebuild it. The main structure was completed over the course of nine years, but the work of the enlargement and decoration was continued over half a century so that the Jews could say to the Lord's followers, "Forty years and six were we in building the Temple" (John 2: 20). Certainly it must have been one of the finest structures ever created by man, and it had nine gates, each of which was richly studded with silver and gold.

Through the eastern gate, called the gate Shushan, and the King's Gate, Altus the centurion must have walked, for this was called the Court of the Gentiles. Gentiles were permitted to walk therein, although not to advance any further. Separated from this court by a low stone wall was the Court of the Israelites, into which foreigners were prohibited to enter. This was divided into two parts – the Court of the Women, in which stood the treasury, and the Court of the Israelites, where Jesus and His disciples walked. Within the precincts of this court was the Court of the Priests, considered so sacred that only they could enter, and from this court twelve steps led to the Temple of God itself.

The most sacred place was divided into three parts – the portico, the outer sanctuary, and the Holy of Holies. In the portico the priests deposited the votive offerings given either by Jews or Gentiles. In the outer sanctuary, into which priests of every degree had ready admission, there stood the altar of incense. But separated from this sanctuary by the great double veil of the Temple was the Holy of Holies, through which none was allowed to pass except the High Priest, and that on only one day per year – *Yom Kippur*, the Day of Atonement. It was on the day of the crucifixion of Christ that the veil of the Temple was torn in two and the Holy of Holies was defiled, a certain sign to the Jews from God.

The scriptures tell us that when Jesus was dead His body was laid in the sepulchre of Joseph of Arimathaea.

> "And the women also, which came with him from Galilee, followed after, and beheld the sepulchre and how the body was laid. And they returned,

> and prepared spices and ointments: and rested the Sabbath day according to the commandment." *(Luke 23: 55–56)*

But on the third day Jesus rose again from the dead as He had said He would, identifying Himself with the Temple in Jerusalem. Then He appeared among those who had deserted Him, and blessed them.

> "And they worshipped Him, and returned to Jerusalem with great joy. And were continually in the Temple, praising and blessing God."
> *(Luke 24: 52–53)*

Simeon had said of Jesus that He was "a light to lighten the Gentiles," and Jesus Himself said, "I am the Light of the World: he that followeth me shall not walk in darkness, but shall have the light of life" (John 8: 12).

So the Light spread from Jerusalem to Rome in the face of first violent Jewish and then Roman opposition. For some among the Jewish people Jesus was illegitimate and a magician, who did not satisfy their criteria for a Messiah. He was an outsider, a stranger in their midst, a man of sorrow and acquainted with grief. Nevertheless He was not crucified for being illegitimate or a magician, but because of the claim that he was the "King of the Jews", and the miracles he wrought were generally thought to be genuine. For the Romans, Christianity became a threat to the State. The historian for both Jews and Romans was Josephus and his record of events obviously reflected their opinions. The history of Jesus was therefore initially ignored.

It has been said that Peter had been designated by Jesus, the Son of Man, as the rock of the Church, and became the Bishop of Rome. A fierce young anti-Christian by the name of Saul was converted to the faith on the road to Damascus and changed his name to Paul. He joined the Christian movement a mere three years or so after the Crucifixion and met James the Just, the brother of Jesus, whom the Lord had designated as his successor and who became the 'Bishop of Bishops' and head of the Apostolic Council. According to the Scriptures, Paul had travelled to Jerusalem when he was young and studied under the great Rabbi Gamaliel the Elder, an influential Pharisee member of the Sanhedrin and son or grandson of Hillel. The remarkable man called Paul was to become, apart from Mary Magdalene, the most persistently loyal friend Jesus ever had. However he was often at variance with the original and authentic Jerusalem church, James the Just and the other pillars of the church, Peter and John. For Paul, the Son of Man had become the actual Son of God, while for the Apostolic Council he was the Jewish Messiah, sent by a Jewish God for a Jewish people.

7

The Declaration of Nazareth

> "He [Jesus] went to Nazareth, where he had been brought up, and on the Sabbath day he went into the synagogue, as was his custom.
>
> And he stood up to read. The scroll of the prophet Isaiah was handed to him. Unrolling it, he found the place where it is written:
>
> 'The Spirit of the Lord is on me, because he has anointed me to preach good news to the poor. He has sent me to proclaim freedom for the prisoners and recovery of sight for the blind, to release the oppressed, to proclaim the acceptable year of the Lord.'
>
> Then he rolled up the scroll, gave it back to the attendant and sat down. The eyes of everyone in the synagogue were fastened on him, and he began by saying to them, 'Today this scripture is fulfilled in your hearing.' " *(Luke 4: 16–21)*

THE GOSPEL OF Mark may well be the first to have been written, by John Mark, the personal secretary of the apostle Peter. The version we have now was certainly composed in 65–70 AD, 35 to 40 years after the events Mark recorded, by a well-educated Greek-speaking Christian. The term Gospel means 'Good News' and the author was concerned with how he was bringing such news to the people rather than writing an actual biography of Jesus.

In Mark's Gospel, Jesus is described as "the Christ, the Son of God" (Mark 1: 1). For most Jewish people at the time this would have been a remarkable statement and to the educated élite would have appeared quite unacceptable. For 'Christ' is Greek for the 'Anointed One', and is the equivalent of the Hebrew term for 'Messiah'. The Jews were awaiting a great military leader or cosmic figure who would deliver them from their enemies, not a person who had just suffered and in their eyes died ignobly on Calvary. And yet that is precisely why the author says Jesus was the Messiah.

One of the significant points about the account is that at the beginning nobody actually seems to have known he was the Messiah. Jesus's family didn't seem to know. The neighbours from his virtually unknown little village of Nazareth wondered what on earth this son of the local carpenter was talking about. But, most of all, his disciples didn't seem to know who he was. God, of course, knew who he was, because Jesus, at his baptism by John the Baptist, and only Jesus, heard a voice from heaven declaring "you are my beloved son" (Mark 1: 11). Mary Magdalene knew, and the demons he cast out knew, but no one else seems to have had a notion.

All this changes in the middle of the Gospel, with the metaphor of the blind man who gradually regains his sight. The disciples at last begin to understand, though Jesus instructs them not to tell anyone. And he continues to predict that he must suffer and die, to take away the sins of the world. Yet, at the very end, even Jesus himself seems not to be so sure after all. He prays to God three times to save him from his fate, and then cries out in total despair before he dies, literally of a broken heart. He had suffered extreme torture and mental anguish, following flogging or scourging with a flagrum, consisting of braided leather thongs with metal balls and pieces of sharp bone woven or intertwined with the braids, causing hypovolaemic shock, so he could no longer carry the cross. On crucifixion his heart finally failed, with massive pulmonary oedema and pericardial effusion, as the description of his death authentically shows, for "one of the soldiers pierced Jesus' side with a spear, bringing a sudden flow of blood and water" (John 19: 34), rupturing his heart and releasing the pleural and pericardial effusions. He was totally, absolutely, completely dead. Yet if anyone had any doubts at all about what happened next, the author does not. Jesus's death and resurrection had inevitably to be such, and in fact, we are all expected to take up our own crosses and follow our beloved Master.

The Gospel of Thomas is of another kind, a 'Sayings' Gospel, which records 114 of Jesus's sayings rather than the story of his life, death and resurrection. Its purpose is to promote the secret teachings of Jesus and explain to the faithful that by understanding his words rather than by believing in his death and resurrection that they would have everlasting life. The Gospel is attributed to Didymus Judas Thomas, whom Jesus says is his 'twin', 'Didymus' being Greek and 'Thomas' Aramaic for 'twin'. If it is not a forgery, as some believe, it may be the closest we ever get to the real Jesus. Yet, as we have seen, the leadership of the church in Jerusalem passed, not to Thomas, but to Jesus's brother, James the Just, who followed the Law, supported the poor against the rich and was deeply respected among the whole Jewish community. He sought to limit the doctrine of Paul, whose mission was essentially to the Gentiles as well as to the Jews. When James was executed in 62 AD, therefore, on the orders of Ananus, a corrupt High Priest who was bathed in luxury, the whole Jewish community were appalled.

The convert Paul was, apart from Jesus Himself, the most important figure in the spread of Christianity. His letters to the young churches were probably written sometime between 50 and 60 AD. Paul's conversion appears to have been the result of an encounter with the living Jesus following his death and resurrection which completely altered Paul's understanding of Jesus, God's Law and the true road to salvation. He became convinced that the end of the world was nigh and people needed to be saved before it was too late. His total belief in the resurrection of the Christ had the clearest implications for the ethical well-being of the community.

The Gospels of Matthew and Luke have been dated to between 80 and 85 AD. The Gospel of Matthew concentrates on Jesus's Jewishness but at the same time demonstrates his opposition to the Jewish leaders of his day. Yet for all that, Jesus was a Jewish Messiah, sent by a Jewish God to a Jewish people to gather Jewish disciples, in fulfilment of Jewish Scriptures. He was merely summing up the Jewish Law into two Commandments: to love God above all else and to love one's neighbour as oneself (Matthew 22: 35–40). Thus he superseded the Scribes and Pharisees and all their works.

Luke was a Gentile physician, known to have been a travelling companion of the apostle Paul, but there is the usual academic debate about whether he wrote the Gospel or not. Nevertheless, Jesus is portrayed as a Jewish prophet, who as the Son of God brought the whole world to salvation, not just Jewish people but Gentiles as well. He was therefore the *Salvator Mundi*, the Saviour of the World. He was born like a prophet, preached like a prophet, and finally died like a prophet. He was even obliged to go to Jerusalem to be killed, for that is where all the prophets die (Luke 13: 33).

The Gospel of John as we have it was written between 90 and 95 AD and has been traditionally ascribed to John, the son of Zebedee, one of Jesus's closest friends. But this ascription cannot be found anywhere until the latter part of the second century. In earlier sources John is described as a countryman from Galilee, who would have spoken, like Jesus, Aramaic, not the literary Greek in which the Gospel is written. Moreover in Acts 4: 13 John is described as illiterate. The Gospel is, in fact, likely to have been translated from oral or written Aramaic sources towards the end of the first century, so that whether John was illiterate or not is of no special significance.

John's Gospel provides a completely different view of Jesus. He is no longer the compassionate and charismatic healer and worker of miracles, proclaiming the coming of the Kingdom of God, a prophet without honour among his own people. Nor even the Jewish Messiah, sent by the Jewish God to fulfil the Jewish Scriptures to physically liberate the Jews from their enemies. He is now the Logos, the Word.

"In the beginning was the Word, and the Word was with God, and the Word was God." The same was in the beginning with God. Jesus had passed from the prophetical to the mystical to the Divine…

8
The Egyptian

OVER FORTY YEARS ago, my father bought me the translation of the *Works of Flavius Josephus* by the remarkable Arian theologian, William Whiston (1667–1752) and I have maintained an abiding interest in the history of my Jewish relatives ever since. When on a visit to the twin cities of St Paul and Minneapolis, Minnesota, USA, in 1990 as founding chairman of the Somme Association I took part in a Passover Seder on 9 April at the home of my Jewish cousins. I had been invited by the highly influential minister Rev Calvin Didier to speak the previous day, Palm Sunday, in the House of Hope Presbyterian Church, one of the finest in the Mid-West of America.

At the Seder we partook of our Hillel sandwiches, according to the Biblical command, and learned much about the famous sage. As a result of their dispersal throughout the world the Jews have played a vital role in a remarkable array of events as diverse as history itself. Indeed, Israel Besht, founder of the Hasidic movement in eighteenth century Russia, has said, "Like the soil, everyone treads on the Jews. But God has put into that soil the power to bring forth all kinds of plants and fruits". The Jewish literary tradition, the oldest in the world, remains unbroken. But, of course, the problems of Jewish identity are most complex since they live in two worlds. There is an external world of the Gentiles and their own remarkable internal one of ancient belief and tradition. Yet today there are too few people in the Jewish community, as well as the Christian one, who are as familiar as they should be with the values, as well as the vitality and indeed the relevance of those thousands of years during which the creativity and achievements of the Children of Israel have been manifested.

Little or nothing is known about Jesus and Paul except that which is written about them in what Christians call the New Testament. But little or nothing is also known of Josephus either except what he tells us of himself in his writings. Nevertheless much of what we think we know of Jewish history from the rise of the Maccabees to the fall of Masada in 73 AD is derived from his books. Titus Flavius Josephus, born Joseph Ben Matthias, (c40–100 AD), informs us that he is of priestly and Hasmonean descent. His *Vita* or Life seems to have been more or less written not only to justify his betrayal of his country to save his own life but to win favour with the Romans. Strangely enough, though a

Romanophile without conscience in Jerusalem, who would not have tolerated the Christians as they were considered a threat to Roman State religion, he was a proud Judeophile in Rome, who would have also thought that Jesus was illegitimate, a false prophet and a magician. He wrote the *Wars of the Jews* to praise the Romans as rulers of the then known world and later *Against Apion* and *Antiquities of the Jews* to praise the Jews and Judaeism.

However, by following the tradition of Greco-Roman historiography, in what he would have considered to have been a quest for historical truth, Josephus in effect has set his work apart from the Biblical authors before him, and Jewish and Christian writers for centuries after him, who regarded the purpose of history as proof of God controlling the destiny of the Universe. His writings contain statements which are obviously biased, erroneous, embellished with outright fabrication, and include legend and folklore presented as fact, yet they are probably as accurate as that of any Hellenistic historian. Although he omits reference to such great exegetes as Hillel, Paul and the Apostles and there are questionable references to Jesus, his chief authority is the everyday life of Judea, its geography, agriculture and the politics of the prominent figures of his day. His work is particularly focused on perhaps two of the most critical centuries of recorded history. Indeed the *Wars of the Jews* must be considered one of the most magnificent literary achievements of all time, which not only affects our emotions and stirs our imagination, but is memorable in a way that only a Jewish composition can be.

On 12 October 1991, Dr Michael Grant wrote to me from his home in Le Pitturacce, Lucca, Italy, wishing me well and saying that he was sending me two of his works under separate cover, namely *The Rise of the Greeks* and *The Fall of the Roman Empire*, which I had not read. Formerly a Fellow of Trinity College, Cambridge, Professor of Humanity at Edinburgh and President and Vice-Chancellor of the Queen's University of Belfast, his other books on the ancient world were to me without equal. I particularly liked *Jesus*, *Saint Paul*, *Saint Peter* and *The Jews in the Roman World*. Dr Grant looked at the Gospels bearing the names of Matthew, Mark, Luke and John with a historian's eye. For him Jesus was not the political revolutionary that those among his followers and adversaries thought he might have been. For although he was raised to passion and indeed anger by the sufferings he witnessed, his every act and admonishment were directed towards his wish to instruct his disciples to prepare for the dawning of the Kingdom of God.

The Authentic Gospel of Jesus by Geza Vermes shows this quite clearly. The women around Jesus, like Mary Magdalene, understood this more than the men, and that is why women would make better Bishops. The question for me regarding the testimony of Josephus is this: why did he leave out Hillel, Jesus and Paul? Or did he really? Like the young Paul, he would have denied Jesus as the Christ or sole Messiah, so reference to Jesus as such in his works must have been added later by Christian copyists. And if material was added later, was any material which was considered offensive removed by the same copyists… perhaps that Jesus was an imposter, the Apostles and Paul deluded, and the Golden Rule of Hillel the real basis of Christian thought?

Yet I do think there is a cryptic or garbled reference to the Life of Jesus in Josephus which does survive. In the Acts of the Apostles, we read that during the time of the infamous Procurator Marcus Antonius Felix (52–58 AD), Paul was arrested following a riot in the Temple:

> "And as Paul was to be led into the castle, he said to the chief captain, 'May I speak to you?' Who said, 'Can you speak Greek? Are you not that Egyptian, which some time ago made an uproar, and led out into the wilderness four thousand men who were murderers (Sicarii)?'" *(Acts 21: 37–38)*

Do we see here perhaps the followers of Jesus reminiscent of Judas of the Sicarii (Dagger-men) and Simon the Zealot? And is it possible that Jesus was the Egyptian, who had indeed returned again, as he said he would, to proclaim the Kingdom of God? What we are sure of, however, is that Paul himself did actually meet the resurrected and living Jesus. For there is no doubt in my own mind that Jesus died on the cross and rose again on the third day and that Paul himself said he had seen the Risen Lord, as did the Apostles and many others before him (1 Corinthians 15: 3–8).

Josephus in the *Wars of the Jews* (2.259) says that during the governorship of Porcius Festus (58–62 AD) there were many people:

> "…who deceived and deluded the people under pretence of Divine inspiration, but were in fact for procuring innovations and changes to the government. These men prevailed with the multitude to act like madmen, and went before them into the wilderness, pretending that God would there show them the signals of liberty."

Do we see here Paul, the Apostles and the early Christians gaining influence among the people and the apparent failure of Jesus's mission gradually changing to triumph. Although for those who had misunderstood his message, and there were many among the "Fourth Philosophy" or Zealots, disaster was about to befall Jerusalem. Josephus then continues:

> "There was an Egyptian false prophet that did the Jews more mischief than the former; for he was a cheat, and pretended to be a prophet also, and he got together thirty thousand men that were deluded by him ; these he led round about from the wilderness to the mount which was called the Mount of Olives. He was ready to break into Jerusalem by force from that place; and if he could but once conquer the Roman garrison and the people, he intended to rule them by the assistance of those guards of his that were to break into the city with him".

In the *Antiquities of the Jews* (20.169–171), Josephus ignores the prophet's alleged threat of violence, writing:

> "About this time, someone came out of Egypt to Jerusalem, claiming to be a prophet. He advised the crowd to go along with him to the Mount of Olives, as it is called, which lay over against the city, at a distance of a kilometre. He added that he would show them how the walls of Jerusalem would fall down at his command, and he promised them that he would procure them an entrance into the city through those collapsed walls. Now when Felix was informed of these things, he ordered his soldiers to take their weapons and came up against them with a great number of horsemen and footmen from Jerusalem, and attacked the Egyptian and the people that were with him. He slew four hundred of them, and took two hundred alive. The Egyptian himself escaped out of the fight, but did not appear anymore."

So, was Jesus still alive at this time, protected by his family and followers? And is that why they wrote nothing about him until it was safe to do so? Furthermore, after his crucifixion, was he protected by the Therapeutae of Egypt until his return to Palestine?

Living through the past fifty years of conflict in Northern Ireland has taught me to be circumspect of journalistic reports on the situation here. Looking back at similar circumstances in Judea all those years ago has also made me appreciate all the more the true story of Jesus in the Gospels. I can remember clearly what happened here since the mid-sixties, so I will stick with the witness of the Apostles, Paul and the Evangelists, who were so close to these happenings. But I will also respect the writings of Josephus regarding

James the Just, the head of the Church of Jesus of Nazareth in Jerusalem. I do not care if there are minor differences in the accounts. It proves their authenticity. The greatest of the exegetes of that time and indeed later, not only Jesus, but James the Just, Hillel, Paul and then Johanan ben Zakkai, Akiba and Augustine emphasised that charity and loving kindness were essential to the interpretation of Scripture. Only when Jews, Christians, Muslims and others accept this can they listen with humility and true understanding to the opinions of others.

9
The Wars of the Jews

Roman persecution of Christians reached its height following the Great Fire of Rome in 64 AD for which, according to Tacitus, Nero's Government blamed the Christians. It is the tradition of the Church that both the often hostile rivals Peter and Paul were imprisoned for nine months under Nero and were put to death in the year 67 AD. St Peter was crucified in Nero's Circus, the site of which is now partially occupied by St Peter's Basilica, while St Paul, because he was a citizen of Rome, was led outside the walls to be beheaded. The following year in Palestine the settlement at Qumran was completely destroyed by the Romans. The Scribes, seeing the approaching legions, hastily stored their scrolls in the nearby caves, where they safely remained.

At this time the Roman Army in Palestine was under the command of Vespasian and his twenty-nine year old son Titus. Vespasian had commanded the Second Legion, the Augusta, which had trained principally in southern Britain. He had quickly subdued the West Country of modern England, carrying the strength of Roman arms from the Solent to the River Exe. Therefore the men chosen to fulfil the prophecy of Jesus Christ that "Jerusalem shall be trodden down by the Gentiles" were trained in Britain itself. While Vespasian was engaging in the Jewish Wars, however, Nero committed suicide. In the civil war which followed, Vespasian became Emperor of Rome, being proclaimed as such at Caesarea on the coast of Palestine. He left the last phase of the Jewish Wars, the actual destruction of Jerusalem, to his son, Titus, and made his way back to Rome to assume control of the Empire.

Herod's splendid Temple was now completed and, although most of the suburbs of Jerusalem had suffered much in rioting and siege, the magnificent edifice stood intact as a wonder of the world, described as such by Josephus in that great work, *Wars of the Jews*.

Many there must have been in Jerusalem who remembered the words of Christ saying that when the time of vengeance was at hand they should not even take up their household goods but should flee to the hills. This the first Christians dutifully did, making their way to Pella, south of the Lake of Galilee.

It was early in May of the year 70 AD that Titus entered the suburbs of the new town of Jerusalem and ordered Josephus to persuade his fellow countrymen to lay down their arms. The reply from Zealots and citizens alike was pure defiance and the city came under a desperate siege. Josephus says of this:

> "Of those who perished by famine in the city the number was prodigious and the miseries which they underwent were unspeakable. So those that were very distressed by the famine were desirous to die and those already dead were esteemed happy for they had not lived long enough either to hear or to see such miseries."

At the beginning of July the castle of Antonia, which stood near the hall in which Pontius Pilate had condemned Jesus to death, was captured by the Romans. This castle was placed on the northern wall of the Temple. For most of that month the battle for the Temple continued, since the Jews were convinced that they would be delivered from their perils at any time by the Lord, who would protect His ancient sanctuary. Titus called repeatedly for surrender and placed the blame for any resultant sacrilege on the Jews themselves, since he had no wish to desecrate their Temple. Nevertheless furious fighting continued unabated and it was to be Titus and his men who were the last to see the Temple of Herod in Jerusalem as Jesus Himself had seen it.

Early in August the Romans reached the Holy of Holies and one soldier, inspired, as Josephus puts it, "by a certain divine fury," snatched a burning torch and, lifting himself on the shoulders of his comrade, threw it through the golden window, so that flames enveloped the Sanctuary of the Lord. Josephus goes on:

> "Then did Caesar, both by calling to the soldiers, who were fighting, with a loud voice and by giving a signal to them with his right hand, order them to quench the fire. But they did not hear what he said, though he spake so loud, having their ears already dinned by a greater noise; neither did they attend to the signal he made with his hand, as some of them were still distracted with fighting and others with passion… And now, since Caesar was in no way able to restrain the enthusiastic fury of the soldiers, and the fire proceeded on more and more, he went into the holy place of the Temple with his commanders, and saw it, with what was in it, which he found to be far superior to the descriptions of foreigners and not inferior to what we ourselves boasted of and believed about it… And thus was the holy house burned down without Caesar's approval."

Even then the Jews would not surrender and once again the battering rams were pushed to the walls of Jerusalem until the city was literally beaten into the dust. Thus had come true the whole prophecy which Jesus had spoken when he said:

> "For there shall be great distress upon the land and wrath unto this people and they shall fall by the edge of the sword and shall be led captive into all nations. And Jerusalem shall be trodden down by the Gentiles until the times of the Gentiles be fulfilled." *(Luke 21: 14)*

Thus were the Jews dispersed throughout the world and the Temple of the Lord in Jerusalem was no more. At this time also the Temple at Leontopolis in Egypt was destroyed by order of Vespasian, and so, excluding perhaps those of the Therapeutae or Essenes of Egypt, none there was to sing the *Laus Perennis* in this world.

There were those who said that the destruction of the Temple was God's retribution for the execution of James the Just. But what we are sure of is that Karl Marx wrote in a letter to Engels: "If Titus had not destroyed my fatherland, I would not have been the enemy of all fatherlands."

10
The True Vine of Egypt

In Jesus's time the Essene calendar was more in vogue than the newer one of the Jerusalem priesthood and was the one used at the Last Supper, as the theologian Pope Benedict XVI has intimated. But it is to Egypt we must look for the origins of our own exegesis. At Christmas we are reminded by the Gospel of Matthew that the child Jesus was taken to Egypt to escape the cruel Herod. This parallels the story of Moses. In addition, Matthew cites the prophet Hosea: "Out of Egypt I called my Son". One does indeed wonder how long Jesus spent in that country during his life.

The ascetic sect of the Therapeutae arose in the first century AD among the Alexandrian Jews in Egypt. The only original account of them is given in *De vita contemplative* (On the contemplative Life) attributed to Philo of Alexandria. The cells of these recluses were situated on the farther shore of Lake Mareotis. Here they lived, men and unmarried women, shut up singly in their cells, giving themselves up to prayer and religious meditation. Thus Menander of Ephesus says of them:

> "The basis of their contemplations was an allegorical interpretation of scripture and they had old Theosophic writings which served to guide them in their more profound investigations of scripture. Bread and water constituted their only diet and they practised frequent fasting. They ate nothing until evening for, through contempt of the body, they were ashamed so long as sunlight was visible to take sensible nourishment to acknowledge their dependence on the world of sense. Many of them fasted for three or even six days in succession."

And it was here that Jesus may have been brought secretly by his faithful followers following his crucifixion and resurrection.

Philo (Greek: *Philon* c25 BC–50 AD) or Philo Judeus was a Hellenistic Jewish philosopher who lived in Alexandria, which was then the intellectual epicentre of the Roman world. He was a contemporary of Jesus and the Apostles but as far as we know said nothing about them, for Philo's family had connections to the Priesthood in Judea, the Hasmonean Dynasty, the Herodian Dynasty and the Julio-Claudian Dynasty in Rome. He had visited the Temple in Jerusalem at least once in his lifetime. Through his brother Alexander he had two nephews, Tiberius Julius Alexander and Marcus Julius Alexander, who was the first husband of the Herodian Princess Berenice. Like Jesus himself there are few biographical details about Philo. Those that have survived are found in his own works, especially in *Legatio ad Gaium* (Embassy to Gaius), and in Josephus. His participation in the embassy to Rome in 40 AD is the only event in his life which we can decisively date, when he represented the Alexandrian Jews before the Emperor Caligula because of civil disorder between the Alexandrian Jewish and Greek communities.

Philo attempted to fuse and harmonize Jewish and the Platonic-Stoic doctrines of Greek philosophy, but this did not result in a good reception within Rabbinic Judaism. He felt that contemporary literal interpretations of the Bible were too narrow to perceive a God who was purely beyond human understanding. Philo thought that the ineffable God had created the world through mediators, the chief of whom was the Logos or Word, the image of God, His spirit, His firstborn son, linking the finite and the infinite. Being the very mind of the Eternal God, Logos is imperishable, neither uncreated as God is, nor created as human beings are, but occupies an entrusted middle position and power in the universe. Some observers believe that Philo's concept of the Logos had a direct influence on early Christianity, others that both Philo and early Christianity are derived from a common source. Is it just possible that the common source was Jesus of Nazareth himself?

There has been some speculation that the name Therapeutae may derive from Theravada (Sanskrit स्थवरिवाद), a branch of Buddhism which uses the teaching of a collection of the oldest recorded Buddhist texts, the Pali Canon, as its doctrinal core, but which also includes a rich diversity of traditions and practices developed over its long history of interactions with various cultures and communities. It remains the most practised form of religion by people in Cambodia, Laos, Sri Lanka, Thailand and by minority groups in Vietnam, Bangladesh and China, as well as important offshoots throughout the world. However Judeo-Christianity is fundamentally different to Buddhism, though it must be said that in the East syncretism between Nestorian Christianity and Buddhism was widespread along the Silk Road in antiquity and the Middle Ages, being especially prominent in the Church of the East in China, as evidenced by the Jesus Sutras.

Every Sabbath Day the Therapeutae came together and, as the number seven was particularly sacred to them, they held a still more solemn convocation once in every seven weeks. They celebrated on this occasion a simple love feast consisting of bread seasoned with salt and hyssop. Mystic discourses were then delivered and hymns which had been handed down from the old tradition were sung. Amidst choral music, dances of mystic import were kept up late into the night. It was among the Therapeutae that the Essene exegesis developed from the prophetic to the mystical and thus scarcely surprising that they were more open to conversion to the Pauline version of Christianity, especially after 70 AD. Most authors fix the background to the Epistle to the Hebrews as Alexandria. Certainly, whatever its geographical setting, in spirit it was addressed to the Essenes.

The Community of Righteousness made an extraordinary cult of angels and the Epistle begins with an affirmation of the superiority of the Word over the angels. The whole Epistle centres on the question of the true priest and indeed we have already seen that the Essenes expressed loyalty only to the line of Aaron as the true priests of Israel. They described themselves as Sons of Zadok, the Aaronite high priest who lived during the time of Solomon. They awaited two Messiahs who would reveal themselves in the last days; one of these would be a high priest, the Messiah of Aaron, and the other of the line of David, the Messiah of Judah, who would be subordinate to him. These doctrines would have provided the main difficulties for the Christian evangelists to the Essenes. For, if Jesus could be presented as the Davidic Messiah, he was not a descendant of Aaron and therefore could not be the priestly Messiah.

The purpose of the Epistle to the Hebrews was to show that the functions of priestly and kingly Messiah could be expressed in one person. Since Melchisedec was at once a priest and king, it was expounded that the true Messiah need not belong to the line of Aaron, but was in fact a "priest for ever after the order of Melchisedec" (Hebrews 5: 6). Such an exposition would appear necessary only to a community for whom the issue of the Aaronite priesthood was of central importance.

Discontent among the Jews in Palestine had continued unabated in the Dispersion and there was again serious rebellion in the reign of the Emperor Trajan during the period 115–118 AD. It is certain that the idea of two Messiahs continued among sections of the Jewish people until at least the second Jewish Revolt against the Romans in 132–135 AD under the Emperor Hadrian for coins at the time speak of El' Azar the High Priest riding side-by-side with Bar Kochba, the Prince of Israel.

During these troubled times there lived in Alexandria one of the greatest of ancient scientists, who was at once an astronomer, mathematician and geographer. He was a native of Egypt called Claudius Ptolemaeus but today is known simply as Ptolemy. The account which Ptolemy gave of Ireland is the oldest known documentary evidence that exists of this island. Ireland and Britain were collectively known to Ancient Greek scholars as the Isles of the Pretani and from this word is developed both the Gaelic word 'Cruthin' and the ancient Welsh word 'Briton' for the inhabitants of these islands. Ptolemy was the first to record the name Uluti (Ulster) and he describes also such Pretanic tribes as the Caledonians, to whom the Romans were to give the name Picts, in that region of Britain now known as Scotland.

It is known from Tertullian that there were Christians living in parts of the British Isles not reached by the Romans in the second century AD but it is equally certain that there were Christians living in Roman Britain itself at this time. Some of these may have been refugees from the southern part of Roman Gaul which is today known as France, where it is known that there was a colony at Lyons under a Bishop Pothinus. In the year 177 AD, during the reign of the Emperor Marcus Aurelius, this colony was attacked and its bishop imprisoned. Before ministering to the Christians of Lyons the presbyter Irenaeus had studied in Asia Minor under Polycarp, who was Bishop of Smyrna and a pupil in his youth of the Apostle John.

11

The Creed of Nicaea

There are many traces of an Eastern origin and connection in the Bangor Antiphonary, including, for example, the festal observance of Saturday as well as Sunday and the presence in the Divine Office of the ceremony of the Kiss of Peace. The philosophy of the Bangor Community, however, was the true vine brought out of Egypt and the single most important influence in this was St Anthony. Anthony is generally considered as having been the first to embrace the life of a monk among the early Christians. He was born in Egypt about the middle of the third century. His spiritual descendents are the Copts and there is a Coptic inscription in Clandeboye Chapel, linked to Bangor Abbey, placed there by the first Marquis of Dufferin and Ava.

While yet a young man, though possessed with a considerable fortune, Anthony distributed the whole among his neighbours and the poor and retired to a place of deep seclusion resolved to lead the life of a hermit. In 285 he took up his residence in a decayed castle among the mountains of eastern Egypt where he spent twenty years in solitude. He thus acquired the reputation of great sanctity. At length, however, yielding to the earnest solicitations of his friends, he returned to the world in 305 and attracted crowds of eager admirers by his preaching and miraculous cures. It was not long nevertheless before he returned to the monastic life and with his followers established two monasteries, one in the mountainous district of eastern Egypt and the other near the town of Arsinoe.

In the year 305, with the resignation of the Emperors Diocletian and Maximian from the sovereignty of the Roman Empire, the two commanders, the Illyrian (Albanian) Constantius and Galvius, assumed control of the State. Constantius and his son Constantine crossed to Britain to assume the government but, following a notable expedition against the Caledonians and other Picts of the North, Constantius became ill and died at York on 25 July of the same year. Constantine was immediately proclaimed Emperor by the Army and when he married Fausta, the daughter of Maximian, in 306 he quickly consolidated his dominions.

Although one historian has calculated that the number of Christians in the Empire at this time was as low as one-fifth of the total population, the Church stood out so well against the backcloth of contemporary pagan society that

Constantine reckoned it to be a force which he would have either to accept or destroy. Being a wise statesman he chose the former course since he knew that the faith would bring a renewal of moral values into the Roman Empire. This adoption of Christianity by the Emperor changed the whole course of world history and made the fourth century a time of development, reconstruction and expansion for the Church. By 314 the British Church had become well enough organised to be able to send three bishops from the Roman cities of York, London and perhaps Lincoln to the famous Council of Arles.

'Correct' belief, the now standard orthodoxy of the Christian Church, was established chiefly at the First Ecumenical Council of Nicaea (now Iznik in Turkey) in May 325. The Council was called by the Roman Emperor Constantine I to settle what he described "as a fight over trifling and foolish verbal differences" between the major Alexandrian ecclesiatics. One group, the followers of Arius, had integrated Neoplatonism, which accented the absolute oneness of the divinity as the highest perfection, with a rationalist and literal approach to the New Testament. Jesus of Nazareth was seen as the most perfect creature of the universe whose standing had caused him to become 'God's Son', but who, as the 'Logos' or 'Word', was created by the uncreated 'Father' and thus subordinate to His will. Arius had published this thesis in the verse of his Thalia (Banquet) around 323, and it spread rapidly by the way of the popular songs of the common people.

The champion of Nicene orthodoxy was Bishop Athanasius of Alexandria in Egypt, and he and his followers eventually won the day. The resultant Nicene Creed was an enlarged and explanatory version of the Apostles' Creed in which the doctrines of Christ's divinity and of the Holy Trinity were defined. The Creed found in the Bangor Antiphonary, which is kept in the Ambrosian Library in Milan, differs in wording from all other versions which are known, and is, in substance, the original creed of Nicaea. For this reason alone the Bangor Antiphonary may be considered one of the most precious relics of Western civilisation. The Bangor School accepted orthodox Christianity as "the true vine brought out of Egypt" and through it Columbanus and his followers helped to wrest Europe from Arianism.

The Lord's Prayer

Our Father who art in heaven, hallowed be thy name,
Thy kingdom come,
Thy will be done
in earth as it is in heaven.
Give us this day our daily bread

And forgive us our trespasses
As we forgive those who trespass against us
And lead us not into temptation
But deliver us from evil.

The Creed
I believe in one God the Father Almighty, Invisible, the Maker of all things visible and invisible.
I believe in Jesus Christ, his only Son, our Lord, Almighty God,
Conceived by the Holy Ghost, born of the Virgin Mary,
Suffered under Pontius Pilate; was crucified, and buried and descended into hell.
On the third day he rose again from the dead,
Ascended into heaven, and sits at the right hand of God the Father Almighty,
From where he shall come to judge the living and the dead:
I believe in the Holy Ghost, Almighty God, having one substance with the Father and Son.
I believe in the holy catholic church, the remission of sins, the communion of saints, the resurrection of the body.
I believe in life after death and life everlasting in the glory of Christ.
All this I believe in the name of God.
Amen.

Following the Reformation, Neoplatonic mysticism rose once more in Italy. Fleeing from the Roman Catholic Inquisition its followers found an equally severe orthodoxy in Calvinist Geneva. One Michael Servetius was burned there as a heretic in 1553. Faustus Socinius was banished during the seventeenth century Counter Reformation and in Poland he founded a group based upon Arian theology. These Polish Socinians had a profound effect on Church and State in the British Isles among Calvinists and Anglicans alike. In Ireland Thomas Emlyn suffered persecution as a Socinian and in 1725 and 1828 trouble over the acceptance of the Westminster Confession of Faith (1646) led to the founding of the Non-Subscibing Presbyterian Church of Ireland which was, ironically, strongest in those modern counties of Antrim and Down, which constituted Ulster in Columbanus' day.

In 367, Athanasius decreed that heretical books should be destroyed. A corpus of writings known to us now as the 'Gnostic Gospels' were among these. Previously known to us through attacks on them by the Presbyter

Irenaeus, the second century Bishop of Lyon, several of these gospels survived by being buried at a monastery founded by a friend of Athanasius called Pachomius. The monastery was at Cheroboskian, now called Nag Hammadi, in Upper Egypt.

One finds much relevance for today in these texts, discovered in 1945, particularly as they relate to Jesus' view of women. Women are indeed regarded more highly in the Gnostics texts than in orthodox texts. The Gnostics allowed women priests and gave a special place to Mary Magdalene above all the disciples. The Gospel of Philip says:

> "...the companion of the Saviour is Mary Magdalene. But Christ loved her more than all the disciples and used to kiss her often... The rest of the disciples were offended by it. They said to him, "Why do you love her more than all of us?" The Saviour answered and said to them;" Why do I not love you as I love her?"

A text called the Dialogue of the Saviour says: "She spake as a woman who knew the call". A Gospel of Mary (Magdalene) contained in a Coptic Codex in Berlin, known as long ago as 1896 was not published until 1955.

Today special and psychological arguments continue to operate against the place of women which was such a feature of Gnosticism. A Vatican 2 document saying "Every type of discrimination... based on sex is to be overcome and eradicated as contrary to God's intent" has not been put into effect. It is remarkable that conditions today are not unlike those which pertained during the formation of the early Church. Now we have the Dead Sea Scrolls and the Nag Hammadi texts. But not only that, we have many women teachers of vision to show us again the Way of the Lord in a manner relevant to our own times.

Such inspired people already know in some mysterious way the true wisdom of human existence. They see out only to see in. Such mystics are never really at home in a lawed and ordered society with its organised Church. The ebb and flow of their exegesis must be allowed that freedom to grow which is necessary for the maturation of the human species. Neither force, nor power, nor autonomy can provide inroads into this process of maturation, for without freedom there will be a holding back in that evolution necessary to prepare us for our rightful place in the universe. I often wonder whether the 'orthodoxy' usually attributed in common Christian heritage to the formulation of the Nicene fathers has been more of an oppression than a safeguard. As a collective phenomenon human beings are still at the stage of the toddler, who is many times distressing, but who, with care and patience, will evolve and progress to maturity.

One of the reluctant soldiers of Constantine was a man names Martin, a native of Pannonia (modern Hungary) and an officer in the Imperial cavalry. Following his conversion to Christianity Martin became the Apostle of Gaul and upheld the rights of the apostolic authority of the Church. St Martin was familiar with monastic ideals of St Anthony and it was through him that these ideals reached the British Isles. Created Bishop of Tours in 371, Martin appointed a monastery or 'White House' at Marmoutiers and an early form of a new *Laus Perennis* was begun there. On his way home from Rome the Romano-Briton Ninian (Uinniau) of Rheged (Galloway) stayed with St Martin at Marmoutiers and studied the new way of life.

And so it was that in 398 St Ninian founded his own White House or 'Candida Casa' at Whithorn in Wigtownshire, Galloway, which resembled, where possible, the parent house in Gaul. Here has been found the Latinus Stone, the earliest Christian monument in Scotland. It bears an inscription written in spoken Latin, rather than in a monastic form. Although little is known about St Ninian or the earliest history of his foundation, it is clear that in the fifth and sixth centuries Candida Casa was to become an important centre of evangelism to both Britain and the north of Ireland. On St Ninian's Day, 16 September 2009, there was a debate in the Scottish parliament which recognised Whithorn as the Cradle of Christianity in Scotland. On the same day in 2010 the Queen welcomed Pope Benedict XVI to Scotland.

But to return to our story, soon the originally Egyptian pattern of monastic life was being practised all over the Western Atlantic seaboard. Mabillon has stated that St Martin's Marmoutiers had early adopted the celebration of the *Laus Perennis* and among those who visited Marmoutiers to take part in it was a young man named Patrick. Before we come again to Ireland however, let us look at the Muslim Jesus.

12
The Muslim Jesus

When I was a Paediatric Registrar in the Belfast City Hospital, I was asked to look after a devout young Muslim from Pakistan. I brought him to the Doctors' home where they were watching a Rugby match on the television. Someone shouted out an obscenity and the young Muslim became deathly white and I practically had to carry him out of the room and gave him water to drink. I asked him: "Brother, what is wrong?" He said: "Beloved Ian, they were blaspheming against the name of our Prophet Jesus."

Despite the obvious stereotypes and pure ignorance that have sometimes obscured it, the long relationship which has existed between Christians and Muslims has also been mutually very appreciative and productive. No more so than that both traditions have for centuries shared a deep love for the Prophet of Galilee, Jesus of Nazareth.

Isa Ibn Maryam (Arabic: عيسى, translit.:□*Īsā*), known as Jesus in the New Testament, is considered to be a Messenger of God and *al-Masih* (the Messiah) in Islam, who was sent to guide the Children of Israel (*banī isrā'īl*) with a new scripture, *al-Injīl* (the Gospel). The belief that Jesus is a prophet is required in Islam, as it is for all prophets named in the Qur'an. This is reflected in the fact that he is clearly a significant figure in the Qur'an (appearing in 93 *ayaat* or verses).

The Qur'an states that Jesus was born to Mary (Arabic: *Maryam)* as the result of virginal conception, a miraculous event which occurred by the decree of God (Arabic: *Allah*). To aid in his ministry to the Jewish people, Jesus was given the ability to perform miracles (such as healing the blind and bringing dead people back to life), all by the permission of God rather than of his own power. The Qur'an emphasizes that Jesus was a mortal human being who, like all other prophets, had been divinely chosen to spread God's message.

The Muslim Jesus, Sayings and Stories in Islamic Literature, edited and translated by Tarif Khalida 2001, presents in English translation the largest collection ever assembled of the sayings and stories of Jesus in Arabic Islamic literature. In doing so it traces a tradition of love and reverence for Jesus that has characterised Islamic thought for more than a thousand years. An invaluable resource for the study of religions, the collection documents how one culture, that of Islam, assimilated the towering figure of another, that of Christianity. As such it is a work of great significance for the understanding of both and of profound implications for modern inter-sectarian relations and ecumenical dialogue. For demeaning of the name of Jesus causes great offence to believers of both.

The People of the Book (Arabic: أهل الكتاب 'Ahl al-Kitāb) is a term used to designate non-Muslim adherents to faiths which have a revealed scripture called, in Arabic, *Ahl-Al-Kitab* (Arabic: أهل الكتاب 'the People of the Book' or 'people of the Scripture'). The three types of adherents to faiths that the Qur'an mentions as *people of the book* are the Children of Israel, including Jews, Karaites and Samaritans, all Christians and Sabians. But some Muslim scholars have also seen the Supreme Creator Being of the Book in Hinduism and even in its Buddhist off-shoot.

In Islam, the Muslim scripture, the Qur'an, is taken to represent the completion of these scriptures, and to synthesize them as God's true, final, and eternal message to humanity. Because the People of the Book recognize the God of Abraham as the one and only god, as do Muslims, and as they practice revealed faiths based on divine ordinances, tolerance and autonomy should be accorded to them in societies governed by sharia (Islamic divine law).

In Judaism the term 'People of the Book' (Hebrew: עם הספר, *Am HaSefer*) was used to refer specifically to the Jewish people and the Torah, and to the Jewish people and the wider canon of written Jewish law (including the Mishnah and the Talmud). Adherents of other Abrahamic religions, which arose later than Judaism, were not added. As such, the appellation is accepted by Jews as a reference to an identity rooted fundamentally in Torah.

In Christianity, the Roman Catholic Church rejects the similar expression 'religion of the book' as a description of the Christian faith, preferring the term 'religion of the Word of God', since the faith of Jesus Christ, according to Roman Catholic teaching, is not found solely in the Christian Scriptures, but also in the Sacred Tradition and Magisterium of the Infallible Church. Nevertheless, members of Protestant denominations, such as the Baptists and Methodists, particularly in the United States of America, forming the Common Identity of all its inhabitants, Episcopalians, Presbyterians, Seventh Day Adventists, as well as the old Puritans and Shakers, have embraced the term 'People of the Book.'

So it is that respect for the Book of God is considered a Divine Ordinance by a large percentage of the people of our world. However the decline of the old aristocracy in the British Isles (Pretania) following the Great War has culminated in the rise of a new group of individuals and the replacement of new money for old. These people control our lives and, worshipping mammon rather than God, they generally despise the Book which tells them otherwise:

> "Lay not up for yourselves treasures upon earth, where moth and rust doth corrupt, and where thieves break through and steal: But lay up for yourselves treasures in heaven, where neither moth nor rust doth corrupt, and where thieves do not break through nor steal: For where your treasure is, there will your heart be also. No man can serve two masters: for either he will hate the one, and love the other; or else he will hold to the one, and despise the other. Ye cannot serve God and mammon." *(Matthew 6: 19–21 and 24)*

13
Patrick of Lecale

To the Irish people the main credit for the introduction of Christianity to Ireland belongs to St Patrick, so that every 17 March we celebrate St Patrick's Day. Yet, despite Patrick's pre-eminent place in the history of the Irish Church, we do not know just how much of his story is historically accurate. Ironically, the only first-hand accounts of Patrick come from two works which he reputedly wrote himself, the Confession and the Epistle to Coroticus (Ceretic Guletic of Alt Clut, modern Dumbarton).

Further, the reference to his arrival in the *Annals* cannot be taken as necessarily factual either, as it is now believed that the *Annals* only became contemporary in the latter part of the sixth century, and fifth century entries were therefore 'backdated'. The question of Palladius and his mission from Rome leads to still more uncertainty, with some scholars even proposing the idea that there could have been two Patricks. Francis Byrne suggested that "we may suspect that some of the seventh century traditions originally referred to Palladius and have been transferred, whether deliberately or as a result of genuine confusion, to the figure of Patrick."

This uncertainty must be borne in mind when we come to look at his story. He was born towards the end of the fourth century in Bannaven Taberniae, a village somewhere in Romanised Britain. His father was Calpornius, a deacon, who was the son of Potitus. Patrick was brought up in a small villa not far away, where, he says, he was made captive at the age of about 16 years and taken to Ulster as a slave and sold to a Dal mBuinne Cruthin chieftain called Milchu, (Miliucc moccu Boin) of the Bonrige, who used him to tend livestock around Mount Slemish near Ballymena in County Antrim. After six years of servitude he managed to escape from Ireland, first going by boat to the Continent, then two years later returning to his parents in Britain. It is thought that during this period he learned the divine wisdom of Marmoutiers.

Despite his parents being anxious that he would now remain at home, Patrick had a vision of an angel who had come from Ireland with letters. In one of these was relayed the message: "We beg you, Holy youth, to come and walk amongst us once again." To Patrick, the letters "completely broke my heart and I could read no more and woke up." Tradition tells that Patrick eventually made the journey back to Ireland, finally landing in Lecale, County

Down in the territory of Dichu (of the Ulaid) who became his first convert. Dichu's barn (*sabhall* or Saul) near Downpatrick was the first of his churches. So deep was the faith of Patrick that it is said that, "each night he sang a hundred psalms to adore the King of Angels."

Not everyone was necessarily overjoyed to see the return of Patrick. His old master Milchu, a convinced pagan, when forewarned of an impending visit by Patrick, set fire to his house and all his property, then perished in the flames rather than risk being converted. Nor was every conversion lasting – King Laeghaire, despite being baptised, remained pagan at heart and was buried at his own request with pagan rites. Estyn Evans wrote that "Professor RAS Macalister of University College, Dublin, a Gaelic enthusiast turned cynic, used to say in private that the number of believing Christians in the early centuries of Christianity could probably be reckoned by counting the number of Irish saints."

Among those who accompanied St Patrick was St Sechnall who was the earliest Christian poet in Ireland. It was in St Sechnall's church of Dunshaughlin that the beautiful eucharistic hymn *Sancti Venite* was first sung. The tradition was that this incomparable hymn was chanted by a choir of angels during the Holy Communion and hence arose the custom ever afterwards in Ireland of singing this hymn at the Communion. Hence, too, the title which the hymn bears in the Bangor Antiphonary, which is the only ancient work in which it is found, 'Hymn during the Communion of the Priests'.

Two stanzas are as follows:

Sancti Venite	Draw nigh, ye Holy ones,
Christi Corpus Sumite	And take the body of the Lord.
Sanctum bibentes	And drink the sacred blood He shed
Quo redempti sanguinum	For your redemption
Alpha et Omega,	The beginning and the end,
Ipse Christus Dominum	The Christ, The Lord,
Venit venturus	Who comes and will come again
Judicare homines.	To judge all men.

14
The Bird of Heaven

AMONG PATRICK'S FIRST converts were Bronagh, daughter of Milchu, and her son Mochaoi (Mahee), whose birthname was Caolàn. St Mochaoi was to found the great monastery of Nendrum on Mahee Island in Loch Cuan (Strangford Lough), and is associated with the saint in the legends which grew around Patrick's name. These legends firmly place Down as the cradle of Christianity in Ireland. Patrick himself is said to have founded Armagh around 444, and the selection of a site so close to Emain Macha would strongly suggest that the Ulster capital was still the most powerful over-kingdom in Ireland at that time. From Down the cult of Patrick spread to Connor in Antrim and then to Armagh, which became the ecclesiastical centre of Ireland.

As far as Nendrum is concerned, the picture of its development is much clearer in the seventh century, for no excavated finds have been found earlier than this. But from 639 onwards the *Annals* record the deaths of Nendrum clergy, including bishops, abbots and a scribe. This would suggest an active, populous monastery, and an early litany says "nine times fifty monks laboured under the authority of Mochaoi of Noendruim." Furthermore, dendrochronology has dated a tide mill on Mahee Island to the year 619, making this one of the oldest excavated tide mills anywhere in the world. The monastery came to an end at some time between 974 and 1178, but its church served a parish until the site was abandoned in the fifteenth century. Some remains of the monastery can still be seen.

But of all the stories told in the old books of Ireland the most strangely beautiful is that of the Bird of Heaven. The story of the Bird of Heaven is this:

> "Mahee was the first man to whom Patrick gave a gospel. And so it was that the grandson of Milchu gathered around him young men to build a church of wood in the manner of the people of Ulster. And as he was about to rest after cutting his portion of timber, he heard a bright bird singing on the blackthorn near him. This bird was more beautiful than all the birds of the world and Mahee, greatly moved by its song, listened enthralled. And the bird said 'Surely this is diligent work, O Holy man.'
>
> The young man was astonished to hear the bird of such wonderful song speak to him in human words and he said, 'Who can thus address

me?' And the bird immediately replied, 'A man of the people of my Lord,' which is to say, an Angel of God from Heaven. 'All hail to Thee,' said Mahee with awe, 'and wherefore hast thou come hither?', 'I am here by command to address thee from my Lord, that I may encourage thee in thy good work, but also because of the love in my heart for thy Lord Jesus to amuse thee for a time with my sweet singing.' "I am glad of that," said the young man.

Thereupon the bird sang to Mahee a song of such singular beauty that he thought that this surely was the Song of God. When he had finished his singing the bird fixed his beak in the feathers of his wing and slept. But Mahee continued to hear the sweetness and perfect harmony of that song for 150 years, standing entranced beside the little bundle of timbers in the middle of the wood in Ulster. And although one and a half centuries were in that angelic song to Mahee the time did not seem any longer than one hour of the day, nor in that hour was there anything but contentment and peace, nor did any age come upon him, nor any withering of the green branches he had gathered for his Lord; nor in the wood itself did a single leaf of a single tree turn to the red and yellow gold of autumn before his eyes. And even the spiders stopped their spinning and the bees gathered not the nectar from the fields before him anymore.

Then suddenly the bird took his beak from his wing and Mahee heard no more his perpetual praise. So the Angel bade him farewell. When the bird was gone Mahee lifted his timbers and made for home as in a dream. And in amazement he looked at that place he had not long left; for there he found a church already built. And a man strange to him passed and told him that this was the church of St Mahee. Then Mahee spoke to the children of God within, but they knew him not. 'Tell us your name and lineage,' they inquired, and he said to them, 'I am Mahee, son of Bronagh, daughter of Milchu the King.' And he told them his tale and they all knew him and knelt to him. And they made a shrine of the wood, and afterwards built a great church at that place. And surpassingly white Angels often alighted there, or sang hymns to it from the branches of the forest trees, or leaned with their foot on tiptoe, their eyes on the horizon, their ear to the ground, their wings flapping, their bodies trembling, waiting to send tidings of prayer and repentance with a beat of their wings to the King of the Everlasting."

It is written that twice was Mahee Abbot of Nendrum. And that little island in Strangford Lough, anciently known as Nendrum and which lies seven miles south-east of the village of Comber and sixteen miles from Belfast, is now called Mahee Island and is surely a holy place. There were many who thought that Mahee was dead when he was seen no more by his fellow monks in the forest of Nendrum in Ulster.

But at first it was written:

> "A sleep without decay of the body,
> Mahee of Nendrum slept;
> Of the people of the congregation where the Sage was
> He did not find the great-great-grandchildren.
> Three melodies of delightful music
> The angel, in the shape of a bird, sang,
> In the middle of a wood, at the foot of a tree,
> Fifty years each melody lasted."

It may only be a story that the song of the Angel of God was sung to Mahee, and that there were two persons of that name, but the truth is that there arose at that place the great monastery of Nendrum. Here was educated Colman who was of the same people of Mahee, the Cruthin of Ulster. Colman was to found the great school of Dromore, but first at Nendrum itself he helped to educate Finnian or Uinnian, British *Uinniau* (495–589) who travelled first to Candida Casa and then to Rome, whence he returned to his native land with the first complete copy of St Jerome's Vulgate version of the Bible. He also founded at Movilla, outside Newtownards in County Down, another great school, the most famous of pupil of which was St Columba, the Light of the Celtic West. Finnian is said to have been of the Dal Fiatach, and thus could be described as Irish, British or both. But one of those who helped Columba in his mission among the Picts or Cruthin of Alba (modern Scotland) was a man, definitely of the Ulster Cruthin, the Ancient British Pretani, whose name was Comgall.

15

Comgall of the Cruthin

The founder of Bangor, Comgall, was born at Magheramorne, County Antrim, in 517, of the people of the Cruthin. He lived in that old kingdom which Milchu had ruled, known now as Dalaradia. His father was Setna, a Pictish warrior, and his mother was known as Briga. Dalaradia (North-West, Mid and South Antrim) was one of the main sub-kingdoms of Ulster, the others being Dalriada (North-East Antrim), Dal Fiatach (North Down and Ards) and Iveagh (South Down). From the fourth century onward Ulster had consisted only of that territory now comprised by the present counties of Down, Antrim, the eastern part of Londonderry and northern Louth.

At the height of its extent of power and influence the kingdom had stretched as far south as the Boyne River but, due to continual invasion by the Southern Gaels under their kings, the "Ui Neill" and their alleged descendants, the above territory only retained the right to the name of Ulster. Donegal (Venniconia) had been completely Gaelicised and the autonomous Cruthin dynasties driven east where they maintained their independence, due no doubt to the proximity of the major Pictish (Caledonian Pretani) kingdom in what is now known as Scotland.

Having shown great promise in his early years of a vocation to the Christian ministry, Comgall was educated under St Fintan at Clonenagh, and is also said to have studied under Finnian at Clonard and Mobhi Clairenach at Glasnevin. Following his ordination as a deacon and priest by Bishop Lugidius, Comgall was imbued with a great missionary zeal and founded in Dal Fiatach the great monastery of Bangor, under the patronage of Cantigern, Queen of Dalaradia, whose life he had saved. To distinguish it from the other Bangors in the British Isles it became known as Bangor Mor, which is to say, Bangor the Great.

The monastic settlement itself and its Rule were very similar to the Community of Righteousness in Palestine and consisted of a large number of huts made of wattles which were like stakes with clay and mortar. These huts were situated around the church or oratory with its refectory, school, scriptorium and hospice. The whole establishment was surrounded by a vallum which consisted of a rampart and ditch.

Life at Bangor was very severe. The food was sparse and even milk was considered an indulgence. Only one meal per day was allowed and that not until evening. Confession was held in public before the whole community and severe acts of penance were observed. There was silence at meal times and at other times conversation was restricted to the minimum. Comgall himself was extremely pious and austere and it is said that he rose in the middle of the night to recite psalms and say his prayers while immersed in the nearby stream.

The strength of the community lay in its form of worship. The choral services were based on the antiphonal singing from Gaul, introduced into the West by Ambrose of Milan in the fourth century. Bangor became famous for this type of choral psalmody and it spread from there throughout Europe. The glory of Bangor was the celebration of a perfected and refined *Laus Perennis* and in singing this the Cruthin of Bangor entered into a convenant of mutual love and service in the Church of Jesus Christ. Because of the 3,000 students and monks in Bangor and its daughter churches, it was possible to have a continuous chorus of the Divine Praise sung by large choirs which were divided into groups, each of which took regular duty and sang with a refinement not possible when St Martin was organising the raw recruits of Gaul.

The *Cursus Psalmorum* in the Divine Office may be exhibited conveniently in tabular form as follows:

Name of Office	Hour	No. of Psalms
1. Ad Secundam	Prime 6 am	3
2. Ad Tertiam	Terce 9 am	3
3. Ad Sextam	Sext Noon	3
4. Ad Nonam	None 3 pm	3
5. Ad Vespertinam	Vespers 6 pm	12
6. Ad initium Noctis	1st Nocturn 9 pm	12
7. Ad medium Noctis	2nd Nocturn Midnight	12
8. Ad Matutinam	3rd Nocturn with Lauds	24 or 36 (Mon–Fri)
	or Matins 3 am	36 to 75 (Sat, Sun)

This shows that the Bangor Rule drew a distinction between Saturday and Sunday nights and the other five nights of the week. On each of these two nights from 1 November to 25 March, 75 psalms were sung, *Ad Matutinam*, with 25 anthems, each anthem being said after three psalms, so that the whole psalter was recited every week during those two nights. From 25 March to 24 June the number of psalms was diminished weekly by one anthem and three psalms, so that on mid-summer day there remained about 12 anthems and 36 psalms. Then, as the nights drew longer, each week brought an additional anthem with three additional psalms so that by 1 November the total was reached again of 25 anthems and 75 psalms. This was the rule for Saturdays and Sundays. The rule for the other five nights seemed to be as follows: it was laid down that 24 or 36 psalms were to be said *Ad Matutinam*. The full number was 36 but in the shorter summer nights only 24 psalms were to be recited.

This arrangement of the *Cursus Psalmorum* in the Church in Ireland was unique and interesting, pointing again to an Eastern origin. The psalms were assigned to each of the day hours which were to be followed by a number of devotions in the form of versicles including collects (i) for our sins; (ii) for all Christian people; (iii) for persons consecrated to God in the grades of the ministry; (iv) for those who give alms; (v) for our enemies. This whole arrangement would have been difficult to carry out under any circumstances and in any place. If practicable in the warm nights of southern Gaul, it must have been almost intolerable in the chilly nights in Ireland.

16
The Bangor Praise

THE SEVENTH CENTURY manuscript already described as the Bangor Antiphonary was given that name by the famous Italian scholar, Muratori. However, the manuscript is not, strictly speaking, a true antiphonary since its contents are as follows:

1	Song of Moses
2	Hymn of St Hilary on Christ
3	Hymn of the Apostles
4–6	Three short canticles
7	Hymn on the Lord's day, the Te Deum with a short preface
8	Hymn during the communion of the priests
9	Hymn when the wax light is blessed
10	Hymn for midnight
11	Hymn on the birthday of the martyrs or on Saturday at Matins
12	Hymn at Matins on Lord's Day
13	Hymn to St Patrick, teacher of the Irish
14	Hymn to St Comgall our Abbot
15	Hymn to St Calemlac
16–34	Collects for the canonical hours
35–36	The Creed, the Lord's Prayer
37–94	Occasional prayers and collects
95	Versicles of the Family of Bangor
96–128	Miscellaneous
129	Commemoration of our Abbots

The Antiphonary was, therefore, more a companion volume to the Psalterium and Lectionarium for use in the Divine Office on either (i) Easter Even and Easter Day or (ii) on Saturdays and Sundays in Eastertide or (iii) on Saturdays and Sundays throughout the year and also on Feasts of Martyrs. Rather than an antiphonary it might be better described as a Book of Praise. Traces of the Spanish-Gaulish influence are further seen in the expression 'Salvator Mundi' which occurs frequently in the Bangor Collects. This title of Jesus Christ as the Saviour of the World is a frequent occurrence in the devotions of the old Gaulish Church. The form of the Nicene Creed and the Eucharistic anthems also show strong Gaulish affinities.

The Bangor Church, however, was hampered by contemporary politics in Ireland. Subject to continuing aggression by the "Ui Neill", their alleged descendants and internal dissension, the Cruthin further declined in Ireland. In an entry in the *Annals of Ulster* it is recorded that in 563 the Cruthin were defeated at the Battle of Moneymore by the "Ui Neill of the North". The opposing armies were led on the one side by "Seven Kings of the Cruthin including Hugh" and on the other side by one Baetan with two kings of the Cruthin in alliance with the "northern Ui Neill". The latter, Clan Connall, who were actually Gaelicised Cruthin, and Clan Owen were rewarded with the territory of Lei and Arda Eolairg, which is today north Antrim (Ballymoney) and east Londonderry.

The influence of St Columba in these events cannot be overestimated. As an important member of the "Ui Neill" and a great ecclesiastic, his position was unique. Though he was not above using their temporal power for his own ends, as shown by the Battle of Cuildrevne in 561, Columba exercised a restraining influence on the "Ui Neill". Comgall was, therefore, at this time able to maintain his friendship with Columba, the two having been fellow students at Glasnevin and Columba having been ordained deacon at nearby Movilla (Newtownards). About 565 Comgall, with St Canice of Kilkenny, accompanied Columba on his great mission to the Pictish King Bridei. Following this, Iona, Columba's foundation, "held for a long time pre-eminence over the monasteries of all the Picts and was their superior in ruling their communities." (Bede) Thus Iona became the centre of the Scottish-Irish cultural province.

At this time the Dalriada dynasty had extended from Ireland into the country of the Epidian Cruthin in western Scotland and in 574 Columba crowned his kinsman Aedan King of the Dalriads on Iona. Columba's friendship with Aedan was of paramount importance for both Church and State in Dalriada. He advised Aedan at the Convention of Druimcett in 575 when Aedan refused to pay tribute to Hugh, King of the "Ui Neill". In his relations with the Cruthin of Dalaradia, with whom he was not apparently related, Columba however showed the prejudices of a scion of the "Ui Neill". About 579 there appears to have been a dispute between Columba and Comgall regarding the Church of Ros-Torathair, a Bangor foundation, which resulted in a battle at Coleraine between the Cruthin and the "Ui Neill".

Political dissension in Ireland had secondary effects in Scotland. As well as Pictland, the natural extension of the Bangor mission was to Galloway, where the population had been greatly leavened by Irish immigration, and the 'Irish Picts' or Cruthin crossing there naturally insisted on having Cruthinic clerics as their instructors in the faith. That was undoubtedly the reason why Galloway came to be considered Pictish. About the year 580 St Donnan, a Cruthin of Bangor, laboured in Galloway and in 590 he was followed by St Dagan who eventually succeeded the Columban cleric, St Euchadius, as Abbot of Candida Casa. It was through such disciples as well as Columbanus and Gall that Comgall became known as, "one of the greatest teachers of missionaries the world has ever seen."

Only one sample of his writings has come down to us and it is found among the literature of his greatest disciple, Columbanus:

> "If the cultivator of the land and husbandman, when preparing the soil to commit to it the seed, does not consider his work all done when he has broken up the earth with a strong shear, and by the action of the plough has reduced the stubborn soil, but further endeavours to cleanse the ground of unfruitful weeds, to clear it of injurious rubbish and to pluck up by the root the spreading shoots of thorns and brambles, fully persuaded that his land will never produce a good crop unless it be reclaimed from mischievous plants, applying to himself the words of the prophet, 'Break up your fallow ground and sow not upon thorns,' how much more does it behove us, who believe the hope of our fruits to be laid up, not on earth but in heaven, to cleanse from vicious passions the field of our heart, and not suppose that we have done enough when we subdue the ground of our bodies by the labour of fasting and of watching, unless we primarily study to correct our vices and reform our morals."

The Rule of Comgall is lost but we may be sure that it was little different from the still extant Rule of Columbanus.

17
Columbanus of Europe

WITH THE FALL of the Western Roman Empire there was a widespread incursion of barbarian tribes such as the Goths, Vandals and Franks into the western and southern parts of Europe and the curtain of the Dark Ages descended upon them. It was the glory of the Bangor Church that during the seventh, eighth and ninth centuries the Light of the Gospel as well as the great learning of Ireland was carried to Gaul, Switzerland, Germany, Austria and Italy, and so Bangor became indeed the light of the Roman World. The piety and learning of the Bangor monks were unrivalled in Christendom and it was mainly due to them that Ireland became known as the island of saints and scholars.

Pope Pius XI has said, "The more light that is shed by scholars in the period known as the Middle Ages the clearer it becomes that it was thanks to the initiative and labours of Columbanus that the rebirth of Christian virtue and civilisation over a great part of Gaul, Germany and Italy took place." The French poet Leon Cathlin concurs in saying, "He is, with Charlemagne, the greatest figure of our Early Middle Ages," and Daniel-Rops of the French Academy has also said that he was "a sort of prophet of Israel, brought back to life in the sixth century, as blunt in his speech as Isaias or Jeremias… For almost fifty years souls were stirred by the influence of St Columbanus. His passing through the country started a real contagion of holiness."

Columbanus was born of the old Leinster Cruthin (Loigis) about the year 543. His *Life*, published by Surius, was written by an Italian monk of Bobbio called Jonas who came from Susa. Although this work is full enough in details regarding his career on the Continent there are few facts of his youth in Ireland. The informants of Jonas were members of Columbanus's own Community at Bobbio, who were the companions of the saint. Therefore, it is an extremely valuable eye-witness account. Columbanus decided as a young man to enter the religious life. Fearful that the ties of matrimony might prevent him from this, he decided to leave home for ever and go north to Ulster. When his mother tried to dissuade him from leaving by throwing herself down across the threshold, Columbanus strode over her prostrate body. It is unlikely he ever saw her again. He travelled first to the island of Cleenish on Lough Erne where he received his early education under the celebrated scholar Sinell. His strength of purpose was that required by Comgall of his monks and so it was natural that Columbanus should come to the Cruthinic foundation at Bangor where he remained for many years as a disciple and friend of Comgall.

At this time the Eastern Roman Empire was ruled and kept intact by Flavius Anicius Justinianus , known to us now as Justinian the Great. Justinian's reign was indeed filled with the greatest of events, both in peace and in war. He was a brilliant soldier and statesman. He codified the law and established the monastic school of St Catherine at Mount Sinai in Egypt. Here resided the celebrated Codex Sinaiticus of the Greek Bible until it was removed by Tischendorf, and it is an important centre of the Greek Orthodox Church until this day. Its library still possesses the oldest of the Wisdom of the Desert Fathers which was learned in the original Greek by Comgall and Columbanus at Bangor.

Bangor missionaries were now spreading throughout Pictland and Ireland and in 589 the greatest mission of all was trusted to Columbanus – the mission to Europe. In that year he set out with twelve companions and from reference in Jonas's and in Columbanus's own letters we have the names of most of them. First, there was Gall, who became almost as well-known as his master; Dogmal, who acted as Columbanus's minister; Cummina, Eunocus, Columbanus the younger, Equonanus, Hugh and Libranus. The original group probably also included Deicola, Lua, Caldwald and Leobard. The latter two monks have Anglo-Saxon names and it is probable that the group included representatives of all the peoples of the British Isles, since the monastery at Bangor was a truly international one. After spending a short time in Britain, possibly in the Thames Valley where Irish monks had settled previously, the group of brothers arrived in the Merovingian kingdom of Burgundy in Gaul in 590.

The Merovingian dynasty of Frankish kings was descended from Clovis, who died on 27 November 511. He was their first Christian ancestor; from his name comes the modern Louis. Gaul had by now been divided into three kingdoms: Neustria, which comprised that territory lying roughly between the Loire and Meuse rivers; Austrasia, which comprised that territory east of this as far as the Rhine and some way beyond it, continuing up the valley of the Rhine into Switzerland; and Burgundy, which comprised the territory to the south as far as the Rhone valley. For the generation following the death of Clovis the three kingdoms were convulsed by civil disorder and internecine feuds, so that of the grandsons of Clovis only one – Gunthram, king of Burgundy and Austrasia – was still alive when Columbanus entered Gaul.

Gunthram warmly received the missionaries and established them at a place called Annegray which was the site of a ruined Roman castle, situated in the modern department of the Haute-Saône. Here the monks repaired the ruined temple of Diana and made it into their first church, rededicating it to St Martin of Tours. The king offered them every appreciation in terms of food and money but they declined, preferring to keep to the monastic ideals to which their lives were committed. Columbanus himself was wont to walk deep into the Burgundian forest, heedless of either starvation or danger, trusting always in the Providence of God. He took with him only the Bible he had transcribed in his beloved Bangor. Thus for weeks, and perhaps months, he led a life identical to that of John the Baptist in the Wilderness. But his spirit was the Spirit of Bangor, his learning was the Learning of Bangor and his rule was the Rule of Bangor.

18
The Community of Luxeuil

Now, as the number of monks in the monastery at Annegray increased daily, it became necessary for the community to seek a more suitable site. King Gunthram had died in 593 and young Childebert II now ruled over Burgundy and Austrasia. Through the offices of Chagneric, one of the courtiers, the king's permission was granted to build a second monastery eight miles west of Annegray, beside the River Breuchin, among the ruins of the former Roman fort at Luxovium, which had been completely destroyed by Attila and his Huns in 451.

Here at the foot of the Vosges mountains, close by a healing stream, there arose the great Community of Luxeuil. Although the site was once completely deserted and overgrown, this exactly suited Columbanus, for he loved manual labour as much as he loved solitude. So great did it become that the most noble youths of the Franks asked to be admitted to its brotherhood. As they grew in holiness so they grew in happiness for surely the blessing of God was upon them and as their community increased it was necessary to make a third foundation at Fontaine, three miles north of Luxeuil.

The Community of Columbanus grew so large that it was necessary for the three centres to have a written Rule. The Columbanus therefore composed for them a *Regula Monachorum* or 'Rule of the Monks', which was an exposition of the basic principles of monasticism. The central discipline of this was obedience. There can be little doubt that the early chapters are a summary of the Good Rule of Bangor written by Comgall himself. As well as this, Columbanus wrote a *Regula Coenobialis* or 'Community Rule' which lists the punishments to be meted out for any breaches of the discipline of the Rule.

The form in which it exists today probably contains later additions by Columbanus's successors in Luxeuil but the opening section must go back to Columbanus himself. For the lay and clerical penitents who came to Luxeuil Columbanus wrote a further Penitential. This, too, was probably a Bangor conscription and shows great similarities to that of Finnian (British Uinnian) of Movilla. Atonement for sin required the practice of the opposite virtue:

> "The talkative is to be punished with silence, the restless with the practice of gentleness, the gluttonous with fasting, the sleepy with watching, the proud with imprisonment, the deserter with expulsion."

Dr JF Kenney has written that the Rule of Columbanus forms a 'Mirror of Perfection' for those who were intent on pursuing the religious life:

> "Acceptance with unflinching logic of the precepts of Christ as preserved in the New Testament is its essential characteristic. A severity seemingly greater than human nature could endure results; absolute obedience to the will of the senior; heavy and unremitting toil, mortification of the flesh to a degree that might be expected to impair the physical strength, are some of its impositions."

It is the only monastic rule of Irish origin, written in the Latin language, which still survives, and it is the earliest and most informative of all the rules which can be regarded as Irish. Luxeuil quickly became the Mother House of the three Communities and the most celebrated, and classical studies were of the utmost importance. The art of music was prominent as in Bangor and was taught at a level at that time unknown in Europe. H Zimmer has written:

> "They were the instructors in every branch of science and learning of the time, possessors and bearers of a higher culture than was at that time to be found anywhere on the Continent, and can surely claim to have been the pioneers – to have laid the cornerstone of western culture on the Continent."

In 597 Columba of the "Ui Neill" died on the island of Iona and in 603 Comgall of the Cruthin, whose Patron had been the beautiful Cantigern, Queen of Dalaradia, died at his monastery in Bangor, in the ninety-first year of his age, in the fiftieth year and third month and tenth day of his presidency, on the sixth of the Ides of May… And of Comgall they wrote in the Bangor Antiphonary:

> **Amavit Christus Comgillum**, Christ loved Comgall
> **Bene et ipse Dominum**, Well, too, did he the Lord.

19
To Bregenz

Now the strict Penitential of Columbanus infringed the authority of the local Frankish bishops. But it was only with his insistence on celebrating Easter according to the British calculation that he was left open to the charge of unorthodoxy. Not even that finest of Popes, Gregory the Great, could convince Columbanus that what had been handed down to his monks by the saints of Ireland could possibly be wrong. They had no wish to impose their usages on others but required to be left alone to themselves. Columbanus was indeed a man of strong will and he remonstrated with the synod of French bishops who objected to his practices with letters both to them and Pope Gregory on the subject, "Surely it is better for you", he wrote, "to comfort rather than disturb us, poor old men, strangers too, in your midst. Let us rather love one another in the charity of Christ, striving to fulfil his precepts and, therefore, secure a place in the assembly of the just made perfect in Heaven." However, the Irish practices were not in accordance with the contemporary discipline of the Church and certainly did not win Columbanus any affectation in the eyes of the Franks who were merely following that discipline.

Further trouble was to follow. Following the death of King Childebert in 595, his two sons became Kings of Austrasia and Burgundy. As both were minors their grandmother Brunhilde acted as Queen Regent and soon Gaul entered again a period of civil disorder. When the new young King of Burgundy, Theuderich (French Thierry, German Dietrich), grew to manhood he put aside his lawful wife and committed himself to a life of debauchery by installing concubines in the Royal household. The infamous Brunhilde instructed Columbanus to confirm Theuderich's illegitimate children, but the Abbot refused and thus incurred the Queen Mother's undying enmity. When Columbanus further denied Theuderich admission to the monastery at Luxeuil the Burgundian king determined to banish the great man and his followers from the kingdom. For the time being, Columbanus was imprisoned at Besançon where he was kept under strict guard. His longing to return to Luxeuil was so great, however, that one day he left Besançon for the monastery without the authority of the king.

When Theuderich heard of this he was furious and ordered that all the monks from both Britain and Ireland should be expelled forthwith to their own countries of origin. To enforce this edict he sent his own chamberlain, Count Bertechar, with a guard of soldiers under a captain named Ragamund. When the soldiers arrived at Luxeuil they found Columbanus chanting the Divine Office. Although at first reluctant to go, Columbanus knew in his heart that the soldiers would be punished if they did not force him out of the monastery and so he called to his brethren and said, "Let us go, my brothers, in the name of God."

And so, with great sadness, in the year 610, almost two decades since the foundation of Luxeuil, Columbanus and the Irish monks left their great monastery and were conducted by Captain Ragamund and his men to Nevers where they embarked on a boat which was to take them to the mouth of the Loire. From there they sailed to Orleans where they found all the churches closed to them by order of the king. They proceeded to Tours where, after some difficulty, Columbanus was able to spend a night in prayer at the tomb of St Martin, and so they all came to Nantes near the mouth of the Loire where they were able to embark on a boat which was to take them back to Ireland.

But it was not the will of God that Columbanus and his companions should return to Bangor, for when they had come to the mouth of the Loire a mighty sea arose and the ship which Columbanus had intended to rejoin was forced to return to harbour. A perfect calm then followed for three days and the captain, being very apprehensive of another storm, caused all the monks and their baggage to be put on shore for he feared that this was a sign from God and so, left to fend for themselves, Columbanus and his friends proceeded to Soissons, to the court of Clothair, King of Neustria, who received them with great kindness and generosity.

Clothair had always disliked Brunhilde and her grandsons and was anxious to keep the monks in his kingdom. However, Columbanus preferred to press on to Metz, seat of the court of Austrasia, where Theudebert, Theuderich's brother, ruled. Theudebert received the monks well and at Metz several of the former brothers from Luxeuil joined Columbanus since they preferred to follow him in his wanderings rather than remain behind in the kingdom of his persecutor. From Metz Columbanus travelled to Mayence, being determined to preach to the pagan populations on the right bank of the Rhine and its tributaries.

During this time Columbanus wrote the famous *Carmen Navale* or 'Boat Song', which has been beautifully translated by Cardinal Ó Fiaich as follows:

Lo, little bark on twin-horned Rhine,
From forests hewn to skim the brine.
Heave, lads, and let the echoes ring.

The tempests howl, the storms dismay,
But manly strength can win the day.
Heave, lads, and let the echoes ring.

For clouds and squalls will soon pass on,
And victory lies with work well done.
Heave, lads, and let the echoes ring.

Hold fast! Survive! And all is well.
God sent you worse, he'll calm this swell.
Heave, lads, and let the echoes ring.

So Satan acts to tire the brain,
And by temptation souls are slain.
Think, lads, of Christ and echo him.

Stand firm in mind 'gainst Satan's guile.
Protect yourselves with virtue's foil.
Think, lads, of Christ and echo him.

Strong faith and zeal will victory gain.
The old foe breaks his lance in vain.
Think, lads, of Christ and echo him.

The King of virtues vowed a prize
For him who wins, for him who tries.
Think, lads, of Christ and echo him.

After great hardship they came as far as Lake Zurich in Switzerland, finally establishing themselves at Bregenz on Lake Constance where they made a new headquarters. The countryside here was wild and beautiful and the tribes living in the region – the Suevi and Alemanni – were pagans who worshipped Wodin as their god. It is said that the impulsiveness of Gall, who set fire to their temples and threw their offerings into the lake, put this mission in jeopardy.

20
Gall of Switzerland

In the spring of 612 war broke out between Austrasia and Burgundy. The Austrasian army was first defeated at Toul and then annihilated at Tolbiac. King Theudebert fled across the Rhine but was captured for his brother Theuderich by Count Bertechar. By order of his grandmother Brunhilde he was committed to a monastery and beheaded shortly afterwards. The death of Theudebert meant that Theuderich was now King of Austrasia and its German provinces as well as Burgundy and, as the Queen mother set up her court at Metz, Columbanus decided that it was time for him to move on.

Among others, Gall was not anxious to go and the resultant separation of the two great saints of Ireland was not effected without acrimony. When Gall threw himself at Columbanus's feet, saying that he was not able for the journey, Columbanus replied, "Brother, I know that now it seems a heavy burden for you to suffer further fatigue for my sake, nevertheless this I enjoin in you before I go so that so long as I live in the body you do not dare to celebrate Communion." This seems to us today as cruel a stricture from Columbanus as that dealt to his mother so many years before, but it underlines that singleness of purpose which was for Columbanus the stamp of his greatness, for we know that at heart he was really a tender and kind man. His personal feelings, however, were not allowed to stand in the way of his duty to God.

And so, although by now more than seventy years of age, Columbanus crossed the snow-covered Alps by the St Gothard's Pass and made his way to the court of the Lombard king, Agilulph, whose queen, Theodelinda, had become famous throughout Europe for her beauty and intelligence. At this time the Lombards, including King Agilulph, were Arians although Queen Theodelinda, was a devout Christian. It is thought that due to her influence the Arian King received Columbanus and his companions with great kindness and consideration and they were able to begin a new mission among the half Christian population of Lombardy.

A place of settlement was, therefore, the first prerequisite and a man named Jucundus reminded the king that there was a suitable place at Bobbio, a ruined church once dedicated to St Peter. This was a fertile and salubrious district near the Trebbia. There, by the grace of God, was built in the Valley of the Appenines a monastery whose name will never be forgotten by those who follow the Way of the Lord – Bobbio the Beautiful. The Bobbio missal preserves a specimen of the liturgy in use in the early Irish Church and is of obvious Bangor origin.

The holy Columbanus lived but one year after the foundation of Bobbio, but the life of the great man was complete for the Bangor Rule had been given to Europe and the world and Bangor had indeed become a Light to the Gentiles and a city set on a hill. During his last days Columbanus's thoughts returned to Gall, the only survivor of that band who had accompanied him from Bangor, a constant and faithful companion over half of Europe whom he had silenced because his obedience had not been to death. On his deathbed, therefore, the great man ordered that the staff on which he had been leaning while travelling through the great mountain ranges of Europe should be taken to Gall as a symbol of forgiveness.

And so the saint died, to the great grief of his companions, on the eleventh day before the Kalends of December, which is to say, 21 November 615, probably in the seventy-third year of his age. He was buried beneath the High Altar of that place. Sometime afterwards his remains were enclosed in a stone coffin and are still preserved in the old monastic church at Bobbio, where I have visited him regularly. It is surely not too much to say that Ireland never sent a greater son than Columbanus to do the work of God in foreign lands. For centuries his influence remained dominant in France and northern Italy. His character was certainly not faultless. He was consumed with a ruthless zeal in the service of his master, Jesus, which was at once the secret of his immense power and the source of his mistakes. It is a measure of his strength of character, however, that when Queen Brunhilde, his constant enemy, was captured by the army of Neustria under Clothair and cruelly done to death following utter public humiliation Columbanus refused a personal invitation from King Clothair to return to Luxeuil from Bobbio.

GSM Walker in his edition of the *Works of St Columbanus* writes of him:

> "A character so complex and so contrary, humble and haughty, harsh and tender, pedantic and impetuous by turns, had as its guiding and unifying pattern the ambition of sainthood. All his activities were subordinate to this one end and with the self-sacrifice that can seem so close to self-assertion he worked out his sole salvation by the wondrous pathway that he knew. He was a missionary through circumstance, a monk by vocation, a contemplative, too frequently driven to action by the world, a pilgrim on the road to Paradise."

21

The Teachers of the World

THE END OF the sixth and beginning of the seventh centuries was indeed the Golden Age of the Bangor monastery, for it became the centre of literature, both sacred and secular, in Europe. Here were compiled the oldest Chronicles of Ireland and the beautiful poetry, the *Voyage of Bran*, which tells also of those great Cruthin Kings of Dalaradia, Mongan and Fiachna.

The *Voyage of Bran* speaks of the Birth of Christ as follows:

A great birth will come after ages,
That will not be in a lofty place,
The son of a woman whose mate will not be known,
He will seize the rule of many thousands.

A rule without beginning, without end,
He has created the world so that it is perfect,
Whose are on earth and sea,
Woe to him that shall be under His unwill!

It's He that made the heavens,
Happy he that has a white heart,
He will purify hosts under pure water,
It's He that will cure your sickness.

Yet the most beautiful poetry of that age is contained in the Bangor Antiphonary. The "Commemoration of our Abbots" in the Antiphonary is perhaps the most valuable in the collection for by it the date of the manuscript can be determined. In itself it is an interesting poem and one can see that after the prefatory verse the lines run in alphabetical order.

Sancta sanctorum opera	The Holy, Valiant deeds
Patrum, fratres, fortissimo,	Of sacred Fathers,
Benchorensi in optima	Based on the matchless
Fundatorum ecclesia,	Church of Bangor;
Abbatum eminentia,	The noble deeds of abbots,

Numerum, tempora, nomina,	Their number, times and names,
Sine fine fulgentia,	Of never-ending lustre,
Audite, magna merita;	Hear, brothers; great their deserts,
Quos convocavit Dominus	Whom the Lord hath gathered
Caelorum regni sedibus.	To the mansions of his heavenly kingdom
Amavit Christus Comgillum;	Christ loved Comgall,
Bene et ipse Dominum;	Well, too, did he the Lord;
Carum habuit Beognoum;	He held Beogna dear;
Dominum ornavit Aedeum;	He graced the noble Aedh;
Elegit sanctum Sinlanum,	He chose the holy Sinlan,
Famosum mundi magistrum	Far-famed teacher of the world.
Quos convocavit Dominus	Whom the Lord hath gathered
Caelorum regni sedibus.	To the mansions of his heavenly kingdom.
Gratum fecit Fintenanum,	He made Finten accepted,
Heredem almum inclitum;	An heir generous, renowned;
Illustravit Maclaisreum,	He rendered Maclaisre illustrious,
Kaput abbatum omnium	The chief of all abbots;
Lampade sacrae Seganum,	With a sacred torch (he enlightened) Segan,
Magnum scripturae medicum,	A great physician of scripture.
Quos convocavit Dominus	Whom the Lord hath gathered
Caelorum regni sedibus.	To the mansions of his heavenly kingdom
Notus vir erat Beracnus;	Beracnus was a distinguished man;
Ornatus et Cuminenus;	Cummian pre-eminent in glory;
Pastor Columba congruous;	Columba a congenial shepherd;
Querela absque Aidanus;	Baithene a worthy ruler;
Summus antestes Crotanus.	Crotan a chief president.
Quos convocavit Dominus	Whom the Lord has gathered
Caelorum regni sedibus.	To the mansions of his heavenly kingdom.
Tantis successit Colmanus,	To these so excellent succeeded Colman,
Vir amabilis omnibus,	A man to be beloved by all;
Xpo (Christo) nunc sedet suprimus	Singing praises to Christ
Ymnos canens. Quindecimus	He now sits on high. That Cronan,
Zoen ut carpet Cronanus,	The fifteenth, may lay hold on life.
Conservet eum Dominus.	The Lord preserve him.
Quos convocavit Dominus	Whom the Lord hath gathered
Caelorum regni sedibus	To the mansions of his heavenly kingdom.
Horum sanctorum merita	The truest merits,
Abbatum fideliddima,	of these holy abbots,
Erga Comgillum congrua,	Meet for Comgal,
Invocamus altissima;	Most exalted, we invoke;

Uti possimus omnia	That we may blot out
Nostra delere crimina,	All our offences
Per Jesum Christum, aeterna	Through Jesus Christ
Regnantem in saecula.	Who reigns for ages everlasting.

To Sinlan, described as "a far-famed teacher of the world", has been attributed the ancient Ulster Chronicle from which the oldest entries of the *Annals of Ulster* have been derived. The harmony that exists between the enumeration of the abbots in the poem and the entries in the Irish annals is remarkable.

22
Molua of Caledonia

SAINT MOLUA, (c530–592), (also known as *Lua, Luan, Luanus, Lugaidh, Moloag, Moloc, Molluog, Moluag, Murlach*), was an Ulster missionary, and a contemporary of Comgall, Columbanus and Columba, who evangelized the Caledonian Pretani or Picts in the sixth century. Saint Molua was the patron saint of Argyll as evidenced by a charter in 1544, from the Earl of Argyll, which states "*in honour of God Omnipotent, the blessed Virgin, and Saint Moloc, our patron*".

Molua, born in Ireland, was a noble of the Dàl nAraide (Dalaradia) or Ulster Cruthin and was educated in Bangor under Comgall. Tradition states that the rock, on which Molua, or Moluag as he was known in the Hebrides, was standing, detached itself from the Irish coast and he drifted across to the island of Lismore, in Loch Linnhe. According to the Irish Annals, in 562 Molua beat Saint Columba in a race to the large island of the Lyn of Lorn in Argyll, now called the Isle of Lismore. WS Skene claims it was the sacred island of the Western Picts and the burial place of their kings whose capital was at Beregonium, across the water at Benderloch.

Molua was accompanied to north Britain by his compatriot Comgall, who presented him to King Brude of the Northern Picts in order to obtain permission to carry on his mission of spreading Christianity. It is likely that King Brude preferred Molua to Columba because of Columba's close relation to the Gaelic-speaking leadership of Dàl Riata and the "Ui Neill". This explains why Molua evangelized largely Pictish areas and Columba stayed within the sphere of Dál Riata or Scottish (Irish) influence.

After founding an island monastery on the Isle of Lismore, Molua went on to found two other great centres in the land of the Picts at Rosmarkie and Mortlach. These were his three centres of teaching, and it is significant that all three were to become the seats of the Roman Catholic Sees of the Isles, Ross and Aberdeen. So it was that St Bernard of Clairvaux wrote of Bangor in his biography of Malachy in the twelfth century:

> "A place it was, truly sacred, the nursery of saints who brought forth fruit most abundantly to the Glory of God, insomuch that one of the sons of that holy congregation, Molua by name, is alone reputed to have been the founder of a hundred monasteries".

Molua died in Rosemarkie, modern Scotland on 25 June 592. The *Annals of Ulster* record the death of Lugaid of Les Mór in 592 "Obitus Lugide Lis Moer."

Molua is said to have been buried at Rosemarkie on the Moray Firth, though his remains were later transported to Lismore, and honoured in the cathedral which bore his name. The Coarb, or successor, of Saint Molua, is the Livingstone chief of the Clan Mac Lea. This Livingstone family of Lismore had long been the hereditary keepers of the crozier of the saint. The bell of Saint Molua was in existence until the sixteenth century when it disappeared during the Reformation. An ancient bell found at Kilmichael Glassary, Argyll, is thought to have been the lost bell. St Molua's parish church at Stormont, Belfast commemorates his name, although he has been totally confused over the centuries with St Molua of Killaloe.

23

The Cruthin Wars and Bishop Congus

IN 627 CONGAL Claen or 'One Eye', a Prince of the Cruthin, became the Over-King of Ulster. He had ruled in Tara until his blinding by bees put him from his kingship (*Bech Bretha*) and the power of the Ulster Cruthin had stretched as far south as the Boyne Valley, with Tara as their ritual centre. The following year Congal slew the High King of the "Ui Neill" and in 629 he strengthened his claim to the whole of Ulster by killing the King of Dalriada who was an ally of the "Ui Neill". This resulted in the Battle of Dunceithirnn in Londonderry later that year, when the north-western Gaels under their new High King, Domnall, son of Hugh, defeated Congal and crushed the Cruthin. Congal was forced to flee to Scotland where he succeeded in reversing the Dalriadan (Epidian Cruthin) alliance with the "Ui Neill".

On 24 June 637 therefore was fought the famous Battle of Magh Rath (Moira) in County Down against Domnall, son of Hugh, by the allies of Ulster. Sadly, however, Congal was killed and Domnall Brecc (Freckled Donald), King of Dalriada, lost all his Ulster territories. In this way the "Ui Neill" consolidated their power in Ulster and the Cruthin further declined. One of the finest passages from the epic of the Belfast poet and antiquarian, Sir Samuel Ferguson, on Congal is the soliloquy of Ardan, the great friend of Congal, to his dead king following the battle.

I stand alone,
Last wreck remaining of a power and order overthrown,
Much needing solace;
And, ah me! not in the empty lore
Of bard or druid does my soul find peace or comfort more;
Nor in the bells or crooked staves nor sacrificial shows
Find I help my soul desires,
Or in the chants of those
Who claim our druids' vacant place.
Alone and faint, I crave,
Oh, God, one ray of heavenly light to help me to the grave,
Such even as thou, dead Congal, hadst;
That so these eyes of mine
May look their last on earth and heaven with calmness such as thine.

The grave of Congal Claen is unmarked today but surely his memory should be kept alive in Ulster for he was the last Cruthinic king to provide an effective opposition to the Gaels in the north of Ireland. Congal had fought above all others for the People of Cruthin. Bangor could only remain strong while the Cruthin remained strong and the complete defeat at the Battle of Moira signalled the inevitable decline of the Bangor monastery. Thus it was that the Cult of Patrick eventually moved from Connor in Dalaradia to Armagh. Abbot Comgall himself had once said that he also would pray only for the People of the Cruthin, his own people, but Comgall was no more. And then in 645 the great and gentle St Gall died quietly beside the River Stinace.

The *Annals* further state that in 663 Segan, son of Uacuinn, died. Segan was described as being "a great physician of scripture." Due to their great understanding and learning, coupled with a deep faith, the Bangor monks, particularly Columbanus himself, were accredited with the powers of healing, both of the body and of the soul. The word 'medicum' (physician or healer) is the Latin equivalent of the Aramaic 'Essene' and of the Greek 'Therapeutae', which exactly describe those communities in Palestine and Egypt upon which the true vine was ultimately modelled.

The story of the Donegal Kingdoms, describing them as Northern "Ui Neill", rather than the Venniconian Cruthin that they actually were, is a later propagandistic fiction and not a summary of what actually happened. Almost certainly it was given its classical form by and on behalf of the Cenel nEogan, during the reign in the mid-eighth century of their powerful and ambitious king, Aed (Hugh) Allan, who died in the year 743. Whatever his actual victories and political successes, they were underlined by a set of deliberately created fictional historical texts which purported to give him and his ancestors a more glorious past than they had actually enjoyed. The same texts projected his dynasty back to the dawn of history and created a new political relationship with the neighbouring kingdoms. Whatever the initial reaction to them, these political fictions were plausible enough to endure and have been ultimately accepted as history by most commentators over the past thirteen hundred years and by those modern 'serious scholars' trapped in nationalist ideologies.

Aed's pseudo-historians were probably led by the Armagh Bishop Congus, who exploited the opportunity provided by the alliance with the King to advance the case for the supremacy of his own church throughout Ireland. Congus was from Cul Athguirt in the parish of Islandmagee, County Antrim. He was descended from Dá Slúaig, the son of Ainmere so he was a member of the Húi Nadsluaga clan who were one of the five prímthúatha of the Dál mBuinne Cruthin, east of Lough Neagh, County Antrim. Congus was a scribe before being elevated to the See of Armagh. He died in 750.

The Bangor Antiphonary itself may be dated from Cronan, the last Abbot listed in the commemoration poem, who, according to the *Annals*, died on 6 November 691. Cronan was alive when the Antiphonary was written so that it follows that it can be dated some year between 680 and 691. The manuscript was given its present title *Antiphonarium Benchorense* by the great Italian scholar, Muratori. It remains the only important relic of the ancient monastery of Bangor and was taken from Bangor to Bobbio at some time between its composition and the plundering of the monastery by the Vikings in the ninth century.

Indirect evidence of the work of the Bangor monks, however, is found in early Christian ornamentation. Pictish artwork is strongly characterised by intricate network interlacing. This is apparent in ornamental stones found on the east coast of Scotland and England from Shetland to Durham and in parts of Ireland. Identical features are also found in the great contemporary illuminated gospels of Durrow, Lindisfarne and Kells. The Book of Durrow is named after the Columban foundation of Durrow near Tullamore in Offaly. It is generally regarded as having been made towards the end of the seventh century, perhaps in the 670s, and Cruthinic influence was outstanding.

But the finest surviving example of the Pictish art form lies in the Lindisfarne Gospels which were written in honour of St Cuthbert by Eadfrith who was made Bishop of Lindisfarne in the year of our Lord 698. These were bound by Bishop Ethilward and ornamented by Bilfrith the anchorite. The great work was preserved with the body of the saint at Lindisfarne and then carried in flight before the fury of the Vikings. Having rested some years at Durham, it was finally returned to Lindisfarne Priory where it stayed until the Dissolution.

The Book of Kells is generally assigned to the early ninth century when it may have been written and illuminated by the scribes of Iona. Subsequently it was brought to Kells where it was known in the eleventh century as 'The great gospel of Colum Cille (Columba)'. There are many influences apparent in its design, notably the Coptic (Egyptian), Pretanic (Pictish) and Celtic, all three of which were prominent in Bangor until its destruction. For example, Christ is symbolised by the Greek letters "Χρ" (Chi Rho) in both the Book of Kells and the Bangor Antiphonary.

Yet because of its location on the shores of Belfast Lough the great monastery lay open to attack by the Vikings. They first came raiding in the year 810 and between 822 and 824 the tomb of Comgall was broken open, its costly ornaments seized and the bones of the great saint "shaken from their shrine" (*The Annals of the Four Masters*). St Bernard related that on one day alone nine hundred monks were killed. It is unlikely that following this time the *Laus Perennis* was ever sung again in Ireland.

24
The Plan of St Gall

Too frail to accompany his abbot, Gallus, or as we know him now, St Gall, left Columbanus's mission in 612 to stay in Swabia and live in a retreat by the Steinach. At this site in 720, an Abbey was eventually formed by the Alemannian Ottmar which bears Gall's name, St Gallen. In 747 Abbot Ottmar was required to convert the community to Benedictine ways. He thus designated buildings for common dining and sleeping with an infirmary and hospice. But the Abbey's lands were totally alienated by greedy neighbours and it ceased to prosper. In 816 however Gozbert arrived as Abbot to find the monk's spiritual life at a low ebb. Through vigorous litigation he reclaimed the estates of the Abbey and regained its fortunes. By 830 he was ready to refurbish the superannuated buildings of the old settlement and for this purpose he requested the guidance of *The Plan of St Gall*, the document created as an instrument of policy to inform and regulate monastic planning throughout the Frankish Empire.

Few documents possess the broad imaginative scope of this parchment, which has become a Swiss national treasure. This manuscript was copied between 820 and 830 from a lost original. It depicts a Benedictine monastery to shelter the work, study and prayers of some two hundred and seventy souls, of whom one hundred and ten were monks. Although Charlemagne (c742–814) had urged adoption of Benedictine custom by Frankish monasteries, the acceptance of this was neither universal nor undisputed. That part of his vision for unity of civil and church affairs was, however, achieved by his son and successor Louis the Pious, who determined to change the Frankish monastic life from the different existing monastic practices, including the Rule of Columbanus, in favour of the Rule of St Benedict.

It is indeed most interesting to visit the library of the great church of St Gallen in Switzerland, the destination to which *The Plan of St Gall* was originally sent some 1200 years ago at the abbot's request. The simple survival of the plan is something of a wonder. And although it describes a self-contained monastic community, it reveals an astonishing congruence with modern concerns of community planning, technology and the efficient use of resources. Indeed essential unity of purpose expressed therein sustains its timeless relevance to human needs and western society.

The Carolingian empire, left to the lesser scions of a great house, broke up after the death of its founder. But the ideals of Charlemagne, and indeed Columbanus before him, survive in a document which became an important force in the shaping of modern Europe. For like the concept of empire itself the scheme transmitted to us in *The Plan of St Gall* was to survive the collapse of that power which first nurtured it and left a permanent imprint on monastic planning for centuries to come.

25
Malachy of Armagh

THE ORDER OF the Columbans did not long survive its founder and merged with the Benedictines in the eighth century. However, in honour of St Gall, as we have seen, there arose a monastery dedicated to him which became one of the most important centres of Irish influence on the Continent. This monastery has been described as, "eminently distinguished as the chief seat of learning of ancient Germany." It reached the height of its fame in the ninth century under Moengal, an Irishman. Although celebrated for its beautiful manuscripts, its carvings and its miniatures, it remained true to the tradition of Bangor in regarding music as the greatest of all the arts. Through the teaching of Moengal the music school of St Gall became "the wonder and delight of Europe."

Moengal has been identified with that abbot of whom the *Annals of Ulster* state, "871 AD Moengal, the pilgrim Abbot of Bangor, brought his old age to a happy close." The famous pupils of Moengal there included Notker Balbulus ('The Stammerer'), who wrote a large series of hymns and is considered one of the greatest musicians of the Middle Ages; Tuotilo who was a painter and sculptor as well as a poet and musician; and Rathpert Waldramon who was a great musician and librarian. These three men were among the finest contributors to European mediaeval hymn-writing.

Finally, in the days of the Cambro-Normans there arose a second Columbanus. In his biography of his friend, Malachy, St Bernard of Clairvaux wrote of Malachy's attempts to revive the Church of Bangor. Mael Maedoc was born at Armagh in 1095 and ordained in 1119. On coming to Bangor as an Abbot in 1124 he took the name of Malachias, the Hebrew for 'My Angel' and this was undoubtedly taken because of the tradition of Bangor being known as the 'Valley of the Angels.'

In 1127 the monastery was attacked by Conor O'Loughlin, king of the "northern Ui Neill", and the "the city was destroyed." Malachy was forced to migrate south with his monks and he set up a new community in County Kerry under the protection of his old friend Cormac McCarthy, king of Desmond. In 1134 he was called back to Ulster to become Archbishop of Armagh and in 1137 he at length returned to his beloved Bangor. Two years later, following a journey to Rome he was made Papal Legate and built a great oratory of stone in Bangor on returning there.

Malachy's influence in Irish ecclesiastical affairs was immense and has been compared to that of Boniface in Germany. He restored the discipline of the Church which had grown lax and had the Roman liturgy adopted. In 1148 he set out once more for Rome but, whilst staying at Clairvaux, died in the arms of St Bernard on All Saints' Day 1148. Of this Bernard wrote "Malachy, Bishop and Legate of the Holy Apostolic See, as if he had been taken up out of our hands by angels, happily fell asleep in the Lord in the fifty-fourth year of his life in the place and at the time he had chosen and foretold."

Bishop Reeves has written that Malachy's foundation at Bangor "like the second temple fell very far short of its primitive greatness, and in the process of time, under civil commotions, dwindled into insignificance and finally became but a name." As for the Bangor Antiphonary it remained at the monastery of Bobbio whence with the Bobbio Missal and other Irish books it was moved to Milan by Cardinal Frederick Borromaeo when he founded the Ambrosian library there. So today there is preserved in Milan a reminder of those days of glory when the *Laus Perennis* was sung in Ireland and Bangor the great was the light of the world.

As for the alleged prophecies of Saint Malachy, these were actually first published in 1595 by a Benedictine named Arnold Wion in his *Lignum Vitæ*, a history of the Benedictine order. Wion attributed the prophecies to Malachy of Armagh. He explained that the prophecies had not, to his knowledge, ever been printed before, but that many were eager to see them. Wion includes both the alleged original prophecies, consisting of short, cryptic Latin phrases, as well as an interpretation applying the statements to historical popes up to Urban VII (pope for thirteen days in 1590), which Wion attributes to Alphonsus Ciacconius. In this scheme the present Pope Francis is Peter of Rome, the last pope.

The Antiphonary of Bangor

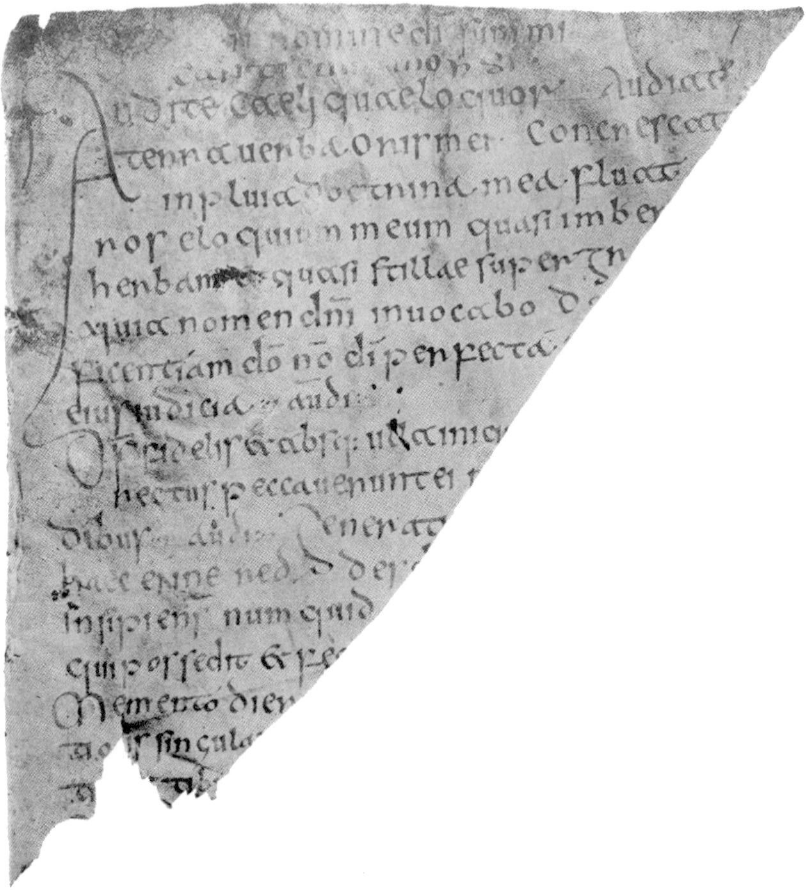

[*Fol. 1 recto.*]

in nomine d*e*i summi

CANTICUM MOYSI.

Audite caeli quae loquor audiat
terra uerba oris mei. concrescat
in pluia doctrina mea fluat *
ros eloquium meum quasi imber *
herbam et quasi stillae super gr *
quia nomen d*omi*ni inuocabo d * *
ficentiam d*e*o n*ostr*o d*e*i perfecta * *
eius iudicia∴, audi*te*∴ * *
D*eu*s fidelis et absq*ue* ulla iniq * *
rectus peccauerunt ei * * *
dibus.., audi*te*∴, Generati * * *
haec enne red d des d * * *
insipiens numquid * * * *
qui possedit et fec * * * *
Memento dier * * * *
tio * is singula * * * * *
ti * tibi * * * * *
* * * * * * *
* * * * * * *
* * * * * * *
* * * * * * *
* * * * * * *
* * * * * * *
* * * * * * *

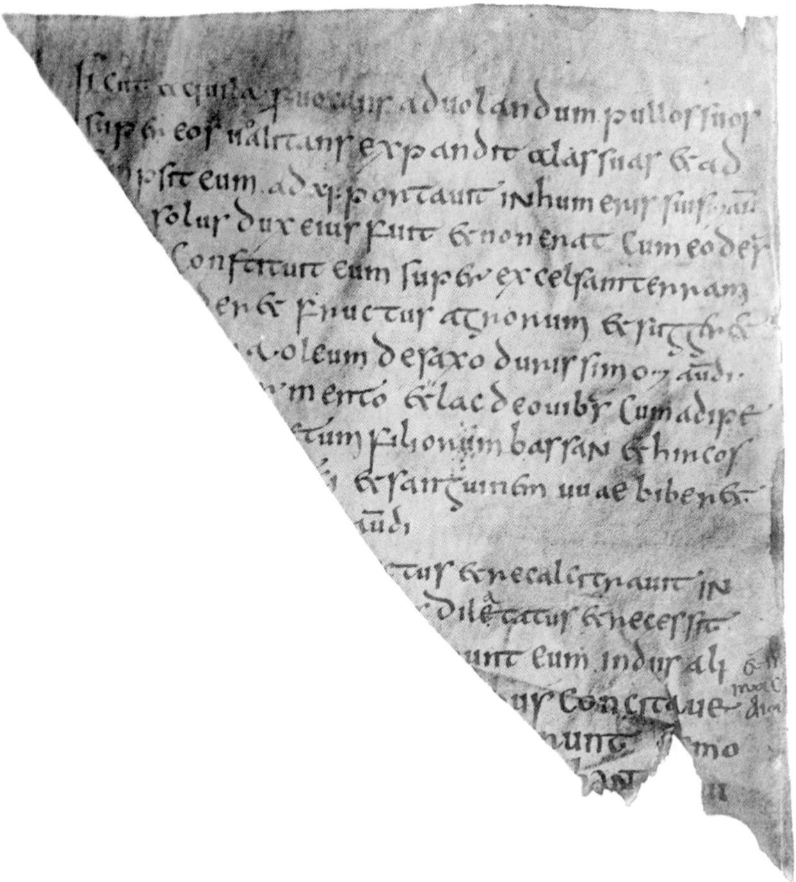

[_Fol. 1 verso._]

Sicut aquila p_ro_uocans ad uolandum pullos suos
super eos ualitans[1] expandit alas suas et ad
* mpsit eum adq_ue_ portauit in humeris suis·.·, au_dite_
* solus dux eius fuit et non erat cum eo deus
* constituit eum super excelsam terram
* * deret fructus agrorum et suggeret
* * * a oleum de saxo durissimo.., audi_te_
* * * rmento et lac de ouibus cum adipe
* * * tum filiorum bassan et hircos
* * * et sanguinem uuae biberet
* * * audi_te_
* * * * tus et recalcitrauit in
* * * * diletatus[2] et recessit
* * * * * unt eum in diis ali
* * * * * us concitaue[3]
* * * * * * runt demo
* * * * * * bant * ui
* * * * * * *
* * * * * * *
* * * * * * *
* * * * * * *
* * * * * * *
* * * * * * *
* * * * * * *

[1] An 'o' has been written subsequently over the second letter of 'ualitans.'
[2] An 'a' has been written subsequently over the fourth letter of 'diletatus.'
[3] On the right margin a later correcting hand has written the accidentally omitted words 'et in iracu[n]dia[m].'

aud

meam ab eis & considerabo nouissima eorū
Generatio enim peruersa est & infideles filii
ipsi me prouocauerunt in uanitatibus suis
& ego prouocabo eos in eo qui non est populus
& in gente stulta inritabo illos.,., audite
Ignis succensus est in furore meo & ardebit
usq. ad inferni nouissima deuorabitq. terram cum germine suo & montium funda-
menta cumburet.,., aud.,. Congregabo
super eos mala & sagittas meas conplebo
in eis consumentur fame & deuorabunt
eos aues amursu amarissimo dentes besti-
arum inmittam in eos cum furore trahen-
tium super terram adq. serpentium..
Foris uastabit eos gladius & intus pa
iuuenem simul ac uirginem lac
homine sene.,., aud.,. Dixi
cer

[*Fol. 2 recto.*]

au*dite*

meam ab eis et considerabo nouissima eoru*m* :· ,
Generatio enim peruersa est et infidelis filii
ipsi me p*ro*uocauerunt in uanitatibus suis
et ego p*ro*uocabo eos in eo qui non est populus
et in gente stulta inritabo illos . . , audite
IGnis succensus est in furore meo et ardebit
usq*ue* ad inferni nouissima deuorabit ter
ram cum germine suo et montium funda
menta cumburet . . , au*dite* : , Congregabo
super eos mala et sagittas meas conplebo
in eis consummentur fame et deuorabunt
eos aues a mursu amarissimo dentes besti
arum inmittam in eos con furore trahen
tium super terram adq*ue* serpentium . . *
Foris uastabit eos gladius et intus p *
iuuenem simul ac uirginem lac * *
homine sene . . , aud*ite* . . , Dixi * *
cessare * * * * * *
* * * * * * *
* * * * * * *
* * * * * * *
* * * * * * *
* * * * * * *
* * * * * * *

prouiderent quomodo persequatur unus
mille et duo fugent decim milia ... audi
Nonne ideo quia ds suus uendidit eos et dns con
clusit illos non enim est ds noster ut ds eorum
et inimici nostri sunt insensati ... audi
De uinea sodomorum uinea eorum et propago
eorum ex gomorra uua eorum uua fellis et
botrus amarissima fel draconum uinum
eorum et uenenum aspedum insanabile ...
Nonne haec condita sunt apud me et signata
in thesauris meis mea est ultio ego retribuam
in tempore ut labatur pes eorum ... audi
Iuxta est dies perditionis et adesse festinant in
tempora iudicabit dns populum suum et ser
uis miserebitur ... audi ... Uidebit quod
...rit manus et clausi quoque defecerunt
...sumpti sunt et dicet ubi nam sunt
... audi

[*Fol. 2 verso.*]

p*ro*uiderent quomodo persequatur unus
mile[1] et duo fugent decim milia.., audi*te*
Nonne ideo quia d*eu*s suus uendidit eos et d*omin*u*s* con
clusit illos non enim est d*eu*s noster ut d*eu*s eoru*m*
et inimici nostri sunt insensati.., audi*te*
De uinea sodomorum uinea eorum et p*ro*pago
eorum ex gomorra uua eorum uua fellis et
butrus amarissima fel draconum uinum
eorum et uenenum aspedum insanabile..,.[2]
Nonne haec condita sunt apud me et signata
in tesauris meis mea est ultio ego retribuam
in tempore ut labatur pes eorum.., audi*te*
IUxta est dies perditionis et adesse festinant
* empora iudicabit d*omin*u*s* populum suum et ser[3]
* is miserebitur.., audi*te*.., UIdebit quod
* * sit manus et clausi quoq*ue* defecerunt
* * sumpti sunt et dicet ubinam sunt
* * * * * * audi*te*
* * * * * * *
* * * * * * *
* * * * * * *
* * * * * * *
* * * * * * *
* * * * * * *

[1] A second 'l' has been written on the left margin.
[2] The presence of this stop and the following capital letter, prove that an 'audite' has been accidentally omitted here.
[3] The word 'in' accidentally omitted before 'seruis' has been written *prima manu* on the right margin after and above the line.

percutiam et ego sanabo et non est qui de
manu mea possit eruere ... audi
Leuabo ad caelum manum meam et dicam
uiuo ego in aeternum et si acuero ut fulgor
gladium meum et arripuerit iudicium ma
nus mea reddam ultionem hostib: meis et
his qui oderunt me retribuam ... audi
Inebriabo sagittas meas sanguine et gla
dius meus deuorabit carnes de cruore
occisorum et de captiuitate nudati inimi
corum capitis ... audi. Laudate gentes popu
lum eius quia sanguinem seruorum ulcis
cetur et uindictam retribuet in hostes eorum
et propitius erit terrae populi sui in saecul
ymnum sci hilari . saeculorum ... aud
de xpo ...
Ymnum dicat turba fr
Ymnum cantus per so
xpo regi concinne
laud
Tu dei d

[*Fol. 3 recto.*]

percutiam et ego sanabo et non est qui de
manu mea possit eruere . . , aud*ite*
Leuabo ad caelum manum meam et dicam
uiuo ego in aeternum et si acuero ut fulgor
gladium meum et arripuerit iudicium ma
nus mea reddam ultionem hostib*us* meis. et
hiis qui oderunt me retribuam . . , aud*ite*
INebriabo sagittas meas sanguine et gla
dius meus deuorabit carnes de cruore
occissorum et de captiuitate nudati inimi
corum capitis.., aud*ite*∴ Laudate gentes popu
lum eius quia sanguinem seruorum ulcis
cetur et uindictam retribuet in hostes eoru*m*
et p*ro*pitius erit terrae populi sui in saecula
YMNU*M* S*ANCTI* HILARI saeculorum∴, aud*ite*
DE *CHRISTO*

Ymnum dicat turba fr * *
ymnum cantus person * *
christo regi concinnent[1] * *
laud * * * * *
Tu d*e*i d * * * * *
* * * * * *
* * * * * *
* * * * * *

[1] An 'a' has been subsequently written over the 'e' in this word, and a dot placed beneath it.

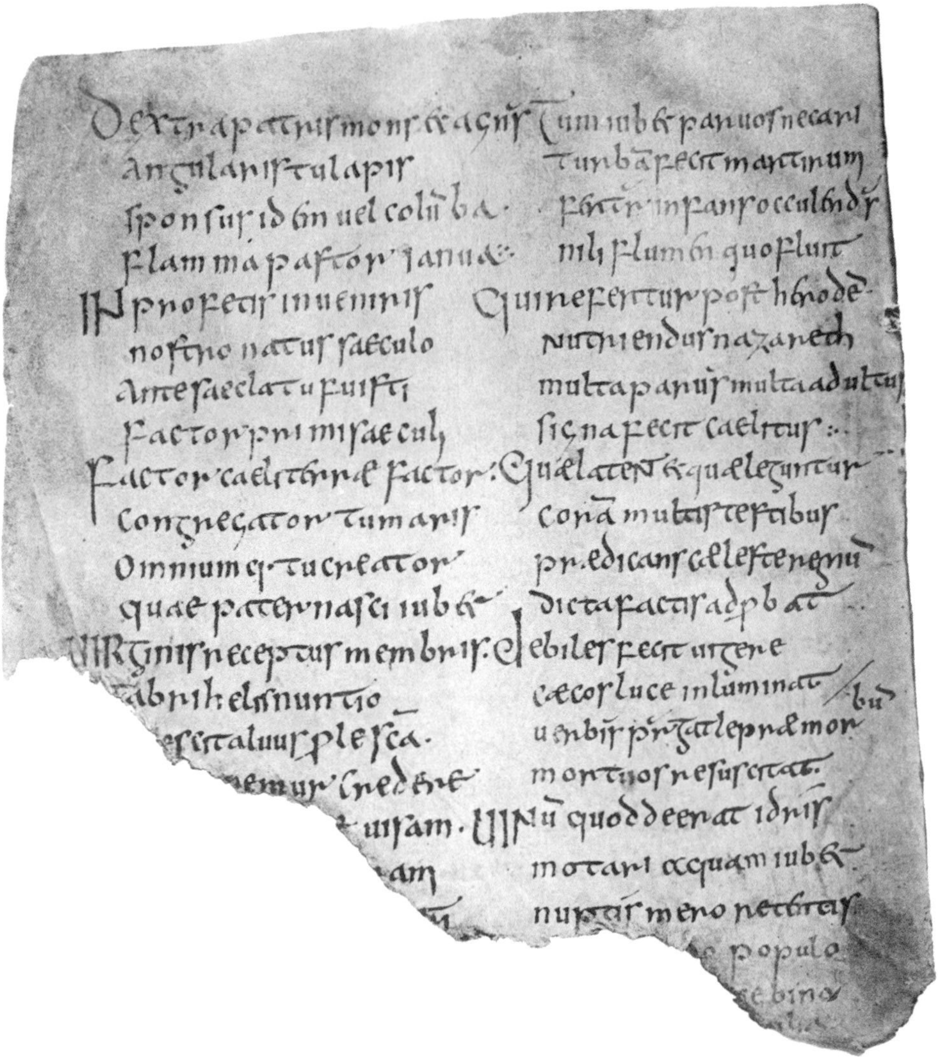

[*Fol. 3 verso.*]

Dextra patris mons et agnus
angularis tu lapis
sponsus idem uel colu*m*ba
flamma pastor ianua :·

IN profetis inueniris
nostro natus saeculo
ante saecla tu fuisti
factor primi saeculi

Factor caeli terræ factor.
congregator tu maris
omniumq*ue* tu creator
quae pater nasci iubet

UIRginis receptus membris.
gabrihelis nuntio
* escit aluus p*ro*le s*anct*a
* * emur credere
* * * uisam.
* * * am
* * * ti
* * * *
* * * *
* * * *
* * * *
* * * *

Tum iubet paruos necari
turba*m* fecit martirum
fertur infans occulendus
nili flumen quo fluit

Qui refertur post herode*m*
nutriendus nazareth
multa paruus multa adultus
signa fecit caelitus :·

Quæ latent et quæ leguntur
cora*m* multis testibus
prædicans cæleste regnu*m*
dicta factis adp*ro*bat

Debiles fecit uigere
cæcos luce inluminat
uerbis purgat lepræ mor / bu*m*
mortuos resuscitat.

UINu*m* quod deerat idris
motari aquam iubet
nuptis mero retentis
* * o populo
* * * e bino
* * * lia
* * * *
* * * *

tur bta ex omni discumbente
uicem lacuo em pertulit
duodecim uiros probauit
per quos uita discitur
ex quib: unus inuenitur
xpi iudas traditur
instruuntur missi ab anna
proditoris osculo
Innocens captus tenetur
nec repugnans ducitur
sistitur falsis grasatur
offerendus pontio
Discerent xpm negandum
turbis seris traditur
impiis uerbis grasatur
sputa flagra sustinet
scandere cruce iubetur
innocens pro noxiis [illegible]
morte carnis qua tenebat
mortem uicit omnium
Tum dm clamore magno
[illegible] pendens inuocat
[illegible]

[illegible] sol [illegible]
nox obscurat saeculum
excitantur de sepulchris
dudum clausa corpora
Adfuit ioseph beatus
corpus mirra perlitum
linteo nudi ligatum
cum dolone condidit
Milites seruare corpus
anna princeps praecipit
ut uideret si probaret
xps quod sponponderat
Angelum dni trementes
ueste amictu candida
quo candore claritatis
uellus uicit sinicum
Demouit saxum sepulchro
surgens xps integer
haec uidit iudaea [illegible]
haec negat cum uideret [illegible]
[illegible]

[*Fol. 4 recto.*]

Turba ex omni discumbente
iugem laudem pertulit
duodecim uiros p*ro*bauit
per quos uita discitur

Ex quib*us* unus inuenitur
*christ*i iuda[1] traditur
instruntur[2] misi ab anna
p*ro*ditoris osculo

INnocens captus tenetur
nec repugnans ducitur
sistitur falsis grasatur
offerentes pontio[3]

Dicerent *christu*m neganduм
turbis s*anct*us traditur
impiis uerbis grasatur
sputa flagra sustinet

Scandere cruce*m* iubetur
innocens pro noxis[4]
morte carnis qua*m* gerebat
mortem uicit omnium

Tum d*eu*m clamore magno
* em pendens inuocat
* * membra *christ*i
* * * a

dunt
Uela templi scisa pen
nox obscurat saeculu*m*
excitantur de sepulchris
dudu*m* clausa corpora

Adfuit ioseph beatus
corpus mirra perlitum
linteo rudi ligatum
cu*m* dolore condidit

Milites seruare corpus
anna princeps praecipit
ut uideret si p*ro*baret
*christu*s quod spoponderat

Angelum d*e*i trementes
ueste amictu*m* candida
quo candore claritatis
uellus uicit siricum ..

Demouit saxum sepulchro
surgens *christu*s intiger
haec uidit iudea mendax
haec negat cum uideret

F * rimum monent *
* * * *
* * * *
* * * *

[1] After and above the 'a' in 'iuda' the letter 's' has been added.

[2] The letter 'e' has been written afterwards over the 'un' in 'instruntur.'

[3] The mark between two points, like an A with the cross stroke lengthened at both ends, prefixed to this line on the margin of the MS., has not been found elsewhere, but it calls attention to the accidental omission of a verse.

[4] After 'noxis,' 'morte' is erased.

Seq: A mortuis paterna
resurrectum dextera
tertia die redisse
nuntiat apostolis
Mox videtur a beatis
quos probavit fratribus
quod redisse ambigentes
intrat januis clausis
Dat docens praecepta legis
dat divinum spm
spiritū di perfectum
trinitatis vinculum
Praecepit totū p orbē
baptizari credulos
nomen patris invocantes
confitentes filium
Mistica fide revelat
tinctos sancto spiritu
fonte tinctos innovatos
filios factos di.
Ante lucē turba[illegible]
Concin[illegible]

Galli cantus galli plausus
proximum sentit diem
nos canentes et praecantes
quae futura credimus
Maiestatē q: inmensam
concinnemus iugiter
ante lucē nuntiemus
xp̄m regem saeculo
Ante lucē nuntiemus
xp̄m regem saeculo
qui in illū recte credunt
regnaturi cum eo
Gloria patri ingenito
gloria unigenito
simul cum sc̄o spiritu
in sempiterna saecula
Ymnum apostolorū
Praecamur patrem
regem omnipotentem
et ihm̄ xp̄m [illegible]
sc̄m quoque spm̄ alle[illegible]
Dm̄ in una [illegible]
perfectum [illegible]
trinum[illegible]

[*Fol. 4 verso.*]

Seq*ue* a mortuis paterna
suscitatum dextera
tertia die redisse
nuntiat apostolis
Mox uidetur a beatis
quos p*ro*bauit fratribus
quod redisset ambigentes
intrat ianuis clausis
Dat docens praecepta legis.
dat diuinum sp*iritu*m
spiritu*m* d*e*i perfectum
trinitatis uinculum
Præcipit totu*m* per orbe*m*
baptizari credulos
nomen patris inuocantes
confitentes filium
Mistica fide reuelat
tinctos sancto spiritu
fonte tinctos innouatos
filios factos d*e*i
ANte lucem turba *
concin * * *
* * * *
* * * *
* * * *

Galli cantus galli plausus
proximum sentet diem
nos canentes et praecantes
quae futura credimus
Maiestate*m*q*ue* inmensam
concinnemus uniter
ante luce*m* nuntiemus
*christu*m regem saeculo :· —
Ante lucem nuntiemus
*christu*m regem saeculo
qui in illum rectæ credunt
regnaturi cum eo . . ,
Gloria patri ingenito
gloria unigenito
simul cum s*anct*o spiritu
in sempiterna saecula·.·—

YMNUM APOSTOLORU*M*

Praecamur patrem
rege*m* omnipotente*m*
et ih*esu*m *christu*m UT ALII
s*anctu*m quoque sp*iritu*m:. alle*luia*
D*eu*m in una DICUNT
perfectum s * *
trinum * * *
* * * *

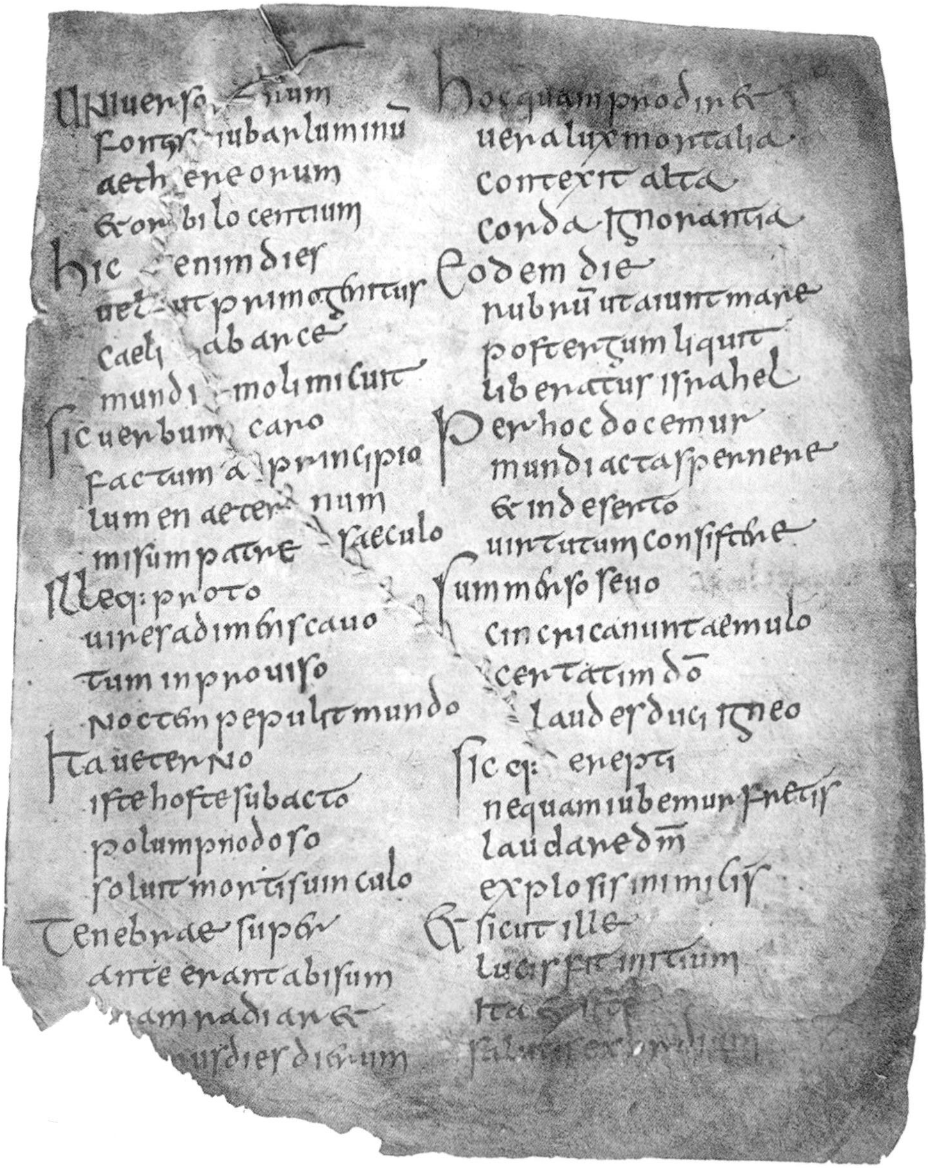

[*Fol. 5 recto.*]

Uniuersorum
fontis iubar lumin*um*
aethereorum
et orbi locentium
Hic enim dies
uelut primogenitus
caeli ab arce
mundi moli micuit
Sic uerbum caro
factum a principio
lumen aeternum
misum patre saeculo
Illeq*ue* proto
uires adimens cauo
tum inprouiso
noctem pepulit mundo
Ita ueterno
iste hoste subacto
polump nodoso
soluit mortis uinculo
Tenebrae super
ante erant abisum
* am radiaret
* us dies dierum

Hoc quam prodiret
uera lux mortalia
contexit alta
corda ignorantia
Eodem die
rubru*m* ut aiunt mare
post ergum liquit
liberatus israhel
Per hoc docemur
mundi acta spernere
et in deserto
uirtutum consistere
Summerso seuo
cincri canunt aemulo
certatim d*e*o
laudes duci igneo
Sicq*ue* erepti
nequam iubemur fretis
laudare d*eu*m
explosis inimicis
Et sicut ille
lucis fit initium
ita et iste
salutis exordium

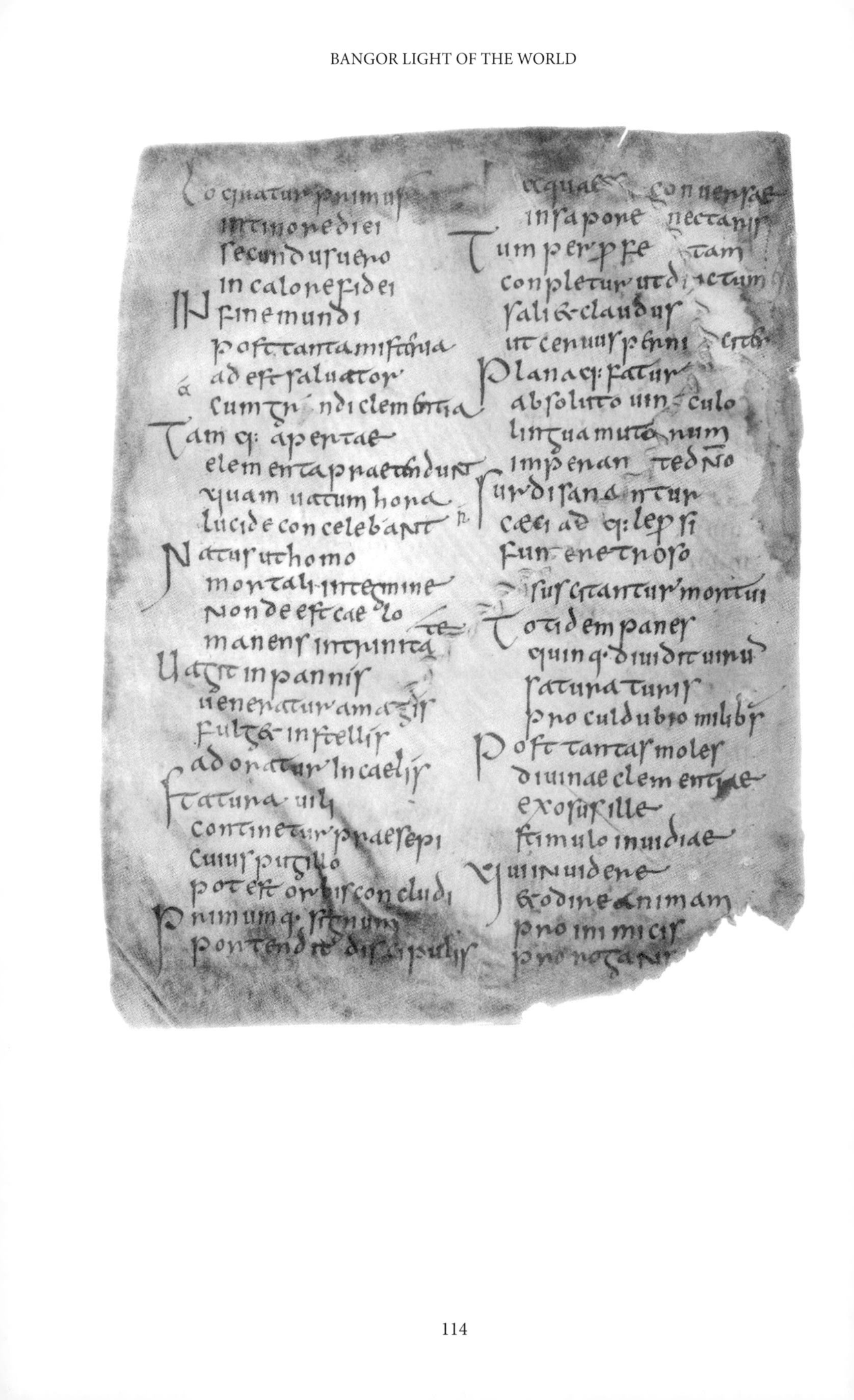

[*Fol. 5 verso.*]

Loquatur primus
in tinore diei
secundus uero
in calore fidei
IN fine mundi
post tanta misteria
adest saluator
cum gr [1]ndi clementia
Tamq*ue* apertae
elementa praetendunt
quam uatum hora
lucide concelebant[2]
Natus ut homo
mortali in tegmine
non deest caelo
manens in trinita /te
Uagit in pannis
ueneratur a magis
fulget in stellis
adoratur in caelis
Statura uili
continetur praesepi
cuius pugillo
potest orbis concludi
Primumq*ue* signum
portendit discipulis
aquae conuersae
in sapore nectaris
Tum per p*ro*fetam
conpletur ut diïctum
saliet claudus
ut ceruus perniciter
Planaq*ue* fatur
absoluto uinculo
lingua mutorum
imperante d*omi*no
Surdi sanantur
cæci adq*ue* lep*ro*si
funere troso
suscitantur mortui
Totidem panes
quinq*ue* diuidit uiru*m*
saturaturis
proculdubio milibus
Post tantas moles
diuinae clementiae
exosus ille
stimulo inuidiae
Qui inuidere
et odire animam
pro inimicis
prorogans

[1] A slanting stroke above this space calls attention to the facts that a letter has been erased, and an 'a' has been written, under a similar slanting stroke, *prima manu* on the left margin.

[2] A slanting stroke has been written over and between the 'b' and 'a' in this word, and an 'r' has been written under a similar slanting stroke by an early correcting hand on the right margin.

Aduersus eum
initur consilium
qui magni dicitur
consilii est nuntius
Accedunt ei
ut latroni cum gladiis
fur enim aeternis
tradituro aestibus
Tandem humano
traditur iudicio
mortali et [illegible]
damnatur probe pe
Cruci confixus
polum mirae concu
lum eque solis
iubar obtenditur
Saxa rumpuntur
uelum scinditur templi
uiui consurgunt
de sepulchris mortui
Con nos sum nodis
annos fere [illegible] milibus
extricat re [illegible]
inferni feralibus
[illegible] to plaustrum
[illegible] osa soboli

Abiectam ali monte
seua ultrice [illegible]
Quem que antiquum
paradiso incolam
recursu suo
clementer restituit
Exaltans caput
uniuersi corporis
in trinitate
locauit aecclesiae
Hoc caelitus
iubet portas principibus
reg cum sociis
aeternales pandere
Errantem propriis
eui chens certissimam
super niuis ouem
humeris ouilibus
Quem expectamus
ad futurum iudicem
iustum cuique
opus suum reddere
Rogo quam taliter
talibus que donaris
uicem condigne
possumus rependere

[*Fol. 6 recto.*]

ADuersus eum
initur consilium
qui magni dictus
consilii est nuntius
Accedunt ei
ut latroni cum gladis
furem aeternis
tradituro aestibus
Tandem humano
traditur iudicio
mortali ege[1]
dampnatur perpe /tuus
CRuci confixus
polum mire concu /tit
lumenq*ue* solis
tribus obtondit oris
Saxa rumpuntur
uelum scinditur templi
uiui consurgunt
de sepulchris mortui
Conrosum nodis
annos fere milibus
extrecat senis
inferi feralibus
* p*ro*toplaustum
* osa soboli

abiecta mali morte
seua ultrice..,
Quemq*ue* antiquum
paradiso incolam
recursu suo
clementer restituit
EXaltans caput
uniuersi corporis
in trinitate
locauit aecclesiae
IN hoc caelitus
iubet portas principes
regi cum socis[2]
aeternales pandere
ERrantem propris
euichens centissimam
supernis ouem
humeris ouilibus[3]
Quem expectamus
adfuturum iudicem
iustum cuique
opus suum reddere
Rogo quam tantes[4]
talibusque donaris
uicem condigne
possumus rependere

[1] The letter 'l' before 'ege' has been erased, and an 'r' under three points has been written on the right margin by an early correcting hand.

[2] A second 'i' has been subsequently written over 'socis.'

[3] The accent over the first syllable of 'ouilibus' was probably intended to be placed over the 'i' of 'humeris.'

[4] A slanting stroke has been placed over the 'e' in 'tantes,' and an 'i' beneath a slanting stroke has been written on the right margin.

Quid tam mortales
temptamus in [illegible]
narrare queunt
quae nullus edicere et
Solum oramus
hoc idemque maximum
nostri aeternae
miserere domine alle
Canticum sci zachariae
Benedictus dominus deus
israhel quia uisitauit
et fecit redemptionem
plebis suae et erexit
cornu salutis nobis in
domu dauid pueri sui
Sicut locutus est per
os scorum prophetarum
suorum qui a
beo sunt. Et liberabit
nos ab inimicis nos
tris et de manu om
nium qui nos oderunt
Ad faciendam mise
ricordiam cum
patribus nostris.

et memorare testa
menti sci sui
Ius iurandum quod
iurauit ad abra
ham patrem nostrum
daturum se nobis
Ut sine timore de ma
nibus inimicorum
nostrorum libera
ti seruiamus illi in
sanctitate et iustitia
coram ipso omnibus
diebus nostris
Et tu puer propheta
altissimi uocaberis
praeibis enim ante
faciem domini parare
uias eius
Ad dandam scientiam
salutis plebi eius in
re missionem
peccatorum meorum
Per uiscera miseri
cordiae dei nostri
in quibus

[*Fol. 6 verso.*]

Quid tam mortales
temptamus migrologi
narrare queuit
quae nullus edicere :·,
Solum oramus
hoc idemq*ue* maximu*m*
nostri aeternae
miserere d*omi*ne.., alle*luia*

BENEDICTIO[1] S*A*NCTI ZACHARIAE

Benedictus d*omi*n*u*s d*eu*s
isr*ahe*l quia uisitauit
et fecit redemptione*m*
plebis suae et erexit
cornu salutis nobis in
domu dauid pueri sui :·,
Sicut loqutus est per
os s*anct*orum p*ro*pheta
rum suorum qui a[2]
b eo sunt et liberabit
nos ab inimicis nos
tris et de manu om
nium qui nos oderunt :·,
AD faciendam mise
ricordiam cum
patribus nostris
et memorari testa
menti s*anct*i sui..,
Iusiurandum quod
iurauit ad abra
ham patrem n*ostru*m
daturum se nobis :·,
UT sine timore de ma
nibus inimicorum
nostrorum libera
ti seruiamus illi in
s*anct*itate et iustitia
coram ipso omnibus
diebus nostris..,_
ET tu puer p*ro*pheta
altissimi uocaberis
præibis enim ante
faciem d*omi*ni parare
uias eius..,
AD dandam scientia*m*
salutis plebi eius in
remisionem
peccatoru*m* meorum..,
Per uiscera miseri
cordiae d*e*i nos *
in quibus[3]

---

[1] We have expanded 'b' into 'benedictio,' but we have not found any title except 'Canticum' (Rom., Moz., Ambros.), and 'Prophetia' (Gallican) for this Canticle in Western Service books. In the Greek Horologion it is entitled *Προσευχὴ Ζαχαρίου.*

[2] The letter 'h' has been erased before 'ab.'

[3] As the 'Canticum Zachariae" breaks off here, and is resumed on fol. 10 recto, it is evident that three leaves of the MS. between fol. 6 and fol. 10 are misplaced.

Cantemus domino gloriose enim hono
rificatus est equum et ascenso
rem proiecit in mare adiutor
et protector fuit mihi in salutem
hic deus meus et honorificabo eum. deus patris mei et exaltabo eum
dominus conterens bella dominus nomen
est illi.

Currus faraonis et exercitum eius
proiecit in mare electos ascen
sores ternos stratores demer
sit in rubrum mare.

Pelago cooperuit eos deuenerunt
in profundum tamquam lapis
dextera tua domine glorificata
est in uirtute dextera manus
tua domine confringit inimicos.
Et per multitudinem maiestatis
tuae

[*Fol. 7 recto.*]

CANTICUM

CANtemus d*omi*no gloriosæ enim hono
rificatus est aequum et ascenso
rem proiecit in mare adiutor
et protector fuit mihi in salutem :·
Hic d*eu*s meus et honorificabo eum[1]
d*omi*n*u*s conterens bella d*omi*n*u*s nomen
est illi . . ,
Currus faraonis et exercitum eius
proiecit in mare electos ascen
sores ternos stratores demer
sit in rubrum mare :·
Pylago cooperuit eos deuenerunt
in profundum tamquam lapis
dextera tua d*omi*ne glorificata
est in uirtute dextera manus
tua d*omi*ne confringet inimicos :·
ETper multitudine*m* maiestatis
/tuæ

[1] These six words, 'd*eu*s patris mei et exultabo eum,' accidentally omitted in the text after 'eum,' have been subsequently written in a small contemporaneous hand-writing on the right margin in an irregularly shaped dotted framework.

Contriuisti aduersarios misisti iram
tuam & comedit eos tā quā stipulā:·
Et per spm irae cundiae tuae diuisa
est aqua gelauerunt tam quam
murus aquae gelauerunt fluctus
in medio maris:·
Dixit inimicus persequens conprae-
hendam partibor spolia neple-
bo animam meam interficiam gla-
dio meo dominabitur manus mea:·
Misisti spm tuum & cooperuit eos
mare merserunt tam quam plum-
bum in aqua ualidissima:·
Quis similis tibi in dis dne quis similis tibi gloriosus in scis mirabiles
in maiestatibus faciens prodigia:·
Extendisti dexteram tuam

[*Fol. 7 verso.*]

contriuisti aduersarios misisti ira*m*
tuam et comedit eos ta*m*qua*m* stipula*m* :·
ETper sp*iritu*m iraecundiae tuae diuisa
est aqua gylauerunt tamquam
muros aquae gylauerunt fluctus
in medio mari . . ,
Dixit inimicus persequens conprae
hendam partibor spolia reple
bo animam meam interficiam gla
dio meo dominabitur manus mea :·
Misisti sp*iritu*m tuum et cooperuit eos
mare merserunt tamquam plum
bum in aqua ualidissima . . ,
Quis similis tibi in diis d*omi*ne quis simi
lis tibi gloriosus in s*an*c*t*is mirabiles
in maiestatibus faciens p*ro*digia :·
Extendisti dexteram tuam

·& deuorauit eos terra· gubernasti iustitiam tuam populo tuo
hunc quem liberasti :·
Exortatus es in uirtute tua inre-
frigerio scō tuo audierunt gentes
& iratae sunt dolores conpraehen-
derunt inhabitantes filistim ...
Tunc festinauerunt duces edom·
& principes moabitarum ad-
praehendit eos timor· tabuerunt
omnes inhabitantes channan ...
Decidat super eos timor & tremor
magnitudinis brachi tui· fiant
tamquam lapis donec transeat
populus tuus dñe usq: dum transeat populus tuus hunc quem dñe
liberasti ...

[*Fol. 8 recto.*]

et deuorauit eos terra. guber
nasti iustitiam tuam populo tuo
hunc quem liberasti :·

Exortatus es in uirtute tua in re
frigerio s*anct*o tuo audierunt gentes
et iratae sunt dolores conpraehen
derunt inhabitantes filistim . . ,

Tunc festinauerunt duces edom
et principes mohabitarum ad
praehendit eos timor. tabuerunt
omnes inhabitantes channan . . . ,

Decidat super eos timor et tremor
magnitudinis brachi tui. fiant
tamquam lapis donec transeat
populus tuus d*omi*ne usq*ue* dum tran
seat populus tuus[1] hunc quem
liberasti . . ,

[1] A point has been placed between 'tuus' and 'hunc,' and a slanting stroke, with a point above it, has been placed above the line, and the word 'd*omi*ne,' with a slanting stroke above it, has been written on the right margin by an early correcting hand.

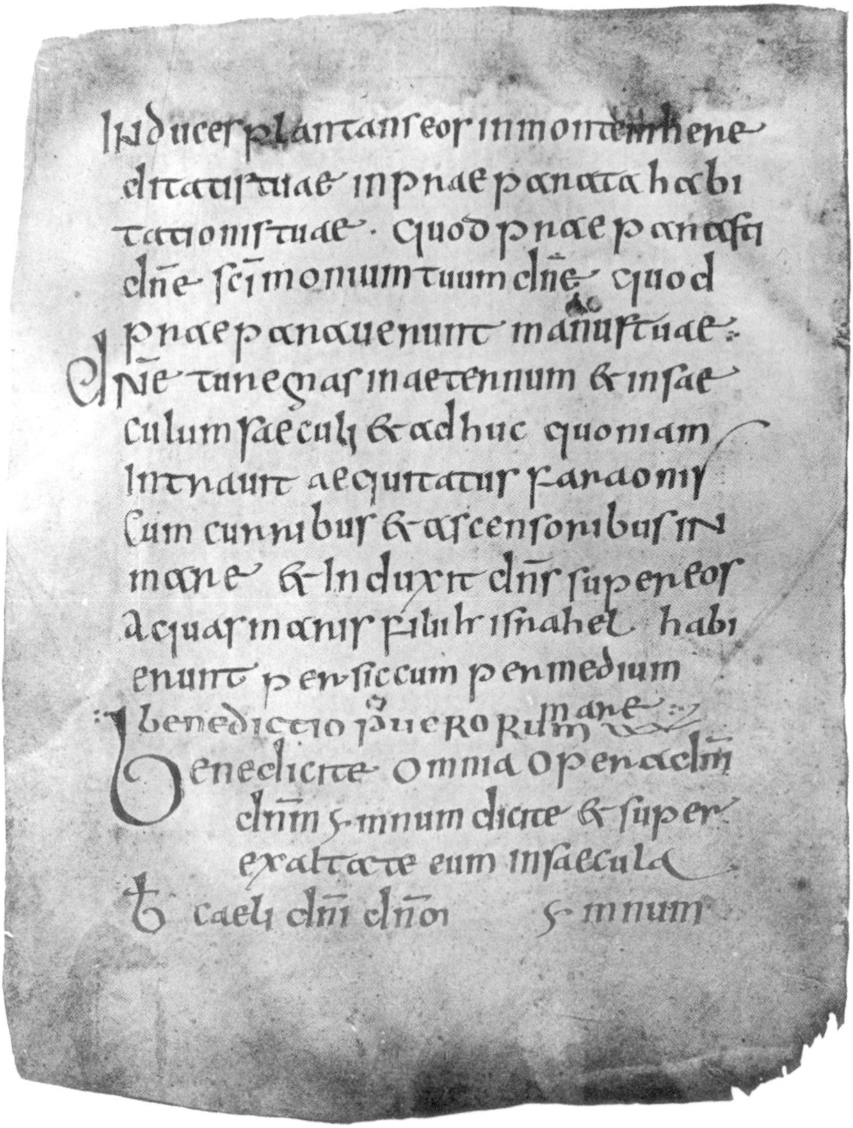
Inducens plantans eos in montem here
ditatis tuae in praeparata habi
tationis tuae. quod praeparasti
dne scimonium tuum dne quod
praeparauerunt manus tuae.
Dne tu regnas in aeternum et in sae
culum saeculi et adhuc quoniam
intrauit aequitatus faraonis
cum curribus et ascensoribus in
mare et induxit dns super eos
aquas maris filii autem israhel habi
erunt per siccum per medium
Benedictio puerorum mane
Benedicite omnia opera dni
dnm ymnum dicite et super
exaltate eum in saecula
Et caeli dni dnm ymnum

[*Fol. 8 verso.*]

INduces plantans eos in montem here
ditatis tuae in praeparata habi
tationis tuae. quod praeparasti
d*omi*ne s*anct*imonium tuum d*omi*ne quod
praeparauerunt manus tuae :·
D*omi*ne tu regnas in aeternum et in sae
culum saeculi et adhuc quoniam
intrauit aequitatus faraonis
cum curribus et ascensoribus in
mare et induxit d*omi*n*u*s super eos
aquas maris filii *autem* israhel habi
erunt per siccum per medium
mare :· ,

BENEDICTIO PUERORUM[1]

Benedicite omnia opera d*omi*ni
d*omi*n*u*m ymnum dicite et super
exaltate eum in saecula
b*enedicite* caeli d*omi*ni d*omi*n*u*m ymnum

[1] Some alteration of this title has begun to be written, without being finished, over the 'P' of 'PUERORUM.' The usual title is 'canticum trium puerorum.'

b angeli dni dnm ẏ·ymnu[m]
b aquae omnes super caelos dnm ẏ·
b omnes potentiae dni dnm ẏ·m
b sol et luna dnm ẏ·m
b stellae caeli dni dnm ẏ·m
b imber et ros dnm ẏ·m
b omnes sps dnm ẏ·m
b ignis et calor dnm ẏ·m
b noctes et dies dnm ẏ·m
b tenebrae et lumen dnm ẏ·m
b frigus et aestas dnm ẏ·m
b pruina et niues dnm ẏ·m
b fulgora et nubes dnm ẏ·m
b dicat terra dnm ẏ·mnum
dicat et super exaltat eum in sae-
b montes et colles dnm ẏ·m
b omnia nascentia terrae dnm ẏ·m

[*Fol. 9 recto.*]

b*enedicite* angeli d*omi*ni d*omi*n*u*m ymnu*m* d*icite*
b*enedicite* aquae omnes super caelos d*omi*n*u*m y*mnum*
b*enedicite* omnis potentias d*omi*ni d*omi*n*u*m ym*num*
b*enedicite* sol et luna d*omi*n*u*m ym*num*
b*enedicite* stellae caeli d*omi*ni d*omi*n*u*m ym*num*
b*enedicite* ymber et ros d*omi*n*u*m ym*num*
b*enedicite* omnis sp*iritu*s d*omi*n*u*m ym*num*
b*enedicite* ignis et calor d*omi*n*u*m ym*num*
b*enedicite* noctes et dies d*omi*n*u*m ym*num*
b*enedicite* tenebrae et lumen d*omi*n*u*m ym*num*
b*enedicite* frigus et aestas d*omi*n*u*m ym*num*
b*enedicite* pruina et niues d*omi*n*u*m ym*num*
b*enedicite* fulgora et nubes d*omi*n*u*m ym*num*
b*ene* dicat terra d*omi*n*u*m ymnum
dicat et superexaltat eum in sæ*cula*
b*enedicite* montes et colles d*omi*n*u*m ym*num*
b*enedicite* omnia nascentia terrae d*omi*n*u*m ym*num*

b maria et flumina dnm ym
b fontes aquarum dnm ym
b bilue et omnia quae mo
uentur in aquis dnm ym
b omnes uolucres caeli dnm ym
b bestiae et iumenta dnm ym
b israhel ete dnm ym
b filii hominum dnm ym
b sacerdotes dni dnm ym
b serui dni dnm ym
b sps et animae iustorum dnm ym
b sci et humiles corde dnm ym
b annanias azarias misael dnm ym
benedicamus patrem et filium
et spm scm dnm ymnum dicamus
et super exaltemus eum in saecula.

[*Fol. 9 verso.*]

b*enedicite* maria et flumina d*omin*u*m* ym*num*
b*enedicite* fontes aquarum d*omin*u*m* ym*num*
b*enedicite* bilue et omnia quae mo
uentur in aquis d*omin*u*m* ym*num*
b*enedicite* omnes uolucres caeli d*omin*u*m* ym*num*
b*enedicite* bestiæ et iumenta d*omin*u*m* ym*num*
b*enedicite* israhelite d*omin*u*m* ym*num*
b*enedicite* filii hominum d*omin*u*m* ym*num*
b*enedicite* sacerdotes d*omin*i d*omin*u*m* ym*num*
b*enedicite* serui d*omin*i d*omin*u*m* ym*num*
b*enedicite* sp*iritu*s et animae iustorum d*omin*u*m* ym*num*
b*enedicite* s*an*c*t*i et humiles corde d*omin*u*m* ym*num*
b*enedicite* annanias azarias misael[1] d*omin*u*m* ym*num*
benedicamus patrem et filium
et sp*iritu*m s*anctu*m d*omin*u*m* ymnum dicamus
et superexaltemus eum in saecula :· ,[2]

[1] A small 'h' has been written *prima manu* above and between the fourth and fifth letters of 'misael' and a point has been placed in a corresponding position below the line.

[2] The apparently erased line at the bottom of this page is only the last line of fol. 9 recto shewing through the skin.

nos:
uisitauit nos oriens ex alto:.
Inluminare his qui
in tenebris et um
bra mortis sedent
ad dirigendos pe
des nostros in uiam
pacis..
Puer autem crescebat
et confortabatur
in spiritu et erat in deser
tis usque ad diem osten
sionis suae ad israhel..
ymnum in die do[minica]
Laudate pueri dominum lau
date nomen
domini te dominum laudamus
te dominum confitemur:
Te aeternum patrem
omnis terra uenera
tur tibi omnes an
geli tibi caeli et uniuer
sae potestates..
Tibi hiruphin et sera
phin incessabili
uoce proclamant
sanctus sanctus sanctus dominus deus
sabaoth.
Pleni sunt caeli et
uniuersa terra
honore gloriae tuae:
Te gloriosus aposto
lorum chorus. Te
prophetarum lau
dabilis numerus:
Te martyrum candi
datus laudat exer
citus. Te per orbem
terrarum sancta con
fitetur aecclesia:
Patrem inmensae
maiestatis uene
randum tuum ue
rum unigenitum
filium..

[*Fol. 10 recto.*]

uisitauit[1] oriens ex alto :·
INluminare hiis qui
in tenebris et um
bra mortis sedent
ad dirigendos pe
des nostros in uiam
pacis . . ,
Puer *autem* crescebat
et confortabatur
in sp*irit*u et erat in deser
tis usq*ue* ad diem osten
sionis suae et isr*ahe*l :· ,

YMNU*M* IN DIE DO M INI CA

Laudate pueri d*omi*n*u*m
laudate nomen
d*omi*ni. te d*eu*m laudamus
te d*omi*n*u*m confitemur :·
Te aeternum patre*m*
omnis terra uenera
tur. tibi omnes an
geli tibi caeli. et uniuer
sae potestates . . ,

Tibi hirubin et syra
phin incessabili
uoce p*ro*clamant
s*anctu*s s*anctu*s s*anctu*s d*omi*n*u*s d*eu*s
sabaoth . ,
Pleni sunt caeli et
uniuersa terra
honore gloriæ tuæ :·
Te gloriosus aposto
lorum chorus. te
p*ro*phetarum lau
dabilis numerus :·
Te martyrum candi
datus laudet exer
citus. te per orbe*m*
terrarum s*anct*a con
fitetur aecclesia :·
Patrem inmensae
maiestatis. uene
randum tuum ue
rum unigenitum
filium . . ,

[1] The word 'nos' has been added above the line followed by two points placed colon-wise (:), and two similar points have been placed between 'uisitauit' and 'oriens.'

This is a continuation of the Canticum Zachariae from fol. 6 verso.

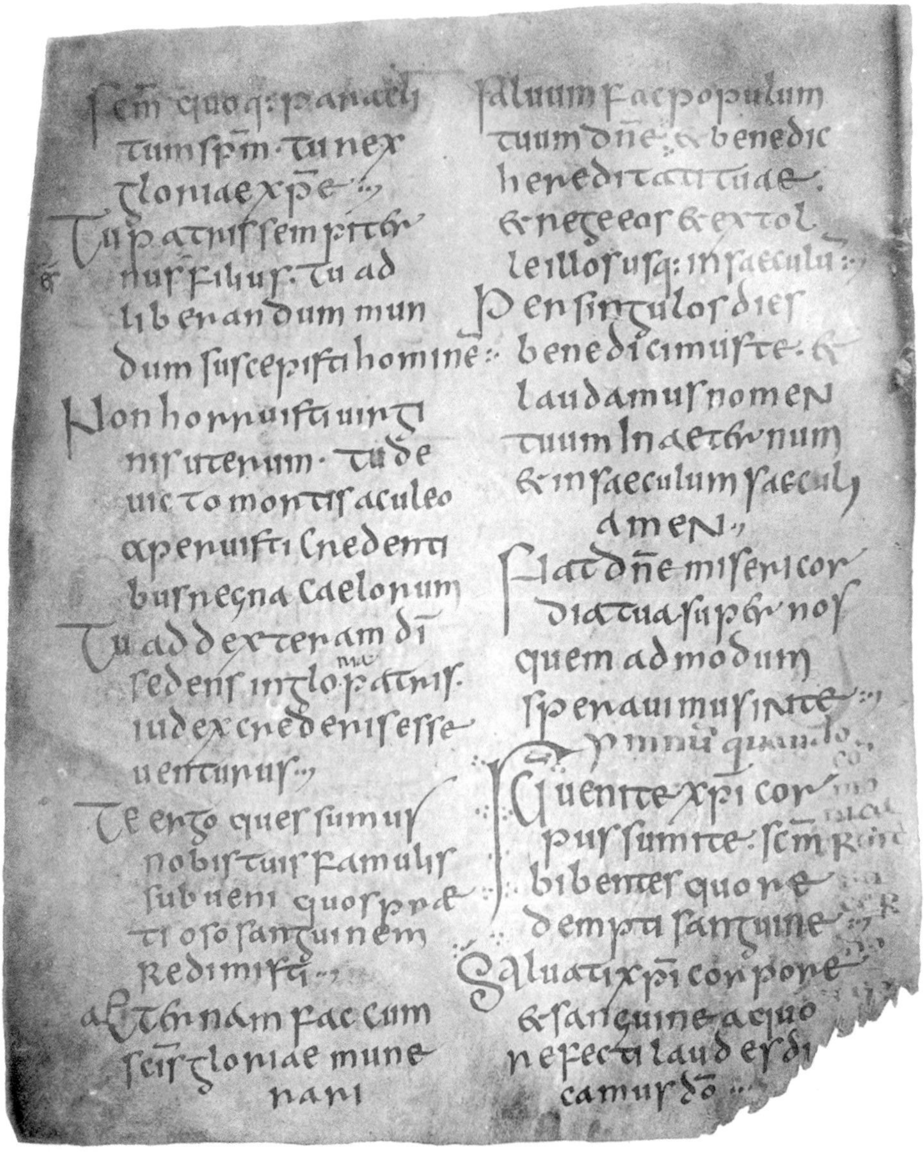

scm quoq: paraclitum spm. tu rex
gloriae xpe.
Tu patris sempiternus filius. tu ad
liberandum mundum suscepisti hominem.
Non horruisti uirginis uterum. tu deuicto mortis aculeo
aperuisti credentibus regna caelorum
Tu ad dexteram di sedens in glo. patris.
iudex crederis esse uenturus.
Te ergo quaesumus nobis tuis famulis
subueni quos pretioso sanguinem
redimisti.
aeternam fac cum scis gloriae munerari

saluum fac populum tuum dne. & benedic
hereditati tuae.
& rege eos & extolle illos usq: in saeculum.
Per singulos dies benedicimus te. &
laudamus nomen tuum in aeternum
& in saeculum saeculi
amen.
Fiat dne misericordia tua super nos
quem admodum sperauimus in te.
ymnu quando commonicarent sacerdotes
Sancti uenite xpi corpus sumite. scm
bibentes quo redempti sanguine.
Saluati xpi corpore & sanguine a quo
refecti laudes dicamus do.

[*Fol. 10 verso.*]

S*anctu*m quoq*ue* paracli
tum sp*iritu*m. tu rex
gloriae *christe*..,
Tu patris sempiter
nus[1] filius. tu ad
liberandum mun
dum suscepisti homine*m* :·
Non horruisti uirgi
nis uterum. tu de
uicto mortis aculeo
aperuisti credenti
bus regna caelorum
Tu ad dexteram d*e*i
sedens in glo[2] patris.
iudex crederis esse
uenturus..,
Te ergo quessumus
nobis tuis famulis
subueni quos præ
tioso sanguinem
redimisti..,
aEternam fac cum
s*anct*is gloriae mune
rari

Saluum fac populum
tuum d*omi*ne[3] et benedic
hereditati tuae.
et rege eos et extol
le illos usq*ue* in saeculu*m* :·,
Per singulos dies
benedicimus te. et
laudamus nomen
tuum in aeternum
et in saeculum saeculi
amen.,
Fiat d*omi*ne misericor
dia tua super nos
quemadmodum
sperauimus in te :·,

YMNU*M* QUANDO COM*M*ONICARENT SACERDOTES

S*anct*i uenite *christi* cor
pus sumite. s*anctu*m
bibentes quo re
dempti sanguine :·,
Saluati *christi* corpore
et sanguine a quo
refecti laudes di
camus d*e*o...,

[1] Two short slanting strokes above and after this word call attention to the word 'es' which has been added in by contemporary hand on the left margin with two similar strokes above it.

[2] A point has been placed after 'glo,' and the letters 'ria' followed by a point have been written by a contemporary hand above and after 'glo.'

[3] Two groups of three points are written after 'domine,' one group above, one group below the line. It is not obvious why they are placed here. A transposition of verses takes place at this verse in some early MSS. of this Canticle, but to mark this the points should have been placed after 'munerari.' See Julian's *Dict. of Hymnology*, p. 1,120.

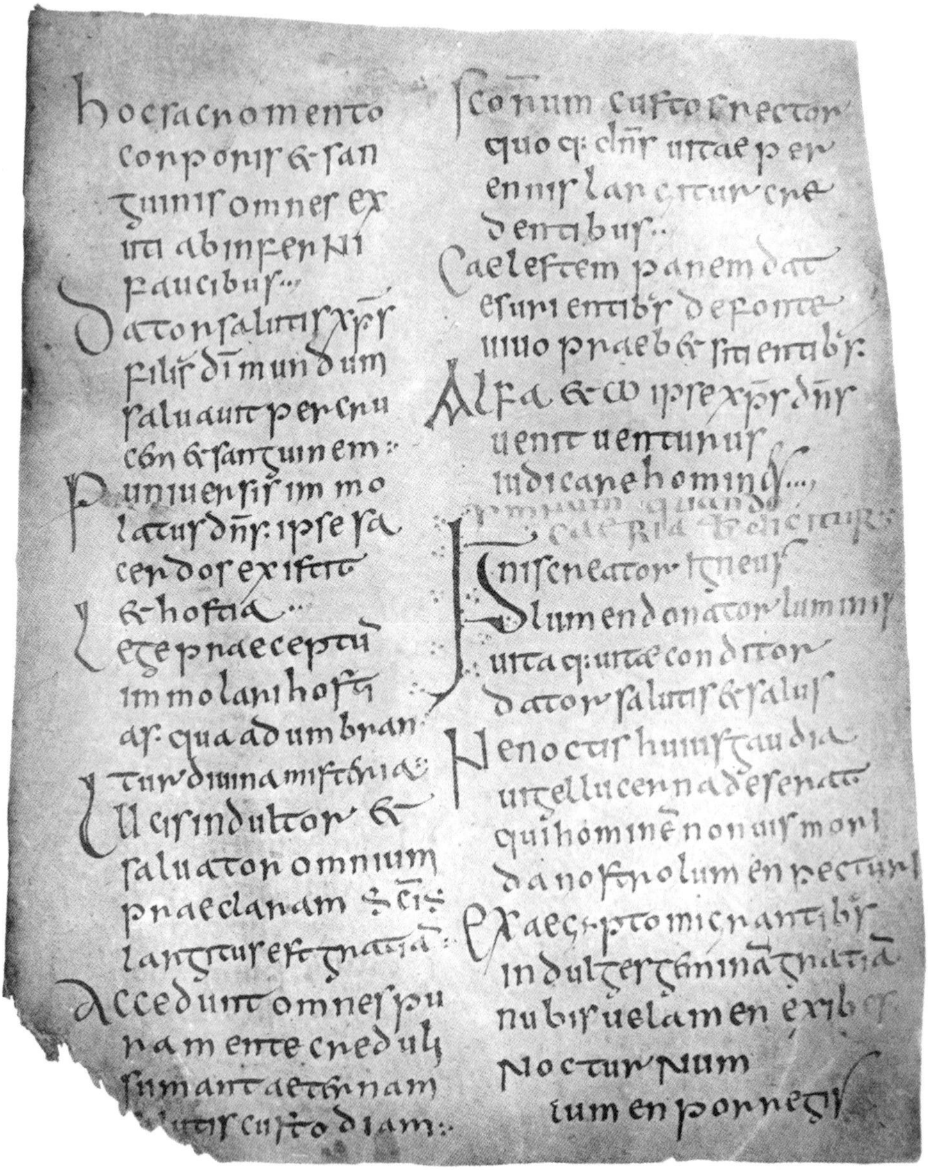

[*Fol. 11 recto.*]

Hoc sacromento
corporis et san
guinis omnes ex
uti ab inferni
faucibus . . ,
Dator salutis *christu*s
filius d*e*i mundum
saluauit per cru
cem et sanguinem :·
P*ro* uniuersis immo
latus d*omi*n*u*s. ipse sa
cerdos existit
et hostia . . ,
Lege praeceptu*m*
immolari hosti
as. qua adumbran
tur diuina misteria :·
LUcis indultor et
saluator omnium
praeclaram s*anct*is
largitus est gratia*m* :·
Accedunt omnes pu
ra mente creduli
sumant aeternam
salutis custodiam :·
S*anct*orum custos rector
quoq*ue* d*omi*n*u*s uitae per
ennis largitur cre
dentibus . . ,
Caelestem panem dat
esurientibus de fonte
uiuo praebet sitientibus.
Alfa et ω ipse *christu*s d*omi*n*u*s
uenit uenturus
iudicare homines . . . ,

YMNUM QUANDO
CAERIA BEN*E*DICITUR·,·

IG nis creator igneus
lumen donator luminis
uitaq*ue* uitæ conditor
dator salutis et salus
Ne noctis huius gaudia
uigel lucerna deserat
qui homine*m* non uis mori
da nostro lumen pecturi
EX aegypto migrantibus
indulges gemina*m* gratia*m*
nubis uelamen exibes
nocturnum
lumen porregis

Nubis columna per die
uenientem plebem protegit
ignis columna ad uesperum
noctem depellis lumine
E flamma famulum prouocas
Rubum non spernis spineam
et cum sis ignis concremans
non uris quod inluminans
Fucodepasto nibulo
tempus decoctis sordibus
feruente sancto spiritu
candore lucet cerea
Secretis iam condit fauum
diuini mellis alitus
cordis replet intimas
uerbo repletis cellolas
Examen ut foetus noui
ore praelectum spiritu
Relectum caelum sarcinis
quaerat securis pinnulis
Gloria patri ingenito
Gloria unigenito
simul cum sancto spiritu
in sempiterna saecula

Mediae noctis
tempus est
prophetica uox
admonet dica
mus laudes ut deo
patri semper
ac filio
Sancto quoque spiritui
perfecta enim
trinitas uniusque
substantiae lau
danda nobis semper est
Terrorem tempus
hoc habet quo
cum uastator an
gelus aegypto
mortem intulit
deleuit primogenita
Haec iustis hora
salus est et quos
idem tunc angelus
ausus punire non
erat signum for
midans sanguinis

[*Fol. 11 verso.*]

Nubis columpna per die*m*
uenient*em* plebe*m* protegis
ignis columna ad uesperu*m*
noctem depellis lumine
E Flamma famulu*m* p*ro*uocas
rubu*m* non spernis spineam
et cum sis ignis concremans
non uris quod inlumnans[1]
Fuco depasto nibulo
tempus decoctis surdibus
feruente s*a*nct*o* sp*iri*tu
carne*m* lucere cercam.
Secretis iam condis[2] faui
diuini mellis alitus
cordis repurgas intimas
uerbo replisti cellolas :·
EXamen ut foetus noui
ore praelectum sp*iri*tu
relectum[3] caelum sarcinis
querat securis pinnulis
Gloria patri ingenito
gloria unigenito
simul cum s*a*nct*o* sp*iri*tu
in sempiterna saecula :··,

YMNU*M* MEDIAE NOC TIS ·.·

Mediae noctis
tempus est
prophetica uox
admonet dica
mus laudes ut d*e*o
patri semper
ac filio..,
S*a*nct*o* quoq*ue* spiritui
perfecta enim
trinitas. uniusq*ue*
substantiae lau
danda nobis semper est :·
Terrorem tempus
hoc habet quo
cum uastatur an
gelus aegypto
mortem intulit
deliuit primogenita
Haec iustis hora
salus est. et quos
idem tunc angelus
ausus puniri non
erat signum for
midans sanguinis

[1] The early correcting hand which added an 'i' over this word should also have erased the second 'n.' The word should evidently be 'inluminas.'

[2] A later correcting hand has written 'en' over the second syllable of 'condis.'

[3] An early correcting hand has placed a point beneath, and an 'i' above, the second 'e' in this word.

a[illegible] ptrus flebat for
titer. tantorum
dino funere. solus
gaudebat isrl. cuius
ptectus sanguine.
Nos uero isrl sumus
laetamur in te dne
hostem spernentes
& malum xpi defen
si sanguine.
Ipsum pfecto tempus
est. quo uoce euange
lica uenturus spon
sus creditur. regni
caelestis conditor.
Occurrunt scae uir
gines obuiam tunc
aduentui. gestantes
claras lampades
magnolaetantes
gaudio.
Stultae uero rema
nent quae extinc
tas habent lampades.

frustra pulsantes
ianuas clausa iam
regni regia.
Quare uigilemus
sobrii gestantes
mentes splendidas
aduentui ut ihu.
digne cum nam obuia.
Noctisque medio
tempore. paulus
quoque & sileas. xpm
uincti in carcere
conlaudantes solu
ti sunt.
Nobis mundus hic
carcer est. te lau
damus xpe ds. sol
ue uincla pecca
torum. in te scē
credentium.
Dignos nos fac rex
o agie. futuri
regni gloriae.
aeternis ut me
reamur.

[*Fol. 12 recto.*]

aEgyptus flebat for
titer. tantorum
diro funere. solus
gaudebat isr*ahe*l agni
p*ro*tectus sanguine :·
Nos uero isr*ahe*l sumus
laetamur in te d*omi*ne
hostem spernentes
et malum *christ*i defen
si sanguine . . ,
IPsum p*ro*fecto tempus
est. quo uoce euange
lica. uenturus spon
sus creditur. regni
caelestis conditor :·
Occurrunt s*anct*æ uir
gines. obuiam tunc
aduentui. gestantes
claras lampades
magno laetantes
gaudio . ,
Stultæ uero rema
nent quae extinc
tas habent lampades.
frustra pulsantes
ianuas clausa iam
regni regia ·.·
Quare uigilemus
subrii. gestantes
mentes splendidas
aduentui ut ih*es*u
digne curramus obuia*m*:
Noctisque medio
tempore. paulus
quoq*ue* et sileas. *christu*m
uincti in carcere
conlaudantes solu
ti sunt
Nobis mundus hic
carcer est. te lau
damus *christ*e d*eu*s. sol
ue uincla[1] pecca
torum. in te s*anct*e
credentium . . ,
DIGnos nos fac rex
agie. futuri
regni gloriae.
aeternis ut me
reamur.

[1] The scribe began to write 'uncla' but changed it to 'uincla.'

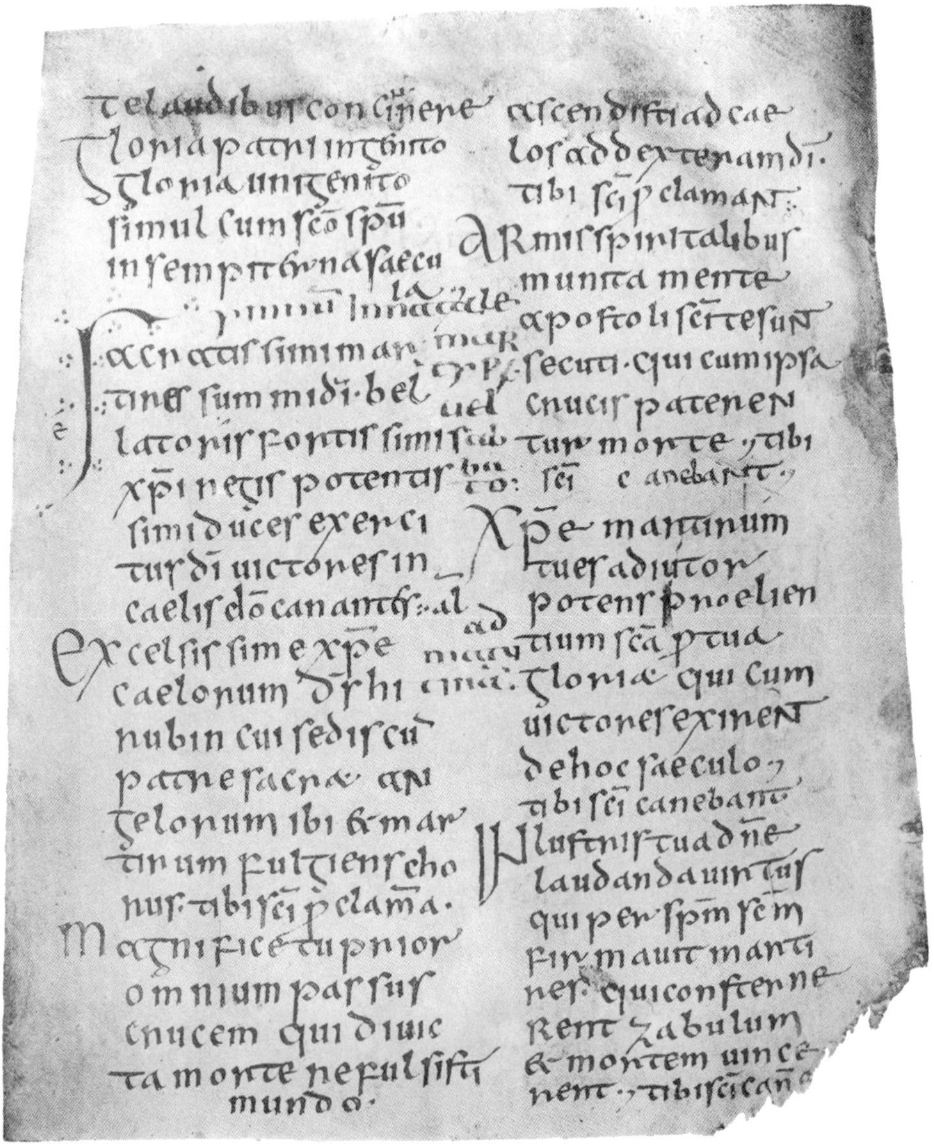

[*Fol. 12 verso.*]

te laudibus concinere[1]
Gloria patri ingenito
gloria unigenito
simul cum s*anct*o sp*irit*u
in sempiterna saecu
la.,

YMNUM IN NATALE MARTYR*UM* UEL SABBATO: AD MATUTINA*M*.

Sacratissimi mar
tires summi d*e*i. bel
latoris[2] fortissimi
*christ*i regis potentis
simi duces exerci
tus d*e*i uictores in
caelis d*e*o canantes :· al*leluia*
EXcelsissime *christ*e
caelorum d*eu*s hi
rubin cui sedis cu*m*
patre sacra. an
gelorum ibi et mar
tirum fulgiens cho
rus. tibi s*anct*i p*ro*clama*nt*.
Magnifice tu prior
omnium passus
crucem qui diuic
ta morte refulsisti
mundo.
ascendisti ad cae
los ad dexteram d*e*i.
tibi s*anct*i p*ro*clamant :·
ARmis spiritalibus
munita mente
apostoli s*anct*i te sunt
secuti. qui cum ipsa
crucis pateren
tur morte., tibi
s*anct*i canebant[3].,
*CHrist*e martirum
tu es adiutor
potens proelien
tium s*anct*a p*ro* tua
gloria. qui cum
uictores exirent
de hoc saeculo.,
tibi s*anct*i canebant
INlustris tua d*omi*ne
laudanda uirtus
qui per sp*iritu*m s*anctu*m
firmauit marti
res. qui consterne
rent zabulum
et mortem uince
rent., tibi s*anct*i can*ebant*[4]

---

[1] An early correcting hand has placed a point between 'i' and 'n,' and has written an 'n' followed by a point over 'concinere.'

[2] A contemporary correcting hand has placed a slanting stroke and a point over the 'i' in this word, and has written an 'e' with a slanting stroke and a point above it in the margin.

[3] 'Canebant' is written over a totally or partly erased 'p*ro*clamant.

[4] The conclusion of this word is doubtful.

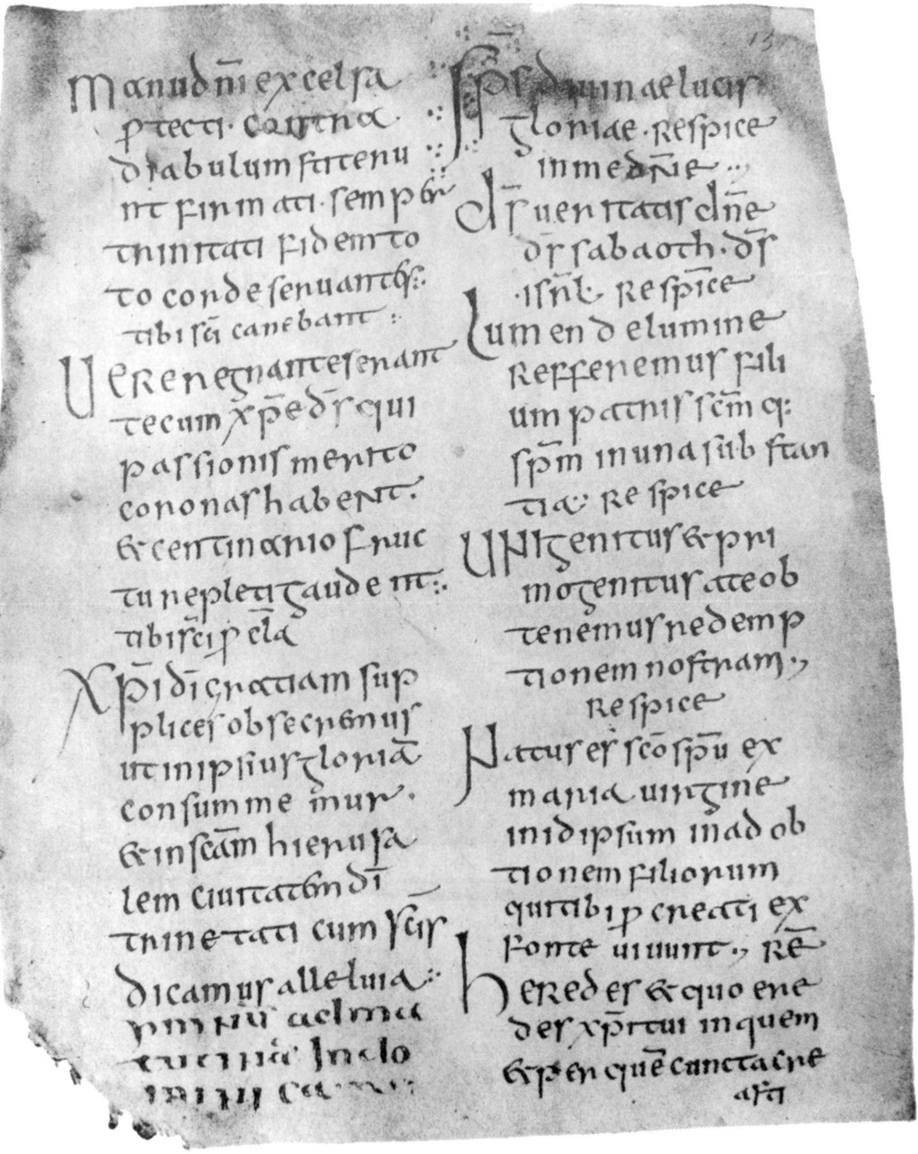

[*Fol. 13 recto.*]

Manu d*omi*ni excelsa
p*ro*tecti. contra
diabulum stiteru
nt firmati. semper
trinitati fidem to
to corde seruantes :·
tibi s*anct*i canebant :·
Uere regnantes erant
tecum *christ*e d*eu*s qui
passionis merito
coronas habent.
et centinario fruc
tu repleti gaudent :·
tibi s*anct*i p*ro*cla*mant*
*CHrist*i d*e*i gratiam sup
plices obsecremus
ut in ipsius gloria*m*
consummemur.
et in s*anct*am hierusa
lem ciuitatem d*e*i
trinetati cum s*anct*is
dicamus alleluia :·

YMNU*M* AD MA
TUTINA*M* IN DO
MINICA

SP*iritu*s diuinae lucis
gloriae. respice
in me d*omi*ne . . ,
D*eu*s ueritatis d*omi*ne
d*eu*s sabaoth. d*eu*s
.isr*ahe*l. respice[1]
Lumen de lumine
refferemus fili
um patris s*anctu*mq*ue*
sp*iritu*m in una substan
tia ·.· respice
UNigenitus et pri
mogenitus a te ob
tenemus redemp
tionem nostram . ,
respice
Natus es s*anct*o sp*irit*u ex
maria uirgine
in id ipsum in adob
tionem filiorum
qui tibi p*ro*creati ex
fonte uiuunt . , re*spice*
Heredes et quo ere
des *christ*i tui in quem
et per que*m* cuncta cre
asti

[1] The mark of abbreviation over 'respice' implies the addition of the remainder of the refrain.

quia in praedistina
tione a saeculis nobis
est datus qui nunc cepit
respice
Unigenito ex mortuis
deo obtenens cor
pus claritatem di
manens in saecula
saeculorum rex ae
ternorum :: respi
Qui a nunc cepit qui
semper fuit natu
ra tuae filius di
uinae lucis gloriae
tuae qui est forma
& plenitudo diuini
tatis tuae sed et quibus:
respice
Persona unigeniti
& primogeniti
qui est totus a toto
diximus lux de lu
mine :: respice
Et deum uerum a deo
uero se se con
fitemur .

tribus personis in
una substantia :: re
spice in me domine
ymnum sancti patricii
Audite omnes amantes
deum sancta merita
uiri in xpo beati
patrici episcupi
quomodo bonum ob actum
similatur angelis
perfectamque propter uitam
aequatur apostolis
Beata xpi custodit
mandata in omnibus
cuius opera refulgent
clara inter homines
sanctumque cuius sequuntur
exemplum mirificum
unde & in caelis patrem
magnificant dominum ::
Constans in dei timore
& fide inmobilis
super quem aedificatur
ut petrum aecclesia
cuiusque apostolatum

[*Fol. 13 verso.*]

quia in praedistina
tione a saeculis nobis
est d*eu*s ih*esu*s qui nunc cepit
respice
Unigenito ex mortuis
d*e*o obtenens cor
pus claritatem d*ei*
manens in saecula
saeculorum rex ae
ternorum :· respi*ce*
Quia nunc cepit qui
semper fuit natu
ræ tuae filius di
uinae lucis gloriæ
tuae qui est forma
et plenitudo diuini
tatis tuae frequens.
respice
Persona unigeniti
et primogeniti
qui est totus a toto
diximus lux de lu
mine ., respice
ET d*eu*m uerum a d*e*o
uero se se[1] con
fitemur.

tribus personis in
una substantia ., re
spice in me d*omi*ne

YMNU*M* S*AN*C*T*I PATRICI.

Audite omnes amantes MA
d*eu*m s*an*c*t*a mereta GIS
uiri in *christ*o beati TER
Patrici episcupi SC
quodo[2] bonu*m* obactu*m* OT
similatur angelis OR*UM*.
perfecta*m*q*ue* p*ro*pter uita*m*
aequatur apostolis
Beata *christ*i custodit
mandata in omnibus
cuius opera refulgent
clara inter homnes[3]
s*an*c*tu*mq*ue* cuius sequuntur
exemplum mirificu*m*
unde et in caelis patre*m*
magnificant d*omi*n*u*m :·
Constans in d*ei* timore
et fide inmobilis
super que*m* aedificatur
ut petrum[4] aecclesia
cuiusq*ue* apostolatum

[1] Muratori read these four letters as 'semper semper,' mistaking the accents for marks of abbreviation; but 'se' is an impossible abbreviation of 'semper.' Another accented 'se' occurs on fol. 21 recto, 1st col., line 22.

[2] A point has been placed over the first 'o,' and the missing syllable 'mo' with a slanting stroke over it has been written on the margin by an early correcting hand.

[3] A small 'i' has been written above this word between 'm' and 'n,' *prima manu.*

[4] A point has been placed beneath the 'm' and an 's' has been written over it by early correcting hand. The correction is a mistake.

a Deo sortitus est
in cuius porte ad uersus
inferni non praeualent
Dominus illum elegit
ut doceret barbaras
nationes et piscaret
per doctrinae retia
et de saeculo credentes
traheret ad gratiam
Dominum qui sequerentur
sedem ad etheream.
Electa Christi talenta
uendit euangelica
quae hibernas inter gentes
cum usuris exigit
nauigi huius laboris
tum operae pretium
cum Christo regni caelestis
possessurus gaudium
Fidelis Dei minister
insignisque nuntius
apostolicum exemplum
formamque praebet bonis
qui tam uerbis quam et factis
plebi praedicat Dei
ut quem dictis non conuertit
actu prouocet bono

Gloriam habet cum Christo
honorem in saeculo
qui ab omnibus ut Dei
ueneratur angelus
quem Deus misit ut Paulum
ad gentes apostolum
ut hominibus ducatum
praeberet regno Dei
Humilis Dei ob metum
spiritu et corpore
super quem bonum ob actum
requiescit Dominus
cuiusque iusta in carne
Christi portat stigmata
et cuius sola sustentans
gloriatur in cruce.
Impiger credentes pascit
dapibus caelestibus
ne qui uidentur cum Christo
in uia deficiant
quibus erogat ut panes
uerba euangelica
et cuius multiplicantur
ut manna in manibus
Castam qui custodit carnem
ob amorem Domini
quam carnem templum parauit
sanctoque spiritui

[*Fol. 14 recto.*]

a d*e*o sortitus est
in cuius porte aduersu*m*
inferni non praeualent
D*omi*n*u*s illum elegit
ut doceret barbaras
nationes et piscaret
per doctrinæ retia
et de saeculo credentes
traheret ad gratiam
d*omi*n*u*m qui seq*ue*rentur
sedem ad etheream .,
ELecta *christ*i talenta
uendit euangelica
quæ hibernas inter gentes
cum usuris exigit
nauigi huius laboris
tum opere praetium
cu*m christ*o regni caelestis
possesurus gaudium
Fidelis d*e*i minister
insignisq*ue* nuntius
apostolicu*m* exemplum
forma*m*q*ue* praebet bonis
qui ta*m* uerbis qua*m* et factis
plebi praedicat d*e*i /tit
ut que*m* dictis non conuer
f * tu p*ro*uocet bono

Gloria*m* habet cum *christ*o
honorem in saeculo
qui ab omnib*us* ut d*e*i
ueneratur angelus
que*m* d*eu*s misit ut paulu*m*
ad gentes apostolum
ut hominib*us* ducatum
praeberet regno d*e*i
Humilis d*e*i ob metum
sp*irit*u et corpore /tum
super que*m* bonu*m* ob ac
requiescit d*omi*n*u*s
cuiusq*ue* iusta in carne
*christ*i portat stigmata
et[1] cuius sola sustentans
gloriatur in cruce .,
Impiger credentes pascit
dapib*us* caelestibus
ne qui uidentur cum *christ*o
in uia deficiant
quib*us* erogat ut panes
uerba euangelica
et[2] cuius multiplicantur
ut manna in manibus
Kasta*m* qui custodit carnem
ob amore*m* d*omi*ni
qua*m* carne*m* te*m*plu*m* parauit
s*an*c*t*oque spiritui

[1] A point has been placed beneath 'et,' a slanting stroke and a point above it, and the word 'in,' under a slanting stroke and a point, has been written on the margin *prima manu*.

[2] Ditto, but without the slanting stroke and point above 'et,' and with slanting stroke only over 'in.'

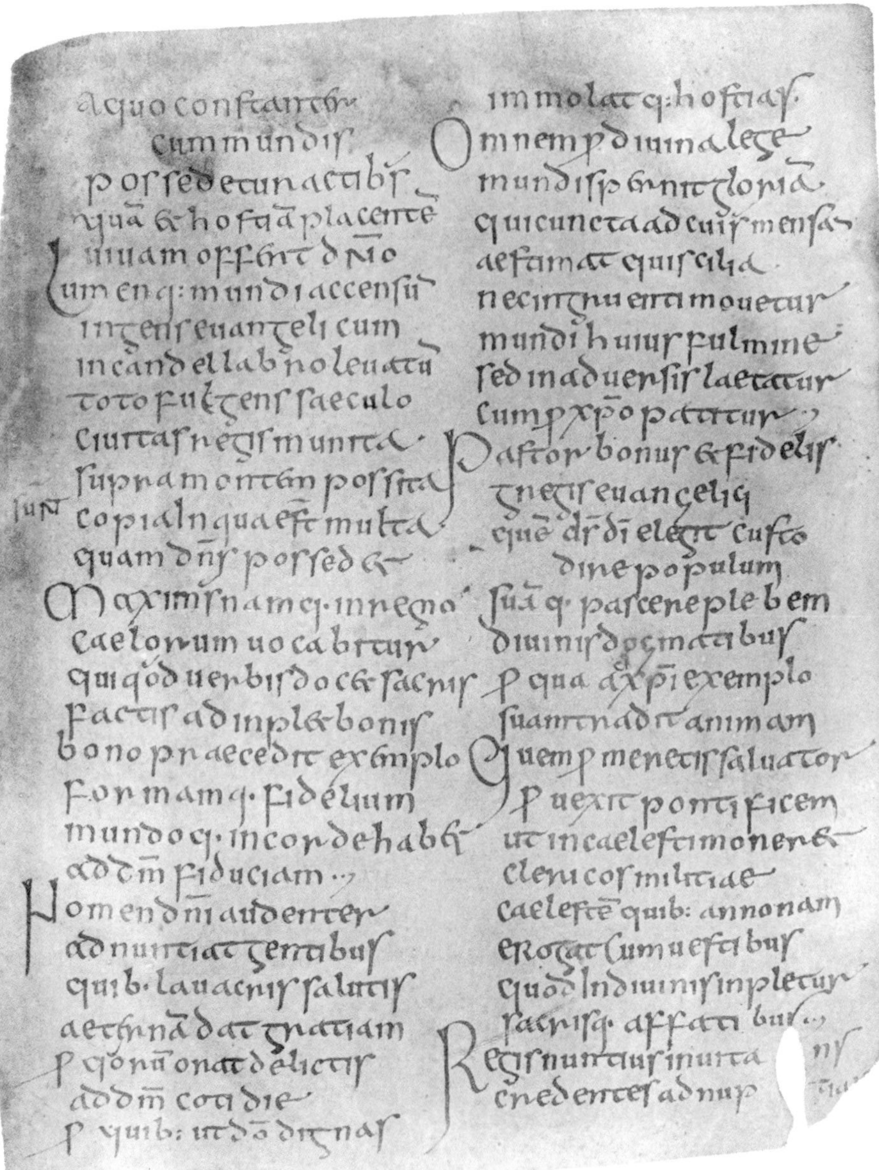

[*Fol. 14 verso.*]

a quo constanter
cum mundis
possedetur actibus
qua*m* et hostia*m* placente*m*
uiuam offert d*omi*no
Lumenq*ue* mundi accensu*m*
ingens euangelicum
in candellabro leuatu*m*
toto fulgens saeculo
ciuitas regis munita
supra montem possita
copia in qua est[1] multa
quam d*omi*n*u*s possedet
Maximus namq*ue* in regno
caelorum uocabitur
qui quod uerbis docet sacris
factis adinplet bonis
bono praecedit exemplo
formamq*ue* fidelium
mundoq*ue* in corde habet
ad d*eu*m fiduciam . . ,
Nomen d*omi*ni audenter
adnuntiat gentibus
quib*us* lauacris salutis
aeterna*m* dat gratiam
p*ro* quoru*m* orat delictis
ad d*eu*m cotidie
p*ro* quib*us* ut d*e*o dignas
immolatq*ue* hostias.
Omnem p*ro* diuina lege
mundi spernit gloria*m*
qui cuncta ad cuius mensa*m*
aestimat quiscilia
nec ingruenti mouetur
mundi huius fulmine
sed in aduersis laetatur
cum p*ro* *christ*o patitur . ,
Pastor bonus et fidelis
gregis euangelici
que*m* d*eu*s d*e*i elegit custo
dire populum
sua*m*q*ue* pascere plebem
diuinis dogmatibus
p*ro* qua a[2] *christ*i exemplo
suam tradit animam
Quem p*ro* meretis saluator
p*ro*uexit pontificem
ut in caelesti moneret
clericos militiae
caeleste*m* quib*us* annonam
erogat cum uestibus
quod in diuinis inpletur
sacrisq*ue* affatibus . . ,
Regis nuntius inuitans
credentes ad nuptias

[1] A slanting stroke has been placed over 'est,' and the word 'sunt,' with a slanting stroke over it, has been written on the margin *prima manu*.

[2] A later correcting hand seems to have written a 'd' over 'a.' If so, the correction is a mistake. Possibly it is the tail of a 'g.' The 'og' in the line above seems to be written *in rasura*, the scribe having first written 'go' by mistake.

quo ornatur ueste in bitto
nuptiali induitur
qui caeleste haurit uinum
in uassis caelestibus
propinansque dei plebem
spiritale poculum
Sacrum inuenit thesaurum
sacro in uolumine
saluatorisque in carne
deitatem peruidit
quem thesaurum emit sanctis
perfectisque meritis
israhel uocatur huius
anima uidens dominum
Testis domini fidelis
in lege catholica
cuius uerba sunt diuinis
condita oraculis
ne humanae putrebit carnes
aessaeque a uermibus
sed caelesti sale aptantur
sapore admixtae
Uerus cultor et insignis
agri euangelici
cuius semina uidentur
christi euangelia

quae diuino serit ore
in aures prudentium
quorumque corda aeternum
sancto arat spiritu
Christus illum sibi legit
in terris uicarium
qui de terrenis captiuos
liberat seruitio
plenosque de seruitute
quos redemit hominum
in numeros de zabuli
absoluit dominio
Hymnos cum apocalypsi
psalmosque cantat dei
quosque ad aedificandum
dei tractat populum
quique legem in trinitate
sacri credit nominis
tribusque personis unam
docetque substantiam
Zona domini praecinctus
diebus ac noctibus
sine intermissione
deum orat dominum
cuius ingenti labore

[*Fol. 15 recto.*]

qui ornatur uestimento
nuptiali indutus
qui caeleste haurit uinu*m*
in uassis caelestibus
p*ro*pinansq*ue*[1] d*e*i plebem
spiritale poculum
Sacrum inuenit thesauru*m*
sacro in uolumine
saluatorisq*ue* in carne
deitatem peruidet
que*m* thesauru*m* emit s*a*n*c*t*is*
perfectisq*ue* meritis
isr*ahe*l uocatur huius
anima uidens d*eu*m :,
Testis d*omi*ni fidelis
in lege catholica
cuius uerba sunt diuinis
condida oraculis
ne humane putent carnes
aessæq*ue* a uermibus
sed caelestis alleantur
sapore ad uictimam :·
Uerus cultor et insignsi
agri euangelici
cuius semina uidentur
*christ*i euangelia
quae diuino serit /ore
in aures prudentiu*m*
quoru*m*q*ue* corda ac men /tes
s*an*c*t*o arat sp*irit*u
*CHristu*s illum sibi[2] legit
in terris uicarium
qui de gemino captiuos
liberat seruitio
plerosq*ue* de seruitute
quos redemit hominu*m*
innumeros de zaboli
absoluit dominio .,
Ymnos cum apocalipsi
salmosq*ue* cantat d*e*i
quosq*ue* ad aedificandu*m*
d*e*i tractat populum
que*m*[3] legem in trinitate
sacri credit nominis
tribusq*ue* personis una*m*
docetq*ue* substantia*m*
Zona d*omi*ni praecinctus
dieb*us* ac noctibus
sine intermisione
d*eu*m orat d*omi*n*u*m
cuius ingenti[4] laboris

[1] A later correcting hand has written another 'n' over the 'i' in 'propinans.
[2] A later correcting hand has written an 'e' over the last letter of 'sibi.
[3] A point has been placed below the 'e,' and an 'a,' with a point above it, has been placed over the 'q' in 'que*m*' by a later correcting hand.
[4] An 's' has been written over the last letter of 'ingenti' by a later correcting hand.

percepturus praemium
Cum apostolis regnabit
sanctus super sedes Israhel

Ymnum sancti Comgilli abbatis nostri

Recordemur iustitiae
nostri patroni fulgidae
Comgilli sancti nomine
refulgentis in opere
adiuti Dei flamine
sancto claroque lumine
trinitatis celsissimae
cuncta tenentes regmine
quem Deus ad aetherea
conduxit habitacula
ab angelis custodita
permansura in saecula

Audite pantes ta erga
allati ad angelica
athletae Dei abdita
a iuventute florida
aucta in lege pagina
alta sancti per viscera
apta fide iustitia
ad Deum ducta gaudia
alti ad lata merita
affatim concordantia
ab angelis

Bonam vitam iustitia
benignitate florida
caritate firmissima
Deo primo adhibetam
iuxta mandatum solida
in regno praestantissima
proximis sepe deditam
condescenso placeta
efficiebat cognitam
in futuro fructifera
quem Deus

Contempnens tum mundialium
voluntatum praesentium
vitiorum firmissimum
infirmos devastantium
verborum contaminum
parte lenia universantium
continebat per viscera
secreta vigilantium
ab angelis

Doctus in Dei legibus
divinis dictionibus
ditatur sanctis opibus
Deo semper placentibus
dedicatur in moribus
Deo Stefanus agius
docebat sic et caeteros
dicta docta operibus

[*Fol. 15 verso.*]

Patri ci lau des sem per dica mus ut nos cum illo sem per ui uamus :·

YM NU*M* S*ANC*TI COM GIL LI

/ mium
percepturus prae
cum apostolis regnabit
s*anctus* super isr*ahe*l . . ,[1]

Patricius aepiscopus oret p*ro* nobis omnib*us* ut deleantur p*ro*tinus peccata quae commisimus :—

AB*BATIS* N*OST*RI

Recordemur iustitiae
nostri patroni fulgidæ
comgilli s*anct*i nomine
refulgentis in opere
adiuti d*e*i flamine
s*ancto* claroq*ue* lumine
trinitatis celsissimae
cuncta tenentes regmine

que*m* d*eu*s ad aetherea
conduxit habitacula
ab angelis custodita
permansura in saecula

Audite pantes ta erga
allati ad angelica
anthlete[2] d*e*i abdita
a iuuentute florida
aucta in legis pagina
alta s*anct*i per uiscera
apta fide iustitia
ad d*e*i ducta gaudia
alti adlata merita
affatim concordantia :·

ab angelis

Bonam uitam iustitia*m*
benignitate*m* florida*m*
caritate*m* firmissima*m*
d*eo* primo adhibetam
iuxta mandatu*m* solida*m*
in regno praestantissima*m*
p*ro*ximis sepe deditam
corde sereno placeta*m*
efficiebat cognitam
in futuro fructifera*m*

quem d*eu*s

Contemptu*m* mundialium
uoluntatu*m* praesentium
uitioru*m* firmissimum
infirmos deuastantium
uerboru*m* cogitaminum
parte leua uersantium
continebat per uisceru*m*
secreta uigilantium

ab angelis.

Doctus in d*e*i legibus
diuinis dicionibus
ditatus s*anct*is[3] opibus
d*eo* semper placentibus
dedicatus in moribus
d*e*i stefanus agius
docebat sic et caeteros
dicta docta operibu[s]

*   *[4]

---

[1] A slanting stroke, with a point over it, is placed at the end of this line, and a similar stroke and point are placed on the margin over 'Patri.'
[2] A small 'a' has been written *prima manu* over the last syllable of 'anthlete.'
[3] The 'i' in this word has been written afterwards below the 'c.'
[4] There are just sufficient indications remaining to shew that the two words 'quem deus' were written here.

Electus a primordio
quod erat in principio
aeternum uerbum patris no
eructatum sanctissimo
corde uerum altissimo
carus eidem lucido
pergnus praeclaro animo
constans opere placido
ab angelis..

Fulgebat alti fulgore
solis uice in uertice
rutulantis meridie
fidei claritudine
confirmatus ex uiscere
indi semper fidere
confidens sanctimoniae
praecipuo munimine
quem deus..

Gaudium sancti spiritus
habebat in uisceribus
regnum quod est sublimibus
deo dignum et fortius
gladium quoque spiritus
leuatum ad nequissimus
quo prosternere superbos
tenens sanctis in manibus..
ab angelis..

Humilis sanctus benignus
probus in dilectibus
humanus iustus commodus
laudabilis in moribus
hilaris uultu sobrius
caritatis in floribus
decoratus ordinibus
factus palam mortalibus
quem deus..

In scripturis eruditus
inspiratus diuinitus
in sacramentis prouidus
canonicis affatibus
ueteris noui actibus
testamenti praefulgidus
feruens spiritu placidus
deo carus et pissimus
ab angelis

Kalcauit mundum subdolum
karitatis per studium
kastitatis firmissimum
contemnens omne uitium
inserbit agnum floridum
pectus adornans lucidum
diuinum habitaculum
trino nomine sanctum
quem deus..

[*Fol. 16 recto.*]

Elegit a primordio
quod erat in principio
aeternu*m* uerbu*m* paterno
eructatu*m* s*anct*issimo
corde ueru*m* altissimo
carus eidem lucido
pignus praeclaro animo
constans opere placido
ab angelis . . ,

Fulgebat alti fulgore
solis uic[1] in uertice
rutulantis meridie
fidei claritudine
confirmatus ex uiscere
in d*e*i semper fidere
confidens s*anct*imoniae
praecipuo munimine
quem d*eus* . . ,

Gaudium s*anct*i sp*iritu*s
habebat in uisceribus
regnu*m* quod est sublimibus
d*e*o dignu*m* et fortius
gladium quoq*ue* sp*iritu*s
leuatu*m* ad nequissimus
quo p*ro*sterneret superbos
tenens s*anct*is in manibus . . ,
ab angelis . . ,

Humilis s*anctu*s benignus
prob*us* in d*e*i legibus
humanus iustus commo/dus
laudabilis in moribus
hilaris uultu subrius
caritatis in floribus
decoratus ordinibus
factus palam mortalibus
quem d*eus* . . ,

INscripturis eruditus
inspiratus diuinitus
in sacramentis p*ro*uidus
canonicis affatibus
ueteris noui actibus
testamenti praefulgidus
feruens sp*irit*u placidus
d*e*o carus et pissimus
ab angelis

Kalcauit mundu*m* subdolu*m*
karitatis per studium
kastitatis firmissimum
contempnens omne uitiu*m*
inserens agru*m* floridum
pectus adornans lucidu*m*
diuinum habitaculum
trino nomine sancitum
quem d*eus* . . ,

[1] An 'e' has been written *prima manu* over and after the last letter of 'uic.'

Lampade sapientiae
constituit in pectore
in tesauro scientiae
condito di munere
ipse flammatus magnopere
luce uende iustitiae
exaltatus munimine
legis spiritalis terre
ab angelis

Magnum adprendit bravium
aeterna uita condignum
adeptus sanctum proemium
post labore firmissimo
cuius perfectum meritum
locamus in auxilium
ut mereamur omnium
uitiorum excidium
quem ds

Notus sanctorum coetibus
abbatum in ordinibus
monachorum militibus
anchoretarum sensibus
sinodum sanctis plebibus
immo uir apostolicus
clarus cunctis in sortibus
ad auctus in sublimibus
ab angelis

Opera solidissimam
in fundamento posita
O contemptorem omnium
rerum nequam praesentium
O ducem sanctum militum
domino militantium
O tironem fortissimum
domino totum deditum
quem ds

Positus muri ferrei
uice in luce populi
dissipare dispendere
cuncta mala distruere
aedificare plantare
bona totali commone
monere sancti Hieremiae
constituti in culmine
ab angelis

Quis contempsit praesentia
huius aeui decidua
quis ascendit ad superna
toto animo gaudia
quis uolebat in ethera
carne uolare posita
qualiter iste talia
adeptus sancta merita
quem ds

[*Fol. 16 verso.*]

Lampade*m* sapientiae
constituit in pectore
in tesauro scientiae
condito d*e*i munere
inflammatus magnopere
luce uerae iustitiae
exaltatus munimine
legis sp*iritu*s littere[1].,.
ab angelis..,

Magnu*m* adpraendit[2] bradium
aeterna uita condignum
adeptus s*anctu*m proemium
post labore*m* firmissimu*m*
cuius perfectum meritu*m*
uocamus in auxilium
ut mereamur omnium
uitiorum excidium..,
quem d*eus*

Notus s*anct*orum coetibus
abbatum in ordinibus
monachorum militibus
anchoretaru*m* sensibus
sinodum s*anct*is plebibus
immo uir apostolicus
clarus cunctis in sortibus
adauctus in sublimibus :·
ab angelis

O petra*m* solidissimam
in fundamento possita*m*
O conte*m*ptore*m* omnium
reru*m* nequa*m* præsentiu*m*
O ducem s*anctu*m militum
d*omi*no militantium
O tironem fortissimum
d*omi*no totum deditum..,
quem d*eus*

Possitus muri ferrei
uice in luce populi
dissipare disperdere
cuncta mala distruere
aedificare plantare
bona tota in commone
more s*anct*i eremiae
constituti in culmine ∴ ∴
ab angelis..,

Quis contempsit praesentia
huius eui decidua
quis ascendit ad superna
toto animo gaudia
quis uolebat in ethera
carne uolare possita
qualiter iste talia
adeptus s*anct*a mereta :·
quem d*eus*.,

[1] A badly formed 'a' has been written by a later hand over and between the last two letters of 'littere.'
[2] A point has been placed after the 'p' in 'adpraendit,' and a small 'b,' with a point before it, has been written *prima manu* above it.

Rexit scam ecclesiam
catholica per regula
retinens fidem solida
mala contra nequitia
suam exercens animam
scae legis per paginam
cuius ex optu gratiam
mihi adornat animam:
ab angelis..

Sapiens suos intra nos
scos elevans oculos
deducebat ad superiores
capite sco intentos
parte sca in dextera
collocans sua in se tra
centorionis opera
habens sca per studia
quem dr

Tulit suam memoriam
ad mansionem supernam
caram do et floridam
suam exercens animam
contemnens terrena subdola
vanem omne insaniam
domuens cum abraham
ad terra illa optimam::
ab angelis..

Vitam aeternam fulgida
adeptus est sub corona
ubi ad sum et praemia
per mansura in saecula
Comitatur virtus agmina
angelorum praecipua
in quirens semper talia
vigilans in ecclesia:
quem dr

Xpm orabat magistrum
suum mum ornans obsequium
xpi tenens officium
actum per apostolicum
huius sequens vestigium
ducens do exercitum
in scam habitaculum
trinitatis lectis simum:
ab angelis..

Hymnum do cum cantico
immolabat altissimo
diei noctis circulo
orans sepe cum triumpho
nunc cantavit sub numero
canticum novum dno
iunctus choro angelico
sum mo ser in nubilo::
quem dr..

[*Fol. 17 recto.*]

Rexit s*anct*am ecclesiam
catholica*m* per regula*m*
retinens fidem solida*m*
mala*m* contra nequitia*m*
suam exercens animam
s*anct*æ legis per paginam
cuius exopto gratiam
mihi adornat animam :
ab angelis . . ,

Sapiens suos internos
s*anct*os eleuans oculos
deducebat ad superos
capite s*anct*o intentos
parte s*anct*a in dextera
collocans sua uiscera
centorionis opera
habens s*anct*a per studia
quem d*eus*

Tulit suam memoriam
ad mansione*m* supernam
caram d*e*o et floridam
suam exercens animam
contempnens terra*m* subdola*m*
uanem omne*m* insaniam
domuens cum abraham
ad terra*m* illa*m* optimam :·
ab angelis . . ,

UItam aeternam fulgida
adeptus est sub corona
ubi adsumet praemia
permansura in saecula
comitaturus agmina
angelorum praecipua
inquirens semper talia
uigilans in æcclesia :·
quem d*eus*

*CHristu*m orabat magistrum
summum ornans obsequium
christi gerens officium
actum per apostolicum
huius sequens uestigium
ducens d*e*o exercitum
in s*anct*am[1] habitaculum
trinitatis lectissimum :· ,
ab angelis . . ,

Ymnum d*e*o cum cantico
immolabat altissimo
diei noctis circulo
orans sepe cum triumpho
nunc cantauit sub numero
canticum nouum d*omi*no
iunctus choro angelico
summo s*anctu*s in iubilo . . ,
quem d*eus* . . ,

[1] Points have been placed below and over the (second) 'a' in 's*anct*am.'

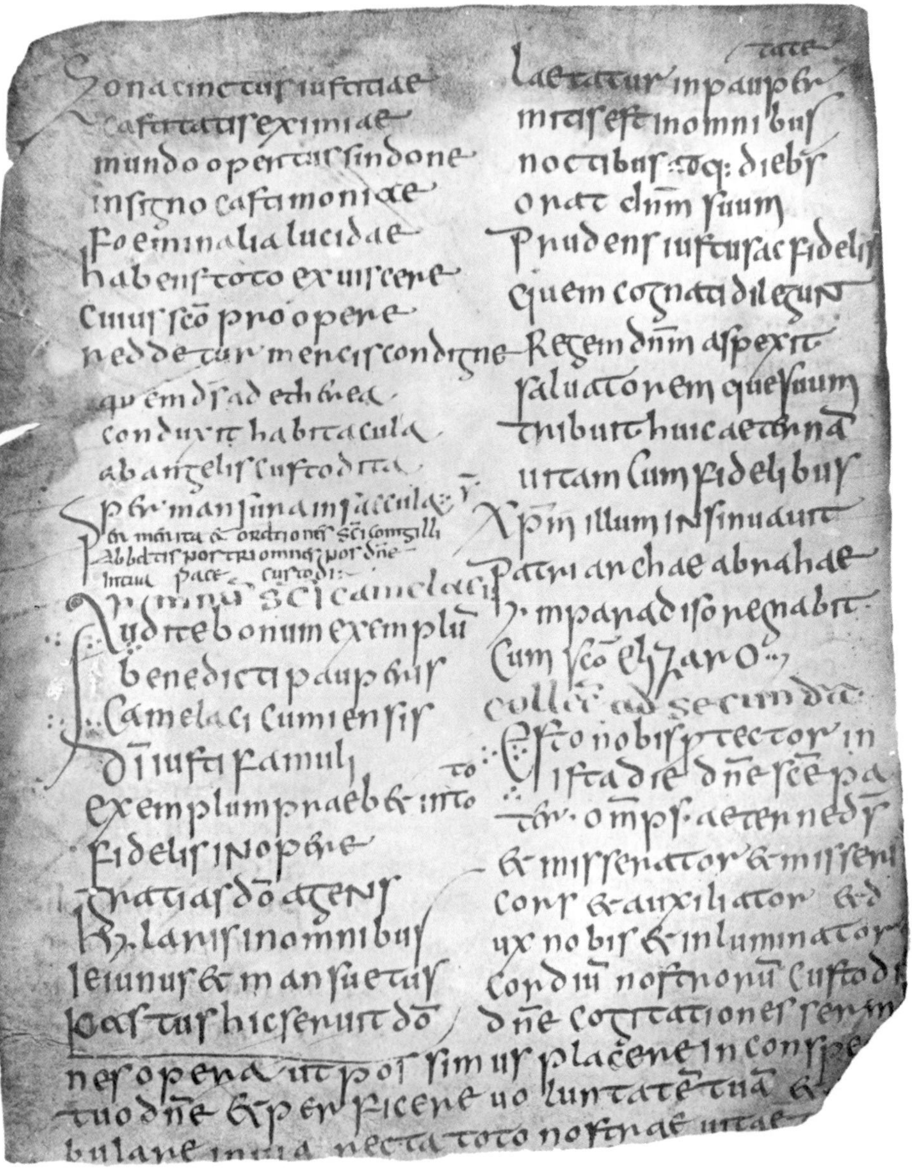

[*Fol. 17 verso.*]

Zona cinctus iustitiae
castitatis eximiae
mundo opertus sindone
insigno castimoniae
foeminalia lucidae
habens toto ex uiscere
cuius s*anct*o pro opere
reddetur mercis condigne
quem d*eu*s ad etherea
conduxit habitacula
ab angelis custodita
permansura in saecula :. [1]

Per merita et orationes s*anct*i comgilli
abbatis nostri omnes nos d*omi*ne
in tua pace custodi :—

YMNU*M* S*AN*C*T*I CAMELACI

Audite bonum exemplu*m*
benedicti pauperis
camelaci cumiensis
d*e*i iusti famuli /to
exemplum praebet in to
fidelis in opere
gratias d*e*o agens
hylaris in omnibus
ieiunus et mansuetus
kastus hic seruit d*e*o /tate
laetatur in pauper
mitis est in omnibus
noctibus adq*ue* diebus
orat d*omi*n*u*m suum
prudens iustus ac fidelis
quem cognati dilegunt
regem d*omi*n*u*m aspexit
saluatoremque suum
tribuit huic aeterna*m*
uitam cum fidelibus
*christu*m illum insinuauit
patriarchae abrahae
ymparadiso regnabit
cum s*anct*o elizaro . . ,

COLLEC*TIO*[2] AD SECUNDA*M*

Esto nobis p*ro*tector in
ista die d*omi*ne s*anct*e pa
ter. om*ni*p*oten*s. aeterne d*eu*s
et misserator et misseri
cors et auxiliator et d
ux nobis et inluminator
cordiu*m* nostroru*m* custodi
d*omi*ne cogitationes serm *
nes opera ut possimus placere in conspe *
tuo d*omi*ne et perficere uoluntate*m* tua*m* et *
bulare in uia recta toto nostrae uitae t *

[1] An 's' with a mark of contraction over it has been written *prima manu* to the right of and slightly above this word.

[2] We have expanded this abbreviation into 'COLLEC*TIO*,' as this form of the word is found on fol. 22 verso, 2nd col., line 8, which is the only place in this MS. where the word is written *in extenso.*

Te oramus altissime
exortu solis lumine
xpe omnes nomine
adesto nobis dne qui
regnas in saecula
Xpi per horam ter
tertiam diprae
camur clementiam
ut nobis perpetuam
suam tribuat gratiam
qui regnas. Sexta.
Tuis parce supplicibus
sexta ora orantibus
qua fuisti pro omnibus
xpe in cruce positus
qui regnas. Nona.
Exaudi praeces omnium
nona ora orantium
in qua xpe cornilium
uisitasti per angelum
qui regnas. Uesper.
Uespertino subtempore
te inuocamus dne nos
tris praeci bus
annuae nostris pec
catis ignosce.

Hoc tempus exi
timus xpe in tuis
laudibus misteriis
omnibus te ex corde
praecantibus qui
regnas. Nocturno.
Ihu clementer uisita
nocte orantes media
qua diuina potentia
petri soluisti uincula
qui regnas.
Ds subueni omnibus
te tersem laudan
tibus unumq: con
fitentibus sacris
ymnorum cantibus
te qui regnas.
Gallorum xpe cantibus
te depraecor son
nantibus petri
ob quondam fletibus
nostris intende
praecibus. qui regnas.

[*Fol. 18 recto.*]

ITEM ALIA AD SECUNDAM

Te oramus altissime
exortu solis lumine
christo oriens nomine
adesto nobis *domine* qui
regnas in saecula

AD TERTIA

CHristi per horam ter[1]
tertiam diprae
camur clementiam
uti nobis perpetua*m*
suam tribuat gratia*m*
qui regnas

AD SEXTA.

Tuis parce supplicibus
sexta ora orantibus
qua fuisti p*ro* omnibus
christe in cruce possitus
qui regnas

AD NONA

EXaudi praeces omniu*m*
nona ora orantium
in qua *christe* cornilium
uisitasti per angelum
qui regnas

AD UESPER*TINA.*

UESpertino sub tempore
te inuocamus *domine* nos
tris praeci bus
annuae nostris pec
catis ignosce :·

COL*LECTIO* AD INITIUM NOCTIS[2]

Noctis tempus exi
gimus *christe* in tuis
laudibus miseriaris
omnibus te ex corde
praecantibus qui
regnas

AD NOCTURNO

IH*es*u clementer uisita
nocte orantes media
qua diuina potentia
petri soluisti uincula
qui regnas

AD MATUTINA

D*eu*s subueni omnibus
te ter *sanctu*m laudan
tibus unumq*ue* con
fitentibus sacris
ymnorum cantibus
qui regnas

ITE*M* MATUTINAS

Gallorum *christe* cantibus
te depraecor so
nantibus petri
ob quondam fleti
bus nostris intende
praecibus. qui reg*nas* :·

[1] A thick stroke has been placed over 'ter' with the view of deleting it.
[2] This title is nearly illegible. Muratori read it 'IN HORA DIMIDII NOCTIS.'

Christe qui pulsis tenebris
diei lucem tribuis
adventum veni lumi
nis tui effunde fa
mulis. qui regnas

Exaudi nos domine sup
plices tuos qui in
hac ora prima diei
referamus tibi gra
tias domino deo nostro qui nos
redemisti tuo sancto san
guine ut preces ad
petitiones nostras
vice primitiarum
tibi oblatas pie cle
menterque suscipias
qui regnas

ad horam tertiam

Tibi subnixis prae
cibus christo domino sup
plicamus qui in hora
tertia diei spiritum sanctum
apostolis orantibus
emisisti eiusdem gra
tiae participationem
nobis poscentibus iu
beas concedi. qui reg.

ad horam sextam

Omnipotens aeterne
deus qui nobis magna
lia fecisti sexta ho
ra crucem ascendisti
et tenebras mundi in
luminasti sic et corda
nostra inluminare
digneris qui regnas

ad horam nonam

Nona agitur diei hora
ad te domine directa sup
plicatione qua cul
toribus tuis divina
monstrantur mira
cula nostra quoque eo
rum imitatione cor
da inluminentur qui reg.

ad vespertinam

Vespertina oratio
nostra ascendat ad
aures divinae maies
tatis tuae et discendat
benedictio tua domine su
per nos quem ad modum
speravimus in te
qui reg nas

[*Fol. 18 verso.*]

ITEM ALIA AD MATUTINA.

D*eu*s qui pulsis tenebris.
diei lucem tribuis
aduentum ueri lumi
nis tuis effunde fa
ITEM[1] mulis ., qui regnas .. ,
AD EXaudi nos d*omi*ne sup
SE plices tuos qui in
CUN hac ora prima diei
DA. refferamus tibi gra
tias d*omi*no d*e*o n*ostr*o qui nos
redemisti[2] tuo s*anct*o san
guine ut praeces ad
petitiones nostras
uice primitiarum
tibi oblatas pie cle
menterq*ue* suscipias
qui regnas

., ad horam tertiam[3] .. ,

TIbi subnexis prae
cibus *christ*o d*omi*no sup
plicamus qui in hora
tertia diei sp*iritu*m s*anctu*m
apostolis orantibus
emisisti eiusdem gra
tiae participatione*m*
nobis poscentibus iu
beas concedi. qui reg*nas*

ad horam sextam

Omnipotens aeternæ
d*eu*s qui nobis magna
lia fecisti sexta ho
ra crucem[4] ascendisti
et tenebras mundi in
luminasti sic et corda
nostra inluminare
digneris qui regnas

ad horam nonam

Nona agitur diei hora
ad te d*omi*ne directa sup
plicatione qua cul
toribus tuis diuina
monstrantur mira
cula nostra quoq*ue* eo
rum imitatione cor
da inlumina ∴ qui reg*nas*

., ad uespertinam .,

Uespertina oratio
nostra ascendat ad
aures diuinae maies
tatis tuae et discendat
benedictio tua d*omi*ne su
per nos quem ad modu*m*
sperauimus in te
qui reg nas

[1] A Greek cross has been placed on the lett margin above this title.

[2] A slanting stroke, with a point above it, has been placed over the space between 'redemisti' and 'tuo,' and the word 'de, under a similar stroke and point, has been written on the margin by a later correcting hand.

[3] From this point it will be noticed that titles are sometimes written by the original scribe in a smaller handwriting, instead of being left to be filled in afterwards by the rubricator.

[4] A point under a slanting stroke has been placed after 'crucem,' and the word 's*anct*am,' under a slanting stroke with a point above it, has been written on the left margin.

ad initium noctis
Deus qui inextricabiles
tenebras inluminas
noctium densitatem ca
liginis inlustras corda
nostra in opere manda
torum tuorum te oramus
dne custodias. qui regnas
ad initium noctis
Evolutis nunc diei tempo
ribus noc turnisque
spatiis supervenientibus
di misericordiam depr
aecemur ut suppliciti di
uinis sensibus tenebra
rum operibus renun
tiare possimus. qui
ad pacem celebrandam
Iniuste egimus.
Redemisti nos dne ds
ueritatis in tuo sco san
guine nunc adiuua nos
in omnibus ihu xpe
qui regnas
pax multa diligentibus

pax tua dne rex
caelestis perma
neat semper in
uisceribus nostris
ut non timeamus
a timore noctur
no. qui regnas.
Incip. hymnum
Credo in dm pa
trem omnipo
tentem inuisibi
lem omnium crea
turarum uisibili
um et inuisibilium
conditorem.
Credo et in ihm xpm
filium eius unicum
dnm nm dm omni
potentem concep
tum de spu sco natum
de maria uirgine
passum sub pontio
pylato qui cruci
fixus et sepultus

[*Fol. 19 recto.*]

ad initium noctis

D*eu*s qui inextrecabiles
tenebras inluminas
noctium densitatem ca
lignis inlustras corda
nostra in opere manda
torum tuorum te oramus
d*omi*ne custodias. qui regnas :· ,

AD INITIUM NOCTIS.

Euolutis nunc diei tempo
ribus noc turnisque[1]
spatis superuenientibus
d*ei* misericordiam dipr
aecemur ut suppliti di
uinis sensibus tenebra
rum operibus renun
tiare possumus., qui r*egnas* :·

.,ad pacem celebrandam :·

INiuste egimus.[2]
Redemisti nos d*omi*ne d*eu*s
ueritatis in tuo s*anct*o san
guine nunc adiuua nos
in omnibus ih*es*u *christ*e :
qui regnas
Pax multa diligentibus :·[3]

Pax tua d*omi*ne rex
caelestis perma
neat semper in
uisceribus nostris
ut non timeamus
a timore noctur
no, qui regnas :·

INCIP*IT* SYMMULU*M*

CRedo in d*eu*m pa
trem omnipo
tentem inuisibi
lem omnium crea
turarum uisibili
um et inuisibilium
conditorem.
CRedo et in ih*esu*m *christum*
filium eius unicum
d*ominu*m n*ostru*m d*eu*m omni
potentem concep
tum de sp*irit*u s*anct*o natu*m*
de maria uirgine
passum sub pontio
pylato qui cruci
fixus et sepultus

[1] Some word like 'nostri' has been first written and afterwards partly altered, partly erased.

[2] There is a mark of abbreviation over 'egimus,' to shew that these two words are only the opening words of a longer sentence, viz., Ps. cv. 6, or Judith vii. 19.

[3] There is a mark of abbreviation over 'diligentibus' to shew these three words are only the opening words of a longer sentence, viz., Ps. cxviii. 165.

discendit ad infe
rnos tertia die re
surrexit a mor
tuis ascendit in
caelis sedit q: ad
dexteram dei pa
tris omnipoten
tis exinde uen
turus iudicare
uiuos ac mortuos.
Credo et in spm scm
dm omnipotente
unam habentem
substantiam cum
patre et filio scam
esse aecclesiam ca
tholicam abremi
sa peccatorum
scorum commoni
onem carnis resur
rectionem credo
uitam post morte
et uitam aeternam

in gloria xpi haec
omnia credo in dm
Oratio dnica amen
Pater noster qui es
in caelis scificetur
nomen tuum adue
niat regnum tuum.
fiat uoluntas tua sicut
in caelo et in terra pa
nem nm cotidianu
da nobis hodie. et
remitte nobis debi
ta nostra. sicut et
nos demittimus de
bitoribus nostris.
et ne patiaris nos
induci in temptati
onem sed libera nos
a malo.
Per horam mediae
noctis tunc a uisi
sunt angeli de nati
uitate dni nri ihu xpi

[*Fol. 19 verso.*]

discendit ad infe
ros tertia die re
surrexit a mor
tuis ascendit in
caelis seditq*ue* ad
dexteram d*e*i pa
tris omnipoten
tis. exinde uen
turus iudicare
uiuos ac mortuos.
CRedo et in sp*iritu*m s*anctu*m
d*eu*m omnipotente*m*
unam habentem
substantiam cum
patre et filio[1] s*anct*am
esse aecclesiam ca
tholicam abremi
sa peccatorum
s*anct*orum commoni
onem carnis resur
rectionem credo
uitam post morte*m*
et uitam aeternam
in gloria *christ*i haec
omnia credo in d*eu*m
amen :· ,

ORATIO DIUI NA . . .

Pater noster qui es
in caelis s*anct*ificetur
nomen tuum. adue
niat regnum tuum.
fiat uoluntas tua sicut
in caelo et in terra. pa
nem n*ostru*m cotidianu*m*
da nobis hodie. et
remitte nobis debi
ta nostra. sicut et
nos demittimus de
bitoribus nostris.
et ne patiaris nos
induci in temptati
onem sed libera nos
a malo

AD NOCTURNO.

Per horam mediæ
noctis tunc gauisi
sunt angeli de nati
uitate d*omi*ni n*ost*ri ih*es*u *christ*i

[1] A group of three points is placed after and above the word 'filio.' The meaning of these points is not obvious. See fol. 10 verso, note 3, and fol. 35 verso, line 14, where the words 'et filio' have been added afterwards to the original text.

ita et nos laetari de
bemur in tua pace
omnipotens deus. qui r
ad matutinam
Tu es domine inlumina
tor caliginum con
ditor elemento
rum remissor cri
minum misericor
dia tua domine mag
na est super eos
qui te toto cor
de nequirunt
maiestas tua domine
mane nos exau
diat et deleat de
licta nostra
quae tibi non sunt
abdita. qui regnas
Tu es spes et salus
tu es vita et vir
tus. tu es adiutor in
tribulationibus

tu es defensor ani
marum nostrarum
deus israhel in omnibus
qui regnas. oratio
Ne memineris iniqui
tatum nostrarum
antiquarum cito
anticipent nos
misericordiae tuae
quia pauperes fac
ti sumus nimis adiu
va nos deus salutaris
noster propter gloriam
nominis tui domine libe
ra nos et propitius esto
peccatis nostris prop
ter nomen tuum Ne
tradas bestiis animam
confitentem tibi
animas pauperum
tuorum ne obliviscaris
in finem Res
pice in testamentum
tuum domine.

[*Fol. 20 recto.*]

ita et nos laetari de
bemus in tua pace
omnipotens d*eu*s., qui r*egnas*

AD MATUTINAM

TU es d*omi*ne inlumna
tor caliginum con
ditorq*ue* elemento
rum remisor cre
minum misericor
dia tua d*omi*ne mag
na est super eos
qui te toto[1] cor
de requirunt
maiestas tua d*omi*ne
mane nos exau
diat et deleat de
licta nostra
quae tibi non sunt
abdita. qui regnas :·

IT*EM* AD MATUTINA*M*

Tu es spes et salus
tu es uita et uir
tus. tu es adiutor in
tribulationibus
tu es defensor ani
marum nostraru*m*
d*eu*s isr*ahe*l in omnibus
qui regnas ORATIO

Ne memineris iniqui CO*M*
tatum nostrarum MO
antiquarum cito NIS.
antecoepent nos FRA
misericordiae tuæ TRO
quia pauperes fac RO*M*
ti sumus nimis adiu
ua nos d*eu*s salutaris
n*oste*r p*ro*pter gloriam
nominis tui d*omi*ne libe
ra nos et p*ro*pitius esto
peccatis nostris p*ro*p
ter nomen tuum ne
tradas bestis anima*m*
confitentem tibi
animas pauperum
tuorum ne obliuis
caris in finem res
pice in testamentum
tuum d*omi*ne.,

[1] An original rent in the membrane causes the spacing after this word, and a somewhat lesser spacing in each of the next ten lines which has not been reproduced in the printed text. The rent also affects fol. 20 verso, naturally.

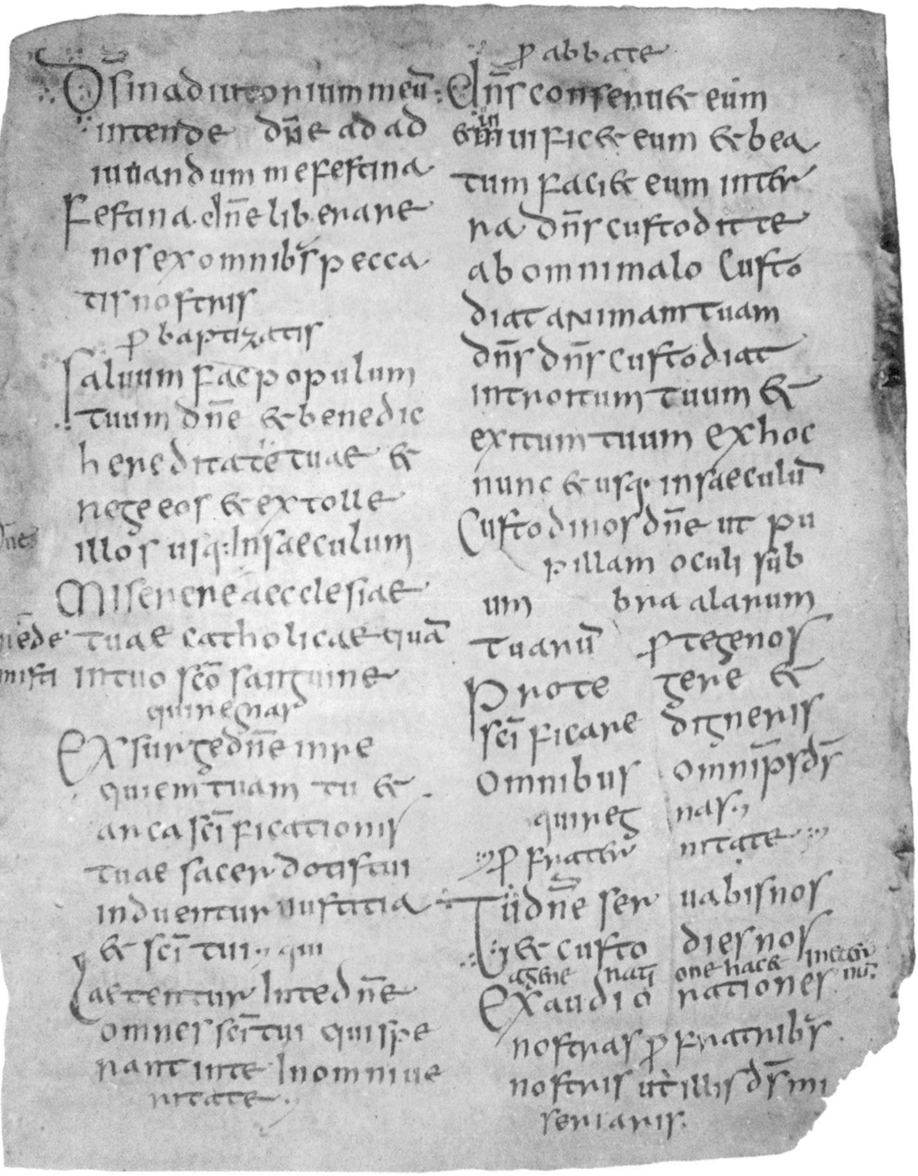

[*Fol. 20 verso.*]

D*eu*s in adiutorium meu*m*
intende d*omi*ne ad ad
iuuandum me festina
Festina d*omi*ne liberare
nos ex omnibus pecca
tis nostris

p*ro* baptizatis

Saluum fac populum
tuum d*omi*ne et benedic
hereditate[1] tuae et
rege eos et extolle
illos usq*ue* in saeculum
Miserere[2] aecclesiae
tuae catholicae[3] qua*m*
in tuo s*anct*o sanguine
qui regnas
EXsurge d*omi*ne in re
quiem tuam tu et
arca s*anct*ificationis
tuae sacerdotis tui
induentur iustitia
et s*anct*i tui ., qui
Laetentur in te d*omi*ne
omnes s*anct*i tui qui spe
rant in te in omni ue
ritate .,

p*ro* abbate

D*omi*n*u*s conseruet eum
et inuificet[4] eum et bea
tum faciet eum in ter
ra d*omi*n*u*s custodit te
ab omni malo custo
diat animam tuam
d*omi*n*u*s d*omi*n*u*s custodiat
introitum tuum et
exitum tuum ex hoc
nunc et usq*ue* in saeculu*m*[5]
Custodi nos d*omi*ne ut pu
pillam oculi sub
um[6] bra alarum
tuaru*m* p*ro*tege nos
Protegere et
s*anct*ificare digneris
omnibus omnip*oten*s d*eu*s
qui regnas .,

:., p*ro* fraternitate :.,

Tu d*omi*ne seruabis nos
et custodies nos[7]
EXaudi orationes ·
nostras p*ro* fratribus
nostris ut illis d*eu*s mi
seriaris.

---

1 A small 'i,' followed by a point, has been written *prima manu* over the last letter of this word.
2 A slanting stroke, with a point over it, written after and above this word, indicates the omission of 'd*omi*ne' which has been added on the left margin by a contemporary correcting hand.
3 A slanting stroke above a point has been placed after and above this word, and the word 'redemisti,' with a point beneath a slanting stroke placed over it, has been added *prima manu* on the left margin. 'Qua*m*' is also an addition to the original text.
4 Two points have been placed within the first two letters of this word, and the syllable 'ui,' under a point and two short vertical strokes has been written over it by an early correcting hand. These strokes form a small 'u,' shewing that the correction itself was not clear.
5 Some such title as 'PRO FRATRIBUS' has been omitted after this line.
6 See fol. 20 recto, note 1.
7 The following words have been written afterwards by a contemporary hand on the space and margin below this line 'a generatione hac et in eternu*m*.'

p pace populorum et regum

Dns uirtutem populo
suo dabit dns benedi
cet populo suo in pace
Pacem praestare digne
ris omnibus omnipotens ds
qui regnas

p blasfemantibus
Dne misericordia tua
in saeculum opera
manuum tuarum
ne dispicias
Dne ds uirtutum ne
statuas illis hoc
in peccatum

p impiis
Iudica illos ds decedant
a cogitationibus suis
[illegible] inritauerunt
te dne

Confundantur illi
qui confidunt in se
et non nos dne qui
confidimus in te

p iter facientibus
O dne saluum fac
o dne bene prospera
re

Prosperitatem
itineris praesta
tuis famulis qui
Confiteantur tibi
dne omnia ope
ra tua et sci tui
confiteantur tibi
Tibi gratias agunt
animae nostrae p
innumeris bene
ficiis tuis dne qui r

p elimosinariis
Dispersit dedit pau
peribus iustitia
eius manet in sae
culum saeculi
cornu eius exaltabi
tur in gloria.
Elimosinas facien
tibus in hoc mundo
retribue dne in
regno tuo sco

[*Fol. 21 recto.*]

p*ro* pace populorum et regum

D*omin*u*s* uirtutem populo
suo dabit d*omin*u*s* benedi
cet populo suo in pace
Pacem praestare digne
ris omnibus omnip*oten*s d*eu*s
qui regnas

p*ro* blasfemantibus

D*omi*ne misericordia tua
in saeculum opera
manuum tuarum
ne dispicias
D*omi*ne d*eu*s uirtutum ne
statuas illis hoc
in peccatum

p*ro* impiis

IUdica illos d*eu*s decedant
a cogitationib*us* suis.[1]
usq*ue* inritauerunt
te d*omi*ne
Confundantur illi
qui confidunt in se
et non nos d*omi*ne qui
confidimus in te.,

p*ro* iter facientibus.

O d*omi*ne saluum fac
o d*omi*ne bene p*ro*spera
re
Prospiritatem
iteneris praesta
tuis famulis. qui[2]
Confiteantur[3] tibi
d*omi*ne omnia ope
ra tua et s*anct*i tui
confiteantur tibi
TIbi gratias agunt
animae nostrae p*ro*
innumeris bene
ficiis tuis d*omi*ne qui r*egnas*

p*ro* elimosi[4]

Dispersit dedit pau
peribus iustitia
eius manet in sae
culum saeculi
cornu eius exaltabi
tur in gloria
Elimoysinas facien
tibus in hoc mundo
retribue d*omi*ne in
regno tuo s*ancto*..,

[1] The mark of abbreviation over 'suis' implies the absence of certain words from this passage which is taken from Ps. v. 11.
[2] The mark of contraction over 'qui' implies the text of the concluding formula.
[3] Above this line some such title as 'PRO GRATIAS AGENTIBUS' should have been inserted.
[4] It looks as if the writer had stopped short, not knowing how to spell the word 'eleemosynariis.'

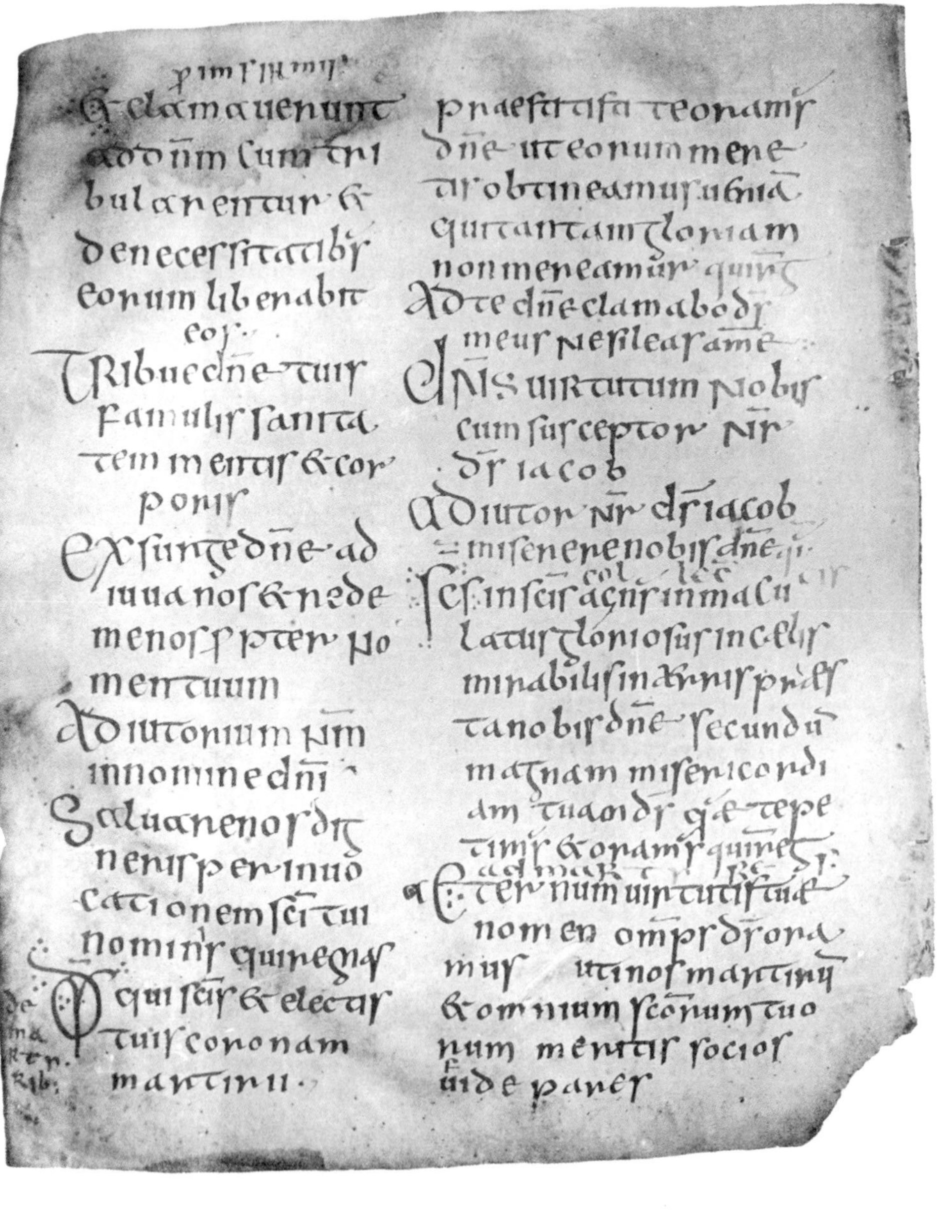

[*Fol. 21 verso.*]

p*ro* imfirmis
Et[1] clamauerunt
ad d*omin*u*m* cum tri
bularentur et
de necessitatibus
eorum liberabit
eos . , .
TRibue d*omi*ne tuis
famulis sanita
tem mentis et cor
poris
EXsurge d*omi*ne ad
iuua nos et rede
me nos p*ro*pter no
men tuum
ADiutorium n*ostru*m
in nomine d*omi*ni
Saluare nos dig
neris per inuo
cationem s*anct*i tui
nomins[2] qui regnas
D*EU*S qui s*anct*is et electis
tuis coronam
martirii . ,[3]
praestitisti te oramus
d*omi*ne ut eorum mere
tis obtineamus ueni*am*
qui tantam gloriam
non mereamur qui r*egnas*[4]
AD te d*omi*ne clamabo d*eu*s
meus ne sileas a me :· [5]
DO*MI*N*U*S uirtutum nobis
cum susceptor n*oste*r
d*eu*s iacob
ADiutor n*oste*r d*eu*s iacob
miserere nobis d*omi*ne qui.[6]
COL LEC[7] TIS
S*ANCTU*S in s*anct*is agnus inmacu
latus gloriosus in cælis
mirabilis in terris præs
ta nobis d*omi*ne secundu*m*
magnam misericordi
am tuam d*eu*s quae te pe
timus et oramus qui reg*nas*
AD MARTYRES.
aEternum uirtutis tuæ
nomen om*ni*p*oten*s d*eu*s ora
mus uti nos martiru*m*
et omnium s*anct*orum tuo
rum meritis socios
uide[8] pares

[1] Ps. cvi. 6. The reference is disguised by Muratori's reading 'Exclamauerunt.'
[2] An 'i' has been written between and above the last two letters of this word *prima manu*.
[3] On the left margin, in a smaller contemporary handwriting, this title has been added 'DE MARTYRIB*US*.'
[4] Some such title as 'PRO TRIBULANTIBUS' has been omitted after this line.
[5] The long mark of abbreviation over 'a me' implies the rest of Ps. xxvii. 1.
[6] The mark over 'qui' implies the remainder of the formula.
[7] The mark of abbreviation over 'LEC' is probably a clerical error.
[8] An 'f' has been written over the first letter of this word *prima manu*.

devotione retinemus
passione consimiles
in resurrectione
felicium facias co
aequari. qui regnas
Miserere mei deus
secundum magnam
Tribue domine peten
tibus te ex fide secun
dum magnam miseri
cordiam tuam deus. qui r[egnas]
ad noc turnam
Media nocte clamo
re facto ut nos in
veniamur parati
sponso. qui regnas
ad matutinam
Deus qui nos a te de luce
vigilare debemus et
tu excita de gravi
somno et libera de so
pore animas nostras
et in cubilibus nostris
conpungamur ut
tui esse memores me
reamur. qui regnas

ad nonam
Tu es spes et salus. Tu es
vita et virtus. Tu es
adiutor in tribulati
onibus. Tu es defen
sor animarum nos
trarum deus israel in
omnibus. qui regnas
ad secundam
Deus qui in altis habitas
et humilia respicis
in caelo et in terra.
in mari et in omnibus
abyssis de profundo cor
dis te deprecamur
ut firmes manus nos
tras ad proelium et
digitos nostros ad bel
lum quo possimus
in matutino interfi
cere omnes peccato
res terrae nostrae
ac nos indeficientes
mereamur et templum sanctum
tuum Christe. qui regnas

[*Fol. 22 recto.*]

deuotione strenuos
passione consimiles
in resurrectione
felicium facias co
aequari. qui regnas[1]
Miserere mei d*eu*s
secundu*m* magnam[2]
TRibue d*omi*ne peten
tibus te ex fide secun
dum magnam miseri
cordiam tuam d*eu*s qui r*egn*as

AD NOCTURNO.[3]

Media nocte clamo
re facto ut nos in
ueniamur parati
sponso qui regnas

AD MATU*TINA*

D*eu*s d*eu*s n*oste*r ad te de luce
uigilare debemus. et
tu excita de graui
sumno et libera de so
pore animas nostras
et in cubilibus nostris
conpuncgamur ut
tui esse memores me
reamur qui regnas ∴

ad ma[tutina][4]

TU es spes et salus. Tu es
uita et uirtus. Tu es
adiutor in tribulati
onibus. Tu es defen
sor animarum nos
trarum d*eu*s isr*ahe*l in
omnibus. qui regnas

AD MATUTINA

O qui in altis habitas
et humilia respicis
in caelo et in terra
in mari et in omnibus
abissis de p*ro*fundo cor
dis te dipraecamur
ut firmes manus nos
tras ad proelium et
digitos nostros ad bel
lum. quo possumus
in matutino interfi
cere omnes peccato
res terrae nostræ
ac nos indefice mere
amur et templum s*anctu*m
tuum *christ*e qui reg*nas*

---

[1] It seems as if some such title as 'PRO PAENITENTIBUS' should have been written after this line.
[2] The long mark of abbreviation over 'magnam' implies the remainder of Ps. l. 3.
[3] A Greek cross has been placed on the left margin opposite this title.
[4] This title has been written afterwards.

Deus qui scos tuos cum
mensura probas et
sine mensura glorifi
cas cuius praecep
ta finem habent et
praemia terminu
non habent exaudi
per illorum mere
ta praeces nostras
et tribue ut eorum
patrocinia adiuuent
nos ad fidei perfectum
ad bonorum operu
fructum ad prosperi
tatis bonum ad sa
lubritatis commo
dum ad religionis
cultum ad diuini
timoris augmentu
per dnm nm ihm
xpm filium tuum
qui est rex regum
et dominus domi
nantium et gloria
futurorum reg
nans et permanebis
una cum aeterno
spu sco in saecula
saeculorum

Collectio post cantemus

Deus qui exeunti
ex aegypto
populo tuo maria
diuisisti et suspen
sis utrimque mar
ginibus in specie
muri erigi flu
enta iussisti animas
quoque nostras a di
luio peccatorum
liberare digneris
ut transire uitiorum
gurgitem ualeamus
hoste contempto

[*Fol. 22 verso.*]

AD MARTYRIBUS[1]

D*EU*S qui s*an*c*t*os tuos cum
mensura p*ro*bas et
sine mensura glorifi
cas cuius praecep
ta finem habent et
proemia terminu*m*
non habent exaudi
per illorum mere
ta praeces nostras
et tribue ut eorum
patrocinia adiuuent
nos ad fidei p*ro*fectum
ad bonorum operu*m*
fructum ad p*ro*speri
tatis bonum ad sa
lubritatis commo
dum ad relegionis
cultum ad diuini
timoris augmentu*m*
per d*omi*n*u*m n*ostru*m ih*esu*m
*christu*m filium tuum
qui est rex regum
et dominus domi
nantium et gloria
futurorum reg
nans et permanens
una cum aeterno
sp*irit*u s*anct*o in saecula
saeculorum . . ,

COLLECTIO
POST CAN

D*EU*S qui exeunti TI
ex aegypto CO
populo tuo maria
diuisisti et suspen
sis utrimq*ue* mar
ginibus in specie
muri eregi flu
enta iusisti animas
quoq*ue* nostras a di
luio peccatorum
liberare digneris
ut transire uitioru*m*
gurgitem ualeamus
hoste contempto

---

[1] This appears to be the wording of this faded title.

salvator mundi qui
cum aeterno patre
uiuis dominaris ac
regnas cum spu sco in
saecula saeculorum ::
col. post

Exaudi praeces nos
tras omps ds &
praesta ut sicut in de
cantato ymno beata
puerorum instituta
sectamur ita tuo mu
nere peccatorum la
queis absoluti aeter
ni ignis non ambiamur
incendiis salvator mun
di qui cum patre uiuis ::
col. post

Te dnm de caelis lau
damus tibi ut canor in
ticum nouum canta
in fine … re

mereamur te dnm
in scis tuis uenera
biliter depraeca
mur ut omnia no
ta nostra suscipi
as peccata dimit
tas salvator mun
di qui regnas ::
col. post euange
lium

Exultantes gau
dio pro reddita
nobis huius diei
luce omnipoten
ti do laudes gra
tiasque referamus
ipsius misericordia
obsecrantes ut die
dominicae resur
rectionis nobis
sollempniter cele
brantibus pacem
& tranquillitatem

[*Fol. 23 recto.*]

saluator mundi qui
cum aeterno patre
uiuis dominaris ac
regnas cum sp*irit*u s*an*ct*o* in
saecula saeculorum :· ,

COL*LECTIO* POST B*ENEDIC*
TIONEM PUERO[1]

EXaudi praeces nos R*UM*
tras om*n*ip*oten*s d*eu*s et
praesta ut sicut in de
cantato imno beata
puerorum instituta
sectamur ita tuo mu
nere peccatorum la
queys[2] absoluti aeter
ni ignis non ambiamur
incendiis saluator mun
di qui cum patre uiuis :·

COL*LECTIO* POST[3] TRES PSA L M OS.

TE d*omin*u*m* de caelis lau
damus tibi ut can
ticum nouum canta
IN FINE. re
mereamur te d*omin*u*m*
in s*an*ct*i*s tuis uenera
biliter dipraeca
mur ut omnia uo
ta nostra suscipi
as peccata dimit
tas saluator mun
di qui regnas . . ,

COL*LECTIO* POST EUANGE
LIUM.

EXsultantes gau
dio p*ro* reddita
nobis huius diei
luce omnipoten
ti d*e*o laudes gra
tiasq*ue* referamus
ipsius misericordia*m*
obsecrantes ut die*m*
dominicae resur
rectionis nobis
sollempniter cele
brantibus pacem
et tranquillitate

---

1 The expansion of the abbreviations has made it necessary to extend this line into two lines in print.

2 The letter before 's' is either a 'y,' or the scribe began a long 's' and left it somewhat like an 'i.'

3 A point under and between the last two letters of 'POST' calls attention to some alteration. Was 'POST RES' on the point of being written instead of 'POST TRES'?

laetitiam praes
tare dignetur
ut a uigilia matuti
na usq: ad noctem
clementiae suae fa
uore protecti exul
tantes laetitia per
petua gaudeamus
per dnm nm ihm xpm s

Super hymnum

Sce dne inluminatio
& salus uera credenti
bus resurrectio
dominicae clari
tatis inlumina cor
dium ut trinitatis sci
entia & unitatis cog
nitione filii lucis &
membra xpi ac tem
plum sci spr esse me
reamur qui regnas
in saecula saeculorum

De martyribus

Hii sunt dne qui fe
lici cruore perfusi
dum blandientem
mundi huius inlecebra
glori ora passione dis
piciunt mortem mor
te uicerunt conside
rantesq: tenebras
huius lucis certo ter
mino ac fine nocturnas
sumpserunt de poena
uitam & de morte uic
toriam Rogamus te xpe
ut eorum praecibus ad
iuuari mereamur quo
rum consortes esse
non possumus per te
xpe ihu qui cum patre uiuis
dominaris & regnas

Super cantemus
dno glo.

[*Fol. 23 verso.*]

laetitiam praes
tare dignetur
ut a uigilia matuti
na. usq*ue* ad noctem
clemenitiae[1] suae fa
uore p*ro*tecti exul
tantes laetitia per
petua gaudeamus
per d*omi*n*u*m n*ostru*m
ih*esu*m *christu*m s*anctum*[2]

SUPER HYMN

S*an*ct*e* d*omi*ne inluminatio U
et salus uera creden M.
tibus resurrectio
dominicae clari
tatis inlumina cor
n*ostru*m ut trinitatis sci
entia et unitatis cog
nitione filii lucis et
membra *christ*i ac tem
plum s*anct*i sp*iritu*s esse me
reamur qui regnas
in saecula saeculorum

DE MARTYRIBUS

Hii sunt d*omi*ne qui fe
lici cruore perfusi
dum blandientem
mundi huius inlecebra*m*[3]
gloriosa passione dis
piciunt mortem mor
te uicerunt conside
rantesq*ue* tenebras
huius lucis certo ter
mino ac fine ruituras
sumpserunt de poena
uitam et de morte uic
toriam rogamus te *christ*e
ut eorum praecibus ad
iuuari mereamur quo
rum consortes esse
non possumus per te
*christ*e qui cum patre uiuis
dominaris et regnas

SUPER CANTEMUS
D*OMI*NO GLO*RIOSE*.

[1] A dot above the first 'i' in this word calls attention to the superfluous letter.
[2] The expansion of contractions has made it necessary to extend this line into two lines in print.
[3] A later hand has written what is apparently a second 'c,' with a point above it, over and above the 'ce' in this word.

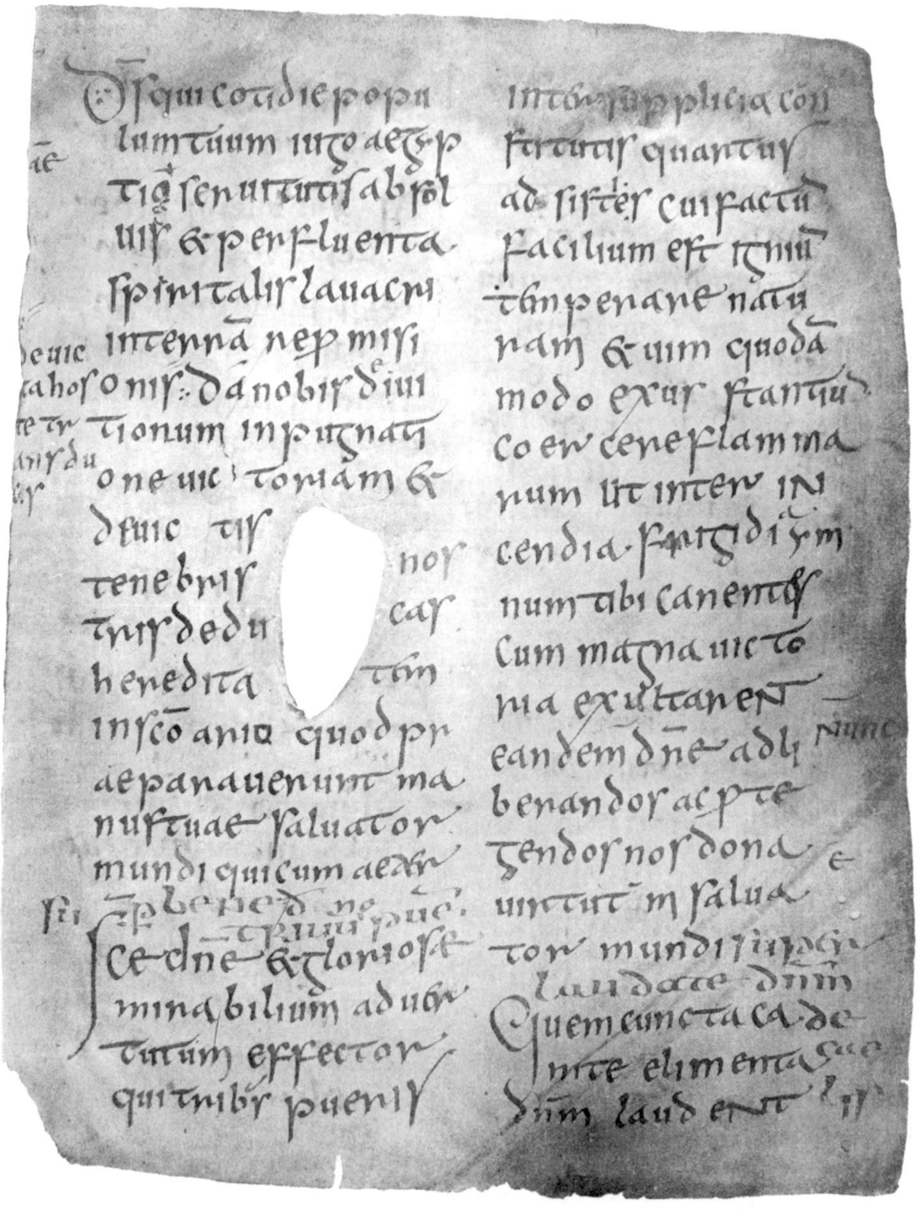

[*Fol. 24 recto.*]

D*EU*S qui cotidie popu
lum tuum iugo aegyp
tio[1] seruitutis absol
uis et per fluenta
spiritalis lauacri
in terra*m* rep*ro*misi
onis :·[2] da nobis diui[3]
tiorum inpugnati
one uictoriam et
deuictis
tenebris nos
tris dedu cas
heredita tem
in s*anct*oario quod pr
aeparauerunt ma
nus tuae saluator
mundi qui cum aeter
SUP*ER* BENED*ICTIONEM* no
TRIUU*M* PUE*RORUM*

S*an*cte d*omi*ne et gloriosæ
mirabilium ad uer
tutum effector
qui tribus pueris
inter supplicia con
stitutis quartus
adsistes[4] cui factu*m*
facilium est igniu*m*
temperare natu
ram et uim quoda*m*
modo exusstantiu*m*
coercere flamma
rum ut inter in
cendia frigidi[5] ym
num tibi canentes
cum magna uicto
ria exultarent
eandem[6] d*omi*ne ad li
berandos ac p*ro*te
gendos nos dona
uirtut m[7] salua
tor mundi SUPER
LAUDATE D*OMI*NUM

Quem cuncta ca DE
nite elimenta CAE
d*omi*n*u*m laudent LIS

[1] A horizontal line has been placed over the last letter of this word, and the letters 'ae,' with a similar line above them, have been written *prima manu* on the margin. Some alteration has also been begun beneath the 'o.'

[2] Two slanting lines have been placed over the last letter of this word, and under two similar lines, preceded by points, these words have been added *prima manu* on the margin, 'deuicta hoste transducis.'

[3] A point has been placed beneath the 'i' in this word, and an 'e' followed by a point has been written *prima manu* above it.

[4] A point has been placed under the 'e' in this word, and an 'i' followed by a point has been written *prima manu* above it.

[5] An 'a' has been written *prima manu* over the last letter of this word.

[6] A horizontal line has been placed over the last letter of this word, and the word 'nunc,' with a similar line above it, has been written *prima manu* on the margin.

[7] A horizontal line has been placed over the vacant space in this word in which a 'u' has been erased, and an 'e,' with a similar line above it, has been written *prima manu* on the margin.

Cuius confessio sa
cra eadem in caelo
et terra et pro regno
nasion nouum to
nanti dicite hymnum
factum iudicium ne
fandus in fine con
scriptum per sacri
pate diuersis spiri
tales melodia modis
ut xpm conlaudet
sps per saecla omnibus
qui cum patre uiuit
super canticum
Deus qui impiam ae
gyptum denis
cum nuptionibus int
cas et diuisu mari
planum iter popu
lo praestetisti prae
cessi [illegible] quaesi
mus nostra [illegible] nos
nostris tali [illegible]

hostibus salua sal
uator mundi qui r
post benedictionem
Deus qui pueris fide
feruentibus for
nacis flammam fri
gidam facis et tribus
inuictis morte diui
to quantus adsistes
prae ca [illegible] mur no
bis aestibus
carnis ta
lem uirtute
pr [illegible] aestes adustis
per te ihu xpe qui r
post laudate
Deus noster et omnium
animarum te ad
oramus ut in hac ui
gilia sollemnitatis
ad missa p [illegible] ue [illegible] nire
praestes quousque
tenebrae iniquitatis

[*Fol. 24 verso.*]

cuius confessio sa
cra eadem in caelo
et terra et pigno
ra sion nouum to
nanti dicite ymnu*m*
facturi iudicium ne
fandiis in fine con
scriptum per stri
pate diuersis spiri
tales melodia[1] modis
ut *christu*m conlaudet
sp*iritu*s per saecla omnes
qui cum patre uiuit

SUPER CANTICO[2]

D*EU*S qui impiam ae
gyptum deniis[3]
curruptionibus mul
tas et diuisu mari
planum iter popu
lo praestes prae
ces exaudi quessi
mus nostras ut nos
nostris taliter
hostibus salua sal
uator[4] mundi qui r*egnas*

POST BENEDICTIONE*M* TRIUU*M* PUERO RU*M*

D*EU*S qui pueris fide
feruentibus for
nacis flammam fri
gidam facis et tribus
inuictis morte· diuic
to[5] quartus adsistes
praecamur no
bis aestibus
carnis ta
lem uirtute*m*
pr aestes adustis
per te ih*es*u *christ*e qui r*egnas*.

POST LAUDATE D*OMI*N*U*M DE CAELIS.

D*EU*S noster d*eu*s omniu*m*
animarum te ad
oramus ut in hac ui
gilia sollempnitatis
admisa[6] p*er* uenire[7]
praestes quousque
tenebrae iniquitatis

---

[1] An 'e' has been written afterwards by a different hand over the 'a' in this word.

[2] A Greek cross, with four points in the spaces made by the central crossing of its limbs, has been placed opposite this title on the margin.

[3] An 'i' has been written *prima manu* over and between the first two letters of this word which are slightly spaced.

[4] An 's' has been erased before the first letter of this line.

[5] A slanting stroke has been placed over the last letter of 'diuicto,' and an 'a,' with a similar stroke above it, has been written on the margin afterwards by a different hand.

[6] A second and round 's,' followed by a point, has been written by a later hand over and between the 'l' and 's' in this word, and a point has been placed below and between the same two letters.

[7] This word seems to have been originally written 'preuenire,' but to have been altered *prima manu*.

nostrae conuer
tetur in lumine
sicut sol in meridie
splendescet salua
tor mundi qui r
post euangelium
Dominicam nos
trae resurrec
tionis initium uene
rantes trinitati d(e)o
n(ostr)o debitas laudes
et grates unito refe
ramus affectu obse
crantes misericordiam
eius ut nobis d(omi)ni et salua
toris n(ostr)i beatae resur
rectionis participium
tam in sp(irit)u quam etiam
in corpore concedat
qui cum patre uiuit
post hymnum.

Respice d(omi)ne ad prae
ces nostras qui in
firmitates uisitas
humanas et tuam no
bis scificationem
largire et immor
talitatem xp(ist)e qui r
item post canticum
Summerso in mari
farao(ne) libera
tur isr(ae)l nos quoque
per baptismi gra
tiam et crucis trium
phum ab omni ma
lo quaesumus libe
rari per te xp(ist)e
item post benedictionem
Deus qui tres pue
ros de fornace
eripuisti sic nos
eripias

[*Fol. 25 recto.*]

nostrae conuer
tantur in lumine
sicut sol in meridie
splendescet salua
tor mundi qui r*egnas*

POST EUANGELIU*M*

Dominicam nos
trae resurrec
tionis initium uene
rantes trinitati d*e*o
n*ostr*o debitas laudes
et grates unito reffe
ramus affectu obse
crantes misericordia*m*
eius ut nobis d*omin*u*s* et salua
toris n*ostr*i beatae resur
rectionis participiu*m*
tam in sp*irit*u quam etiam
in corpore concedat
qui cum patre uiuit..,

POST HYMNUM.

Respice d*omi*ne ad prae
ces nostras qui in
firmitates uisitasti
humanas et tuam no
bis s*anct*ificationem
largire et inmor[1]
talitatem *christ*e qui r*egnas*

ITEM POST CANTICO.[2]

Summerso in mari
faraone libera
tur isr*ahe*l nos quoq*ue*
per baptismi gra
tiam et crucis trium
phum ab omni ma
lo quessumus libe
rari per te *christ*e

ITEM POST BENEDI

D*EU*S qui tres pue TE[3]
ros de forna
ce eripuisti sic nos
eripias

---

[1] The 'n' in this word is '*in rasura.*'
[2] A roughly shaped Greek cross has been prefixed to this title on the margin.
[3] The fourth syllable of this word has been accidentally omitted.

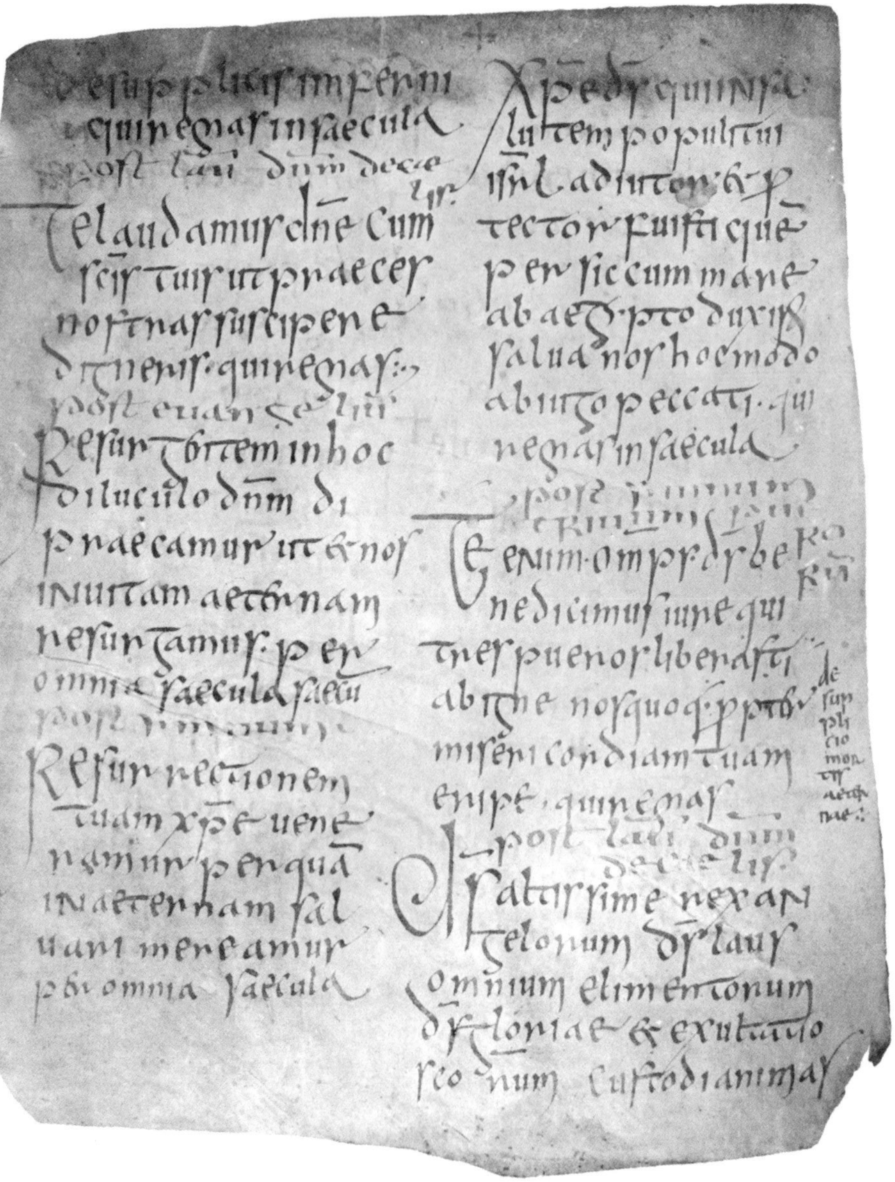

[*Fol. 25 verso.*]

de supplicis imferni
qui regnas in saecula

POST LAU*DATE* DO*MI*N*UM* DE CÆ LIS.

Te laudamus d*omi*ne cum
s*anct*is tuis ut praeces
nostras suscipere
digneris. qui regnas :· ,

POST EUANGELIU*M*

Resurgentem in hoc
diluculo d*omi*n*u*m di
praecamur ut et nos
in uitam aeternam
resurgamus. per
omnia saecula saecu*lorum*

POST YMNUM

Resurrectionem
tuam *christ*e uene
ramur per qua*m*
in aeternam sal
uari mereamur
per omnia saecula

*CHrist*e[1] d*eu*s qui in sa
lutem populi tui
isr*ahe*l adiutor et p*ro*
tector fuisti que*m*
per siccum mare
ab aegypto duxisti
salua nos hoc modo
ab iugo peccati. qui
regnas in saecula

POST YMNUM TRIUUM PUE RO RU*M*

Te enim. om*nipo*te*n*s. d*eu*s be
nedicimus iure qui
tres pueros liberasti
ab igne nos quoq*ue*[2] p*ro*pter
misericordiam tuam
eripe. qui regnas

POST LAU*DATE* DO*MI*N*UM* DE CAELIS.

D*EU*S altissime rex an
gelorum d*eu*s laus
omnium elimentorum
d*eu*s gloriae et exultatio
s*anct*orum custodi animas

[1] A Greek cross has been placed upon the top margin above and to the left of the opening word of this collect. Some such title as 'Post Cantemus' has been omitted after the cross.

[2] A slanting stroke, with a point above it, has been placed after and above this word, and under similar marks on the margin the following words have been added in a smaller contemporary handwriting, 'de supplicio mortis aeternae . ·.'

seruorum tuorum
qui regnas in saecula
post euangelium
Canticis spiritalibus
Dilectati hymnos
xpe consonantes
canimus tibi quibus
tua maiestas possit
placari oblata lau
dis hostia spiritali
qui tecum uiuit
item post euange
Deluculo lucis auc
tore resurgente
exultemus in dno de
uicta morte quo
peccata possimus
semper obdire uitae
q; ambulemus in noui
tate. qui tecum uiuit

post hymnum
Lux orta est in lu
ce prima exor
dio dierum antiquo
facta. uincentur
tuus dne. qui nostra
abluere uenit per
crucem peccata
qui tecum uiuit.
de martyribus.
Triumphalium me
mores martyrum
tuorum qui pro te tol
lerare uixilla pas
sionum praecamur
ut per sca menta ip
sorum nostrorum ue
niam mereamur pecca
torum. qui regnas.

[*Fol. 26 recto.*]

seruorum tuorum
qui regnas in saecula :·

POST EUANGE LIUM[1]

CANticis spiritalibus
dilectati imnos
christe consonantes
canimus tibi quibus
tua maiestas possit
placari oblata lau
dis hostia spiritali :·,
qui tecum uiuit

ITEM POST EUANGE LIUM[1]

Deluculo lucis auc
tore resurgente
exultemus in d*omi*no de
uicta morte quo
peccata possimus
semper obire uitae
q*ue* ambulemus in noui
tate. qui tecum uiuit

POST YMNUM

Lux[2] orta est in lu
ce prima exor
dio dierum antiquo
facta unigenitus
tuus d*omi*ne qui nostra
abluere uenit per
crucem peccata
qui tecum uiuit

DE MARTYRIBUS.

TRiumphalium me
mores martirum
tuorum qui p*ro* te tol
lerare uixilla pas
sionum praecamur
ut per s*anct*a merita ip
sorum nostrorum ue
niam mereamur pecca
torum. qui regnas ..,.

---

[1] For the exact position of the last four letters of these titles see collotype.

[2] This column commences in a larger style of handwriting which is continued by different scribes till fol. 29 recto, inclusive.

+ post cantemus
Plebs isrl in figu
ram nostri libera
tur in transitu ma
ri. nos renati per gra
tiam baptismi. libe
rati ab exterminan
di. qui regnas
post benedicite
Qui tres pueros in
flamma saluasti.
discensu in fornacem
caelestis nuntii. sic
nos per angelum mag
ni consilii. liberare
digneris ab igne in
ferni, qui regnas
post laudate dominum
Te quem exercitus de
canit caelorum cae
quemque aecclesia
laudat sanctorum
quem et ministrat
spiritus uniuersorum
miserere obsecro
omnium nostrorum
qui regnas
super cantemus
+ Cantemus tibi
domine exerci
tuum xpe oran
ter ut quem ad
modum exemis
ti dilectum po
pulum tuum cap
tiuitatis aeterni
mae iugo iter
demonstrante
eis nubis colump
na

[*Fol. 26 verso.*]

POST CANTEMUS[1]

Plebs isr*ahe*l in figu
ram nostri libera[2]
tur in transitu ma
ri. nos ergo per gra[2]
tiam baptismi. libe
ra tu ab exitis mun
di. qui regnas

POST BENEDICITE

Ut tres pueros in
flamma saluasti.
discensu in fornacem
caelestis nuntii. sic
nos per angelu*m* mag
ni consilii. liberare
digneris ab igne im
ferni, qui regnas..,

POST LAU*DATE* DO*MI*N*U*M

D*EU*S quem exercitus DE
canit caelorum CAE
quemq*ue* aecclesia LIS
laudet[3] s*an*c*t*orum
quem ymnizat
sp*iritu*s uniuersorum
miserere obsecro
omnium nostroru*m*
qui regnas

SUPER CANTEM[4]

Cantemus[5] tibi U
d*om*ine exerci S.
tuum *christ*e oran
tes ut quem ad
modum exemis
ti dilectum po
pulum tuum cap
tiuitatis acerri
mae iugo iter
demonstrante
eis nubis colump
na

---

[1] A roughly shaped Greek cross has been prefixed on the margin to this title.
[2] The final 'a' in these lines has been written above the line.
[3] An early correcting hand has written an 'a' over the 'e' in 'laudet.'
[4] A roughly shaped Latin cross has been prefixed on the margin to this title.
[5] The handwriting changes here. The new hand uses accents more frequently, especially over vowels long by nature and not by position.

per diem eadem ignis quoque per noc
tem fenditur en comane dextera
levaque in abruptum decesas acervos
stupens unda solidatur tuus popu
lus navigat plantas minantes iter
eius nec eques potest sequi nec natis
maria tympanum quatit hymnus
iste cantatur tu ex peculius tuetur.
tuere nos ab infestatione veteris ini
mici et ab omni periculo mundi li
berare digneris salvator mundi qui
cum aeterno patre vivis dominaris
ac regnas una cum aeterno spiritu sancto in sae
cula saeculorum.

Super benedictionem
trium puerorum.

[*Fol. 27 recto.*]

per diem eadem ignis quoq*ue* per noc
tem fenditur[1] ergo mare dextera
leuaq*ue* in abruptum degestis acerribus
stupens unda solidatur tuus popu
lus nauigat plantis mira res iter
eius nec eques potest sequi nec ratis
maria tympanum quatit ymnus
iste canitur grex peculius tuetur.
iter[2] nos ab insectatione ueteris ini
mici et ab omni periculo mundi li
berare digneris saluator mundi qui
cum aeterno patre uiuis dominaris
ac regnas una cum aeterno sp*irit*u s*anct*o in sæ
cula saeculorum :· ,

SUPER BENEDICTIONEM
TRIUUM PUERORUM :

[1] An 'i' has been written *prima manu* over the 'e' in this word.
[2] An 'a' has been written by an early correcting hand over this word.

Tris ebrei uenerabiles numero sacra
mento muniti aetate teneri sed
fidei soliditate robusti amone diui
nae religionis regis adorare ima
ginem contempserunt utpute qui
ipsum contempserant necem quin a
sufflatur solito septies amplius camini
iussit incendi ac pice & stuppa anima
tum citani in cendium aestuantibus
globis enuberet quoque ipsum alienis
ignibus caelum illo praecipitantur
insontes ibidemque te propter quem
praecipitantur inueniunt xpe
taliter nos & tyranni intellectu alis
furore & ab ingenito igni digneris
liberare saluator mundi qui cum aeter
no patre in iiij

[*Fol. 27 verso.*]

Tris[1] ebrei uenerabiles numero sacra
mento muniti aetate teneri sed
fidei soliditate robusti amore diui
nae relegionis regis adorare ima
ginem contempserunt utpute qui
ipsum contempserant regem qui ira
sufflatus solito septies amplius caminu*m*
iusit incendi ac pice et stuppa arma
tum citari incendium aestuantibus
globis erubescit quoq*ue* ipsum alienis
ignibus caelum illo praecipitantur
insontes ibidemq*ue* te propter que*m*
praecipitantur inueniunt *christ*e
taliter nos et tyranni intellectualis
furore et ab ingenito igni digneris
liberare saluator mundi qui cum aeter
no patre uiuis

[1] A point has been placed over the 'i' of this word, and an 'e,' under a point, has been written above it by a later correcting hand.

post laudate dnm de caelis
Laudent te dne angeli uirtutes sidera
potestates & quae omnium suum tibi de-
bent officio tuae laudationis exsultent
ut per uniuersitatis armonia tibi in &
concinnentem fiat ut in caelo ita & in
terra uoluntas tua sit tibi praecamur
dne beneplacitum in populo tuo ut
per exaltationes tuas in eius faucibus
collocatas maneat in singulis & uer
bi tui animatura quo doceas & uitae
nostrae ueritas quia semper aspicias
& salus qua mansuetos exaltes quia se
cundum multitudinem magnitudinis
tuae te laudamus dne gratia lau
dationis ostensae

[*Fol. 28 recto.*]

POST LAUDAT[1] D*OMI*N*U*M DE CAELIS.

Laudent te d*omi*ne angeli uirtutes sidera potestates et quae ortum suum tibi de bent officio tuae laudationis exsultent ut per uniuersitatis armonia*m* tibimet concinnentem fiat ut in caelo ita et in terra uoluntas tua sit tibi praecamur d*omi*ne beneplacitum in populo tuo ut per exaltationes tuas in eius faucibus collocatas maneat in singulis et uer bi tui armatura qua doceas et uitae nostrae ueritas quia[2] semper aspicias et salus qua mansuetos exaltes quia se cundum multitudinem magnitudinis tuae te laudamus d*omi*ne gratia lau dationis ostensae

---

[1] The final 'e' of this word has been accidentally omitted.

[2] The 'i' of this word is marked by a point above it for erasure.

immolatione per psalterium morti
ficatione per tympanum congrega
tione per chorum exultatione
per citharam iubilatione per cym
balum ut semper misericordiam tua
habere mereamur xpe saluator
mundi qui cum aeterno patre uiuis
super cantemus dño
Dne qui in chorum fugientes tueris
bis senas per lnuis satnibus emulum
terrena primis fluctibus in binis mon
tium utrimque redactis celsorum ceu
iugis abruptae arentibus talis regione
munum quasi et de petra limphas p
ducens meretatur ergo ut olim priorum
supplicium hostias aeterni quaesumus
sitatores cunnum quod est cuius a fra
tur

[*Fol. 28 verso.*]

immolatione per psaltirium morti
ficatione per tympanum congrega
tione per chorum exsultatione
per urganum iubilatione per cym
balum ut semper misericordiam tua*m*
habere mereamur *christ*e saluator
mundi qui cum aeterno patre uiuis..,

SUPER CANTEMUS D*OMI*NO[1]

D*OMI*NE qui cinchrim fugientes tueris
bis senas per inuissa tribus emulum
itenera prius fluctibus in binis mon
tium utrimq*ue* redactis celsorum ceu
iugis abrupte arentibus talis equore
murum quasi et de petra limphas. p*ro*
ducens mergatur ergo ut olim piorum
supplicium hostis aeterni quaesumus
statores currum quod est cuius affa
tus

[1] A roughly shaped Greek cross has been prefixed on the margin to this title.

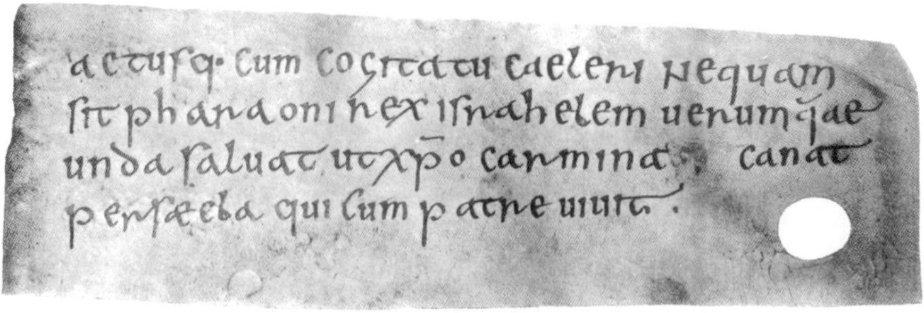

actusq· cum cogitatu caeleri nequam
sit pharaoni rex israhelem uenumqae
unda saluat ut xpo carmina canat
per saecla qui cum patre uiuit.

[*Fol. 29 recto.*]

actusq*ue* cum cogitatu caeleri nequam sit pharaoni rex israhelem uerum quae unda saluat ut *christ*o carmina[1] canat per saecla qui cum patre uiuit.[2]

---

[1] The letter 't' has been erased after 'carmina.'

[2] Fol. 29 verso is blank. This slip, which is an original insertion in the MS., never had any writing *prima manu* on its reverse side. For unimportant later entries on it see Introduction.

uersiculi familiae benchuir

benchuir bona regula
recta atq. diuina
stricta sca sedula
summa iusta ac mira

munther benchuir beata
fide fundata certa
spe salutis ornata
caritate perfecta

nauis numquam turbata
quamuis fluctibus tonsa
nuptiis quoque parata
regi dno sponsa

domus deliciis plena
super petram constructa
necnon uinea uera
ex aegipto transducta

certe ciuitas firma
fortis atque munita
gloriosa ac digna
supra montem
posita

arca chirubin tecta
omni parte
aurata
sacrosanctis referta
uiris quatuor portata

xpo regina apta
solis luce amicta
simplex simulq. docta
undecumq. inuicta

uere regalis aula
uariis gemmis ornata
gregisq. xpi caula
patre summo seruata

uirgo ualde fecunda
haec et mater intacta
laeta ac tremebunda
uerbo di subacta

[*Fol. 30 recto.*]

UERSICULI. FAMILIAE. BENCHUIR.

Benchuir bona regula
recta atq*ue* diuina
stricta s*anct*a sedula
summa iusta ac mira.
Munther benchuir beata
fide fundata certa
spe salutis ornata
caritate perfecta :·
Nauis numqua*m* turbata
qua*m*uis fluctibus tonsa
nuptis quoq*ue* parata
regi d*omi*no sponsa . . ,
Domus dilicis plena
super petra*m* constructa
necnon uinea uera
ex aegipto transducta
Certe ciuitas firma
fortis atq*ue* munita
gloriosa ac digna
supra montem
possita :· ,

ARca hirubin tecta
omni parte
aurata
sacros*anct*is referta
uiris quattuor porta /ta
*CHrist*o regina apta
solis luce amicta
semplex simulq*ue* docta
undecumq*ue* inuicta
Uere regalis aula
uaris gemmis ornata
gregisq*ue* *christ*i caula
patre summo seruata
UIRgo ualde fecunda
haec et mater. intacta
leta ac tremebunda
uerbo d*e*i subacta :·

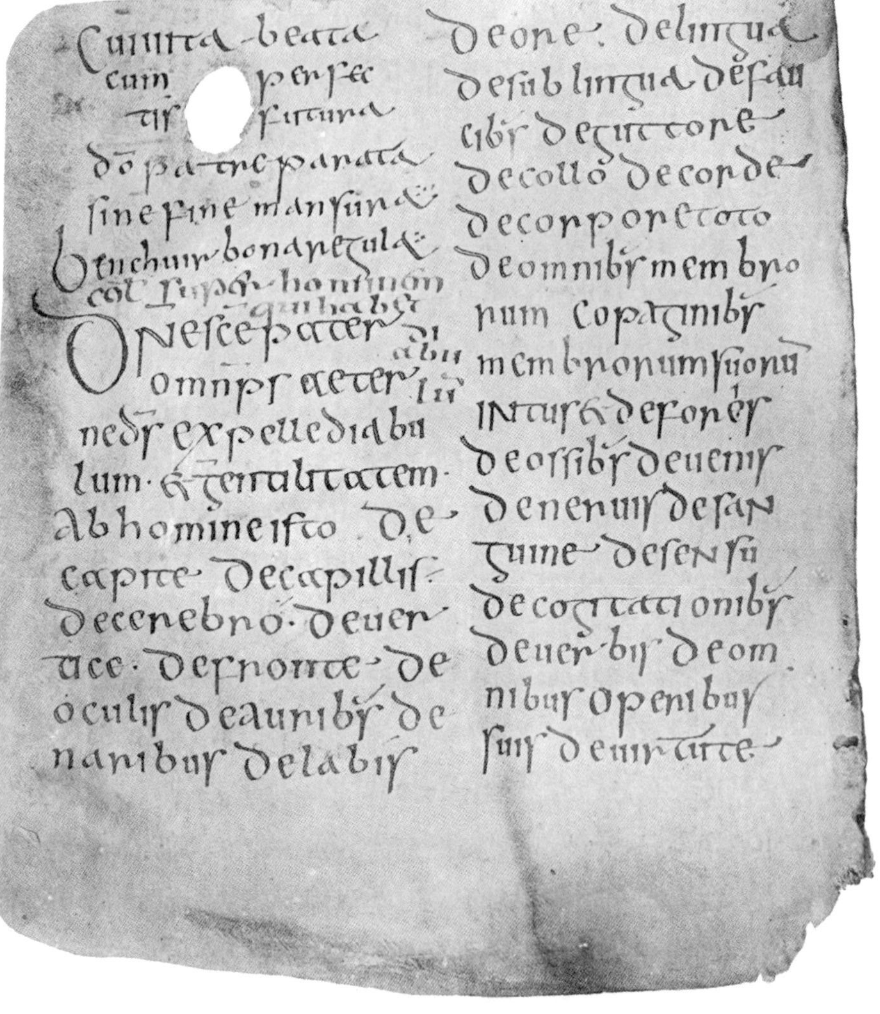

[*Fol. 30 verso.*]

Cui uita beata
cum perfec
tis futura
d*eo* patre parata
sine fine mansura :· ,
Benchuir bona regula :·

COL*LECTIO* SUPER HOMINEM QUI HABET DIABU LU*M*

D*omi*ne s*anct*e pater
omn*ipotens* aeter
ne d*eu*s expelle diabu
lum. et gentilitatem.[1]
ab homine isto de
capite de capillis[2]
de cerebro.[2] de uer
tice. de fronte de
oculis de auribus de
naribus de labis
de ore. de lingua
de sublingua de fau
cibus de guttore
de collo de corde
de corpore toto
de omnibus membro
rum copaginibus
membrorum suoru*m*
intus et defores[3]
de ossibus de uenis
de neruis de san
guine de sensu
de cogitationibus
de uerbis de om
nibus operibus
suis de uirtute

[1] A mark of contraction has been placed by mistake over the first letter of this word.

[2] A slanting stroke, with a point beneath it, has been placed after 'capillis,' and a slanting stroke, with a point above it, has been placed after and above 'cerebro.' The meaning of these marks is probably to indicate some variation in the order of the part of the body enumerated. The order varies in the same collect in the Stowe Missal. *Liturgy and Ritual of the Celtic Church*, p. 207.

[3] A point has been placed under the loop of the 'e' in this word, and an 'i' has been written *prima manu* over it.

De omni conuer
satione eius hic
et in futuro sed
operatur inte
uirtus xpi ihu
qui passus est
ut uitam aeter
nam mereamur
per dnm nm ihm
xpm filium suum
oratio de mar
tyribus.
Sci qui mar
tiribus
tuis largitur
et regnum no
bis peccatori
bus ueniam
prestare

dignetur. hii cho
ronam suam pas
sione perficientes me
ruerunt nos tamen
iniquitatibus et pre
uaricationibus
nostris remissi
onem et mise
ricordiam pos
tulamus.
per te ihu xpe
Incipit anti
fano in na
tale dni. sis
dne refugi
um adse
cunda.

[*Fol. 31 recto.*] [1]

de omni conuer
satione eius hic
et in futuro sed
operatur in te
uirtus *christ*i in eo
qui p*ro*passus est
ut uitam aeter
nam mereamur
per d*omin*u*m* n*ostru*m ih*esu*m
*christu*m filium suum

ORATIO DE MAR
TYRIBUS.

D*eu*s qui. mar
tiribus
tuis lagitus[2]
es regnum. no
bis *autem* peccati[3]
bus ueniam
prestare
digneris. hii cho[4]
ronam suam pas
sione per fide*m* me
ruerunt. nos *autem* p*ro*
iniquitab*us*[5] et pr
aeuaricationib*us*
nostris remisi
onem a te et mise
ricordam pos
tulamus :·
per te ih*es*u *christ*e

INCIPIT ANTE
FANO IN NA
TALE D*OMI*NI. SUP*ER*
D*OMI*NE REFUGI
UM. AD SE
CUNDA.

[1] There are three different handwritings on this page, the first extending from 'de'—'suum,' the second extending from 'D*eu*s'—'*christe*,' the third being employed in the rubrical headings.

[2] A slanting stroke has been placed over the 'a' in 'lagitus,' and an 'r,' with a slanting stroke over it, has been written on the margin *prima manu.*

[3] A slanting stroke, with a point above it, has been placed over the 'a' in 'peccatibus,' and an 'n,' under a slanting stroke with a point above it, has been written on the margin *prima manu.*

[4] A Greek cross has been placed on the margin to the right of this line.

[5] The letters 'ti' have been written over the letter 'a' in this word by a contemporary correcting hand. They are preceded and followed by a fine point, and another fine point has been placed in the concave space formed by the second stroke of the 'a.'

ab hodierno die nox
minuitur dies crescit
conciuntur tenebrae
lumen augitur et in lu
cro lucis nocturnae
dispendia transferun
tur. incipiunt
ante famulus super cantemus.

Educti ex aegypto
patres nostri et bene
pertransierunt pedibus
rubrum mare dixerunt laudem
domino nostro.

Tres pueri in ca
mino missi sunt
et non timu
erunt flam
mam ignis
dixerunt

laudem domino nostro.

Filii ebreorum
pertransierunt
israhelitae ple
bes transierunt
per siccum mare
laudem dixerunt.

Tres pueri ora
bant de medio ignis
ad te clamabant
ex uno ore hymnum
dicebant.

Gloriosus in sanctis
mirabilis in ma
iestatibus faciens
prodigia.

Benedicamus dominum
patrem et filium
et spiritum sanctum dominum

[*Fol. 31 verso*] [1]

Ab[2] hodierno die nox
minuitur dies crescit
concutiuntur tenebræ
lumen augitur. et in lu
cro lucis nocturnae
dispendiae transferen
INCIPIUNT tur . . . ,
ANTEFANI[3] SUP*ER* CANTEMUS.

EDucti ex aegypto
patres nostri et
pertranisierunt
pedibus rubrum ma
re dixerunt lau
dem d*omi*no nostro :· ,

ET BE NE DI CI TE.

TRIS[4] pueri in ca
mino misi sunt
et non timu
erunt flam
mam ignis
dixerunt
laudem d*omi*no nostro :· ,

Filii ebre eorum
penitrauerunt
israhelitae ple
bes transierunt
per siccum mare
laudem dixerunt :· ,

TRIS[4] pueri te ora
bant de medio ignis
ad te clamabant
ex uno[5] uoce ymnu*m*
dicebant

Gloriosus in s*anct*is
mirabilis in ma
iestatibus faciens
prodigia . . ,

Benedicamus d*eu*m
patrem et filiu*m*
et sp*iritu*m s*anctu*m d*omi*nu*m*

---

[1] A fresh but contemporaneous handwriting commences on this page.

[2] A Latin cross has been placed on the margin to the left of this line.

[3] A little lower down on the left margin the remains are visible of a cross with points placed in the spaces formed by the central intersection of its limbs.

[4] A point has been placed beneath the 'i' in this word, and an 'e' has been written by an early correcting hand above it.

[5] A point has been placed in the central space of the 'o' in 'uno,' and an 'a' has been written by an early correcting hand above it.

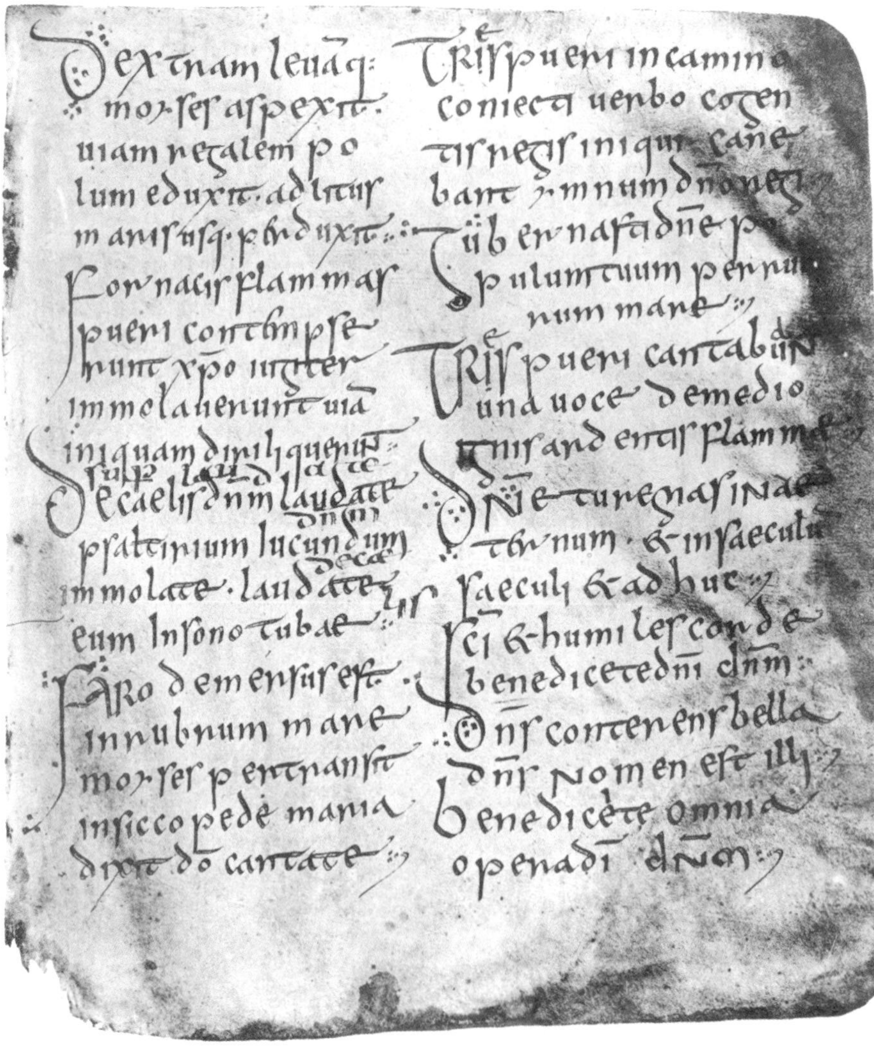

[*Fol. 32 recto.*]

DEXtram leua*m*q*ue*
moyses aspexit.
uiam regalem po
lum eduxit. ad litus
maris usq*ue* perduxit :·
Fornacis flammas
pueri contempse
runt *christ*o iugiter
immolauerunt uia*m*
iniquam diriliquerunt :·

SUP*ER* LAUDATE[1]

DE caelis d*omi*n*u*m laudate
psaltirium iucundum D*OMI*N*U*M
immolate. laudate DE CÆ
eum in sono tubae :· LIS
FARo demersus est
in rubrum mare
moyses pertransit
in sicco pede maria
dixit d*e*o cantate :· ,

TRIS[2] pueri in camino
coniecti uerbo cogen
tis regis iniqui. cane
bant ymnum d*omi*no regi :· ,
Gubernasti d*omi*ne po
pulum tuum per rub
rum mare :· ,
TRIS[2] pueri cantabunt[3]
una uoce de medio
ignis ardentis flammæ :· ,
D*omi*ne tu regnas in ae
ternum. et in saeculu*m*
saeculi et adhuc :· ,
S*anct*i et humiles corde
benedicete d*omi*ni d*omi*n*u*m :·
D*omi*n*u*s conterens bella
d*omi*n*u*s nomen est illi :· ,
Benedicete[4] omnia
opera d*e*i d*omi*n*u*m :· ,

---

[1] No space has been left in the MS. for this title; of the rest of it 'DOMINUM' has been inserted below 'laudate,' 'DE CÆ' below 'iucundum,' 'LIS' below and after 'laudate.'

[2] A point has been placed below the 'i' in 'Tris,' and an 'e' has been written above it by an early correcting hand.

[3] An 'a' has been written over the 'u' in this word by an early correcting hand.

[4] An 'i' has been written over the third 'e' in this word *prima manu*.

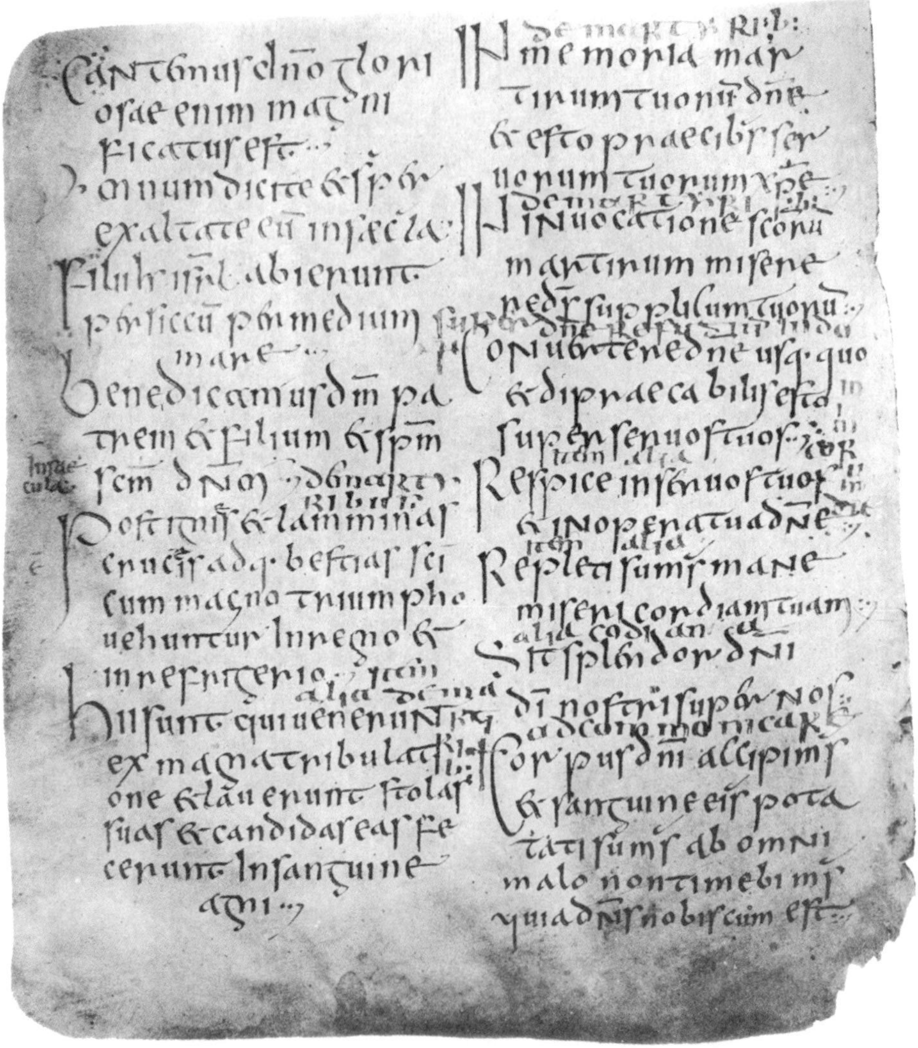

[*Fol. 32 verso.*]

Cantemus[1] d*omi*no glori
osae enim magni
ficatus est. . . ,
Ymnum dicite et super
exaltate eu*m* in sæcula :·
Filii *autem* isr*ahe*l abierunt
per siccu*m* per medium
mare . . ,
Benedicamus d*eu*m pa
trem et filium et sp*iritu*m
s*anctu*m d*omi*n*u*m[2] . . , DE MARTY
RIBUS.

Post ignis[3] et lamminas
crucis[4] adq*ue* bestias s*anct*i
cum magno triumpho
uehuntur in regno et
in refrigerio . . , ITEM
ALIA DE MA
RTI
RI
B*US*

Hii sunt qui uenerunt
ex magna tribulati
one et lauerunt stolas
suas et candidas eas fe
cerunt in sanguine
agni . . ,

DE MARTYRIB*US*

IN memoria mar
tirum tuoru*m* d*omi*ne
et esto praecibus ser
uorum tuorum *christ*e :· ,

DE MARTYRIB*US*

IN inuocatione s*anct*oru*m*
martirum misere
re d*eu*s supplicum tuoru*m* :· ,

SUPER DO*MI*NE REFUGIU*M* IN DO
M
I
NI
COR
U
M
DIE

Conuertere[5] d*omi*ne usq*ue* quo
et dipraecabilis esto
super seruos tuos . . ,

ITEM ALIA.

Respice in seruos tuos
et in opera tua d*omi*ne :· ,

ITEM ALIA.

Repleti sumus mane
misericordiam tuam :· ,

ALIA CODIANA

Sit splendor d*omi*ni
d*e*i nostri super nos :·

AD COMMONICARE

Corpus[5] d*omi*ni accipimus
et sanguine eius pota
tati[6] sumus ab omni
malo non timebimus
quia d*omi*nus nobiscum est :· ,

---

[1] A roughly shaped Latin cross has been placed before the commencement of this line.

[2] A slanting stroke and a point have been placed after and above this word, and also on the left margin where the words 'in saecula' have been added below them.

[3] An 'e' has been written by an early correcting hand over the second 'i' in 'ignis.'

[4] An 'e' has been written by an early correcting hand over the 'i' in 'crucis,' and an 'e,' below a slanting stroke, has been written likewise on the margin. A corresponding slanting stroke runs beneath the upper part of the interlinear 'e.'

[5] A roughly shaped Latin cross, with ornamental terminations to its horizontal bar, has been placed before the commencement of these two lines.

[6] [illegible]

Item alia
Gustate et uidete alle.
quam suauis est dns. al.
Item alia
In labiis meis medita
bor ymnum. alle.
Cum docueris me ego
iustitias respondebo. al.
alia
Hoc sacrum corpus dni
et saluatoris sanguinem
sumite uobis in uitam
perennem. alle
Item alia
Quam dulcia faucibus meis
eloquia tua dne.
Item alia
Hic est panis uiuus qui
de caelo discendit. al.
Qui manducat ex eo
uiuet in aeternum. al.
alia
Refecti xpi corpore
et sanguine tibi semper
dne dicamus. alle.
[illegible]
Gloria in excelsis deo
et in terra pax homi
nibus bonae uoluntatis.
Laudamus te benedici
mus te adoramus te

glorificamus te magni
ficamus te. gratias
agimus tibi propter
magnam miseri
cordiam tuam dne
rex caelestis ds pa
ter omnipotens.
Dne fili unigeni
te ihu xpe sce sps
di et omnes dicimus
amen. Dne
fili di patris agne
di qui tollis pecca
tum mundi mise
rere nobis. Sus
cipe orationem
nostram qui sedes
ad dexteram di pa
tris miserere nobis.
Quoniam tu solus scs
tu solus dns tu so
lus gloriosus cum
spu sco in gloria
di patris amen.

[*Fol. 33 recto.*]

ITEM ALIA

Gustate et uidete , alle*luia*
quam suauis est d*omin*u*s*., al*leluia*

ITEM ALIA

IN labiis meis medita
bor ymnum. alle*luia*.
cum docueris me ego
iustitias respondebo ∴ al*leluia*.

ALIA

Hoc sacrum corpus d*omin*i
et saluatoris sanguine*m*
sumite uobis in uitam
perennem ., alle*luia*

ITEM ALIA

Quam dulcia faucibus meis
eloquia tua d*omin*e,

ITEM ALIA

Hic est panis uiuus qui
de caelo discendit, al*leluia*
qui manducat ex eo
uiuet in aeternum. al*leluia*

IT*EM* ALIA

Refecti *christ*i corpore
et sanguine tibi semper
d*omin*e dicamus ., alle*luia* .,

AD UESPERU*M* ET AD[1] MATUTINAM

Gloria in excelsis d*e*o
et in terra pax homi
nibus bonae uoluntatis :·,
laudamus te benedici
mus te adoramus te
glorificamus[2] te magni
ficamus te .., gra
tias agimus tibi p*ro*p
ter magnam miseri
cordiam tuam d*omin*e
rex caelestis d*eu*s pa
ter omnipotens :·,
D*OMI*NE filii unigeni
te ihe*s*u *christ*e s*anct*e sp*iritu*s
d*e*i et omnes dicimus
amen .., D*OMI*NE
filii d*e*i patris agne
d*e*i qui tollis pecca
tum mundi mise
rere nobis ., SUS
cipe orationem
nostram qui sedes
ad dexteram d*e*i pa
tris miserere nobis :·,
Quoniam tu solus s*anctu*s
tu solus d*omin*u*s* tu so
lus gloriosus cum
sp*irit*u s*anct*o in gloria
d*e*i patris amen :·,[3]

[1] A roughly shaped Latin cross has been placed before the commencement of this title.

[2] The cursive 'u' above the line is nearly all cut off.

[3] The discrepancy in length between the two columns on this page as compared with the corresponding collotype, is due to the insertion of the first six titles in the left column on the margin or between the lines.

Cotidie benedici
mus te et laudamus
nomen tuum in ae
ternum et in saecu
lum saeculi amen:
Digna re dne die
ista sine peccato
nos custodire: bene
dictus es dne ds pa
trum nostrorum,
et laudabile et glo
riosum nomen tuum
in saecula amen:
Miserere nobis dne:
miserere nobis,
Uerba mea auribus
usq· et ds meus,
mane et exaudies
uocem meam·
Mane oratio mea
prae ueniet te dne:
Diebus adq· nocti
bus horis adq· mo
mentis, miserere
ne nobis dne,

Orationibus ac meri
tis scorum tuorum: mise
Angelorum archange
lorum patriarcha
rum prophetarum,
miserere nobis dne
Apostolorum marty
rum et confessorum
adq· uniuersa gnadus
scorum, miserere
Gloria et honor patri
et filio et spiritui sco, et
nunc et semper et in sae
cula saeculorum amen:

[*Fol. 33 verso.*] [1]

Cotidie[2] benedici
mus te et laudamus
nomen tuum in æ
ternum et in saecu
lum saeculi amen :·
Dignare d*omi*ne die
ista sine peccato
nos custodire. bene
dictus es d*omi*ne d*eu*s pa
trum nostrorum .,
Et laudabile et glo
riosum nomen tuu*m*
in saecula amen :·
Miserere nobis d*omi*ne.
miserere nobis ..,
Uerba mea auribus.
usq*ue* et d*eu*s meus .,
mane et exaudies
uocem meam .,
mane oratio mea
praeueniet te d*omi*ne :·
Diebus adq*ue* nocti
bus horis adq*ue* mo
mentis ., misere
re nobis d*omi*ne,

Orationibus ac mere
tis s*anct*orum tuoru*m* :· mise*rere*
Angelorum archange
lorum patriarcha
rum p*ro*phetarum .,
miserere nobis d*omi*ne
Apostolorum marti
rum et confessorum
adq*ue* uniuersa gradus
s*anct*orum ., miser*e*re
Gloria et honor patri
et fili[3] et sp*irit*ui s*anct*o, et
nuc[4] et semper et in sae
cula saeculorum. amen :·,

[1] This page is in a different handwriting from fol. 33 recto. From this page onwards considerable variety of handwriting occurs, but all the handwritings are contemporaneous, or nearly so, with the body of the MS. There are no additions of a distinctly later date.

[2] For the connection of this and some of the following verses with 'Te Deum Laudamus,' see Julian's *Dict. of Hymnology*, p. 1,120. See fol. 10 verso.

[3] A later correcting hand has added a small 'o' after the last letter in this word.

[4] The same correcting hand has written a small 'n' after and above the second letter of 'nuc.'

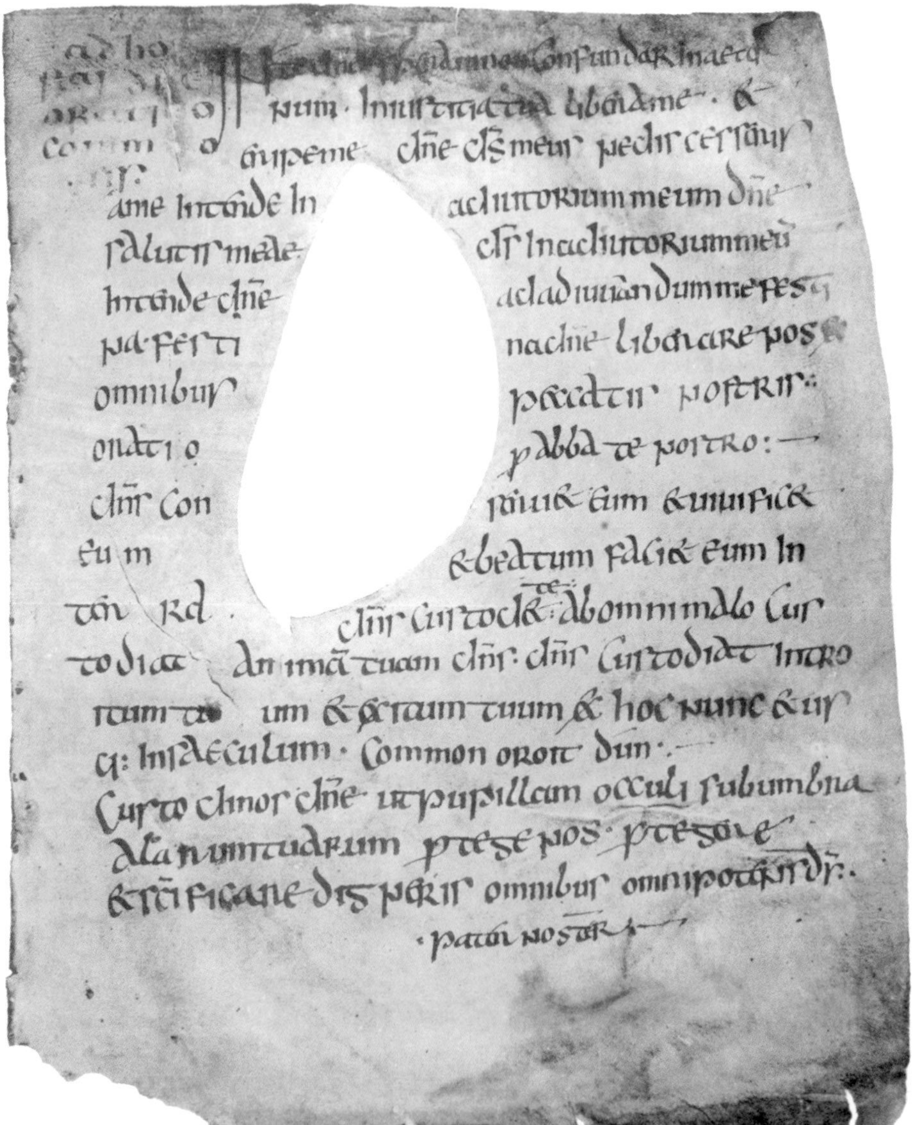

[*Fol. 34 recto.*]

AD HORAS DIEI ORATIO COMMONIS.

IN te d*omi*ne speraui non confundar in aeter
num. in iustitia tua libera me. et
eripe me d*omi*ne d*eu*s meus ne discesseris
a me intende in adiutorium meum d*omi*ne
salutis meae d*eu*s in adiutorium meu*m*
intende d*omi*ne ad adiuuandum me festi
na · festi na d*omi*ne liberare nos ex
omnibus peccatis nostris ∴
ORATIO P*RO* ABBATE NOSTRO:—
d*omi*n*u*s con seruet eum et uiuificet
eum et beatum faciet eum in
ter ra. d*omi*n*u*s custodet[1] ab omni malo cus
todiat anima*m* tuam d*omi*n*u*s. d*omi*n*u*s custodiat intro
itum tu um et exitum tuum ex hoc nunc et us
q*ue* in saeculum. COMMON OROIT DUN:—
custodi nos d*omi*ne ut pupillam occuli sub umbra
alarum tuarum p*ro*tege nos. p*ro*tegere
et s*an*c*t*ificare digneris omnibus omnipotens d*eu*s..
. pater noster:—[2]

---

[1] Two points, one above the other, are placed after 'custodet,' and the word 'te,' followed by two similar points, has been written *prima manu* interlineally above it.

[2] The mark of contraction over 'noster' implies the remainder of the 'oratio diuina,' the text of which has already been given on fol. 19 verso.

[illegible]
Ds summe ad te delicti [illegible] pe-
debemus & tu exercita de regno in
summo & libera [illegible] de propone
animas nostras [illegible] & in cubi
libus nostris [illegible] conpunc
tamur ut tui [illegible] esse memores mere[illegible] amur
ad horam [illegible] qui regnas
nonam ..

Conuenienter fra[illegible]
dilectissimi ad
orationem nonam
in quo tempore latro
conuersus est & regnum paradisi
pollicetur ei ita & nos dne con
fitemur peccata nostra & reg
num caelorum consequamur
& uitam aeternam mereamur
qui regnas.

[Fol. 34 verso.]

AD MATUTINA.

D*eu*s d*eu*s n*oste*r ad te de luce uigilare
debemus. et tu excita de graui
sumno et libera de sopore
animas nostras et incubi
libus nostris conpunc
gamur ut tui esse me
mores mere amur
qui regnas

AD HORAM
NONAM.

Conuenientes fr*atre*s
dilectissimi ad
orationem nonam
in quo tempore latro
confessus est et regnum paradisi
pollicetur ei ita et nos d*omi*ne con
fitemur peccata nostra et reg
num caelorum consequamur
et uitam aeternam mereamur
qui regnas :· ,

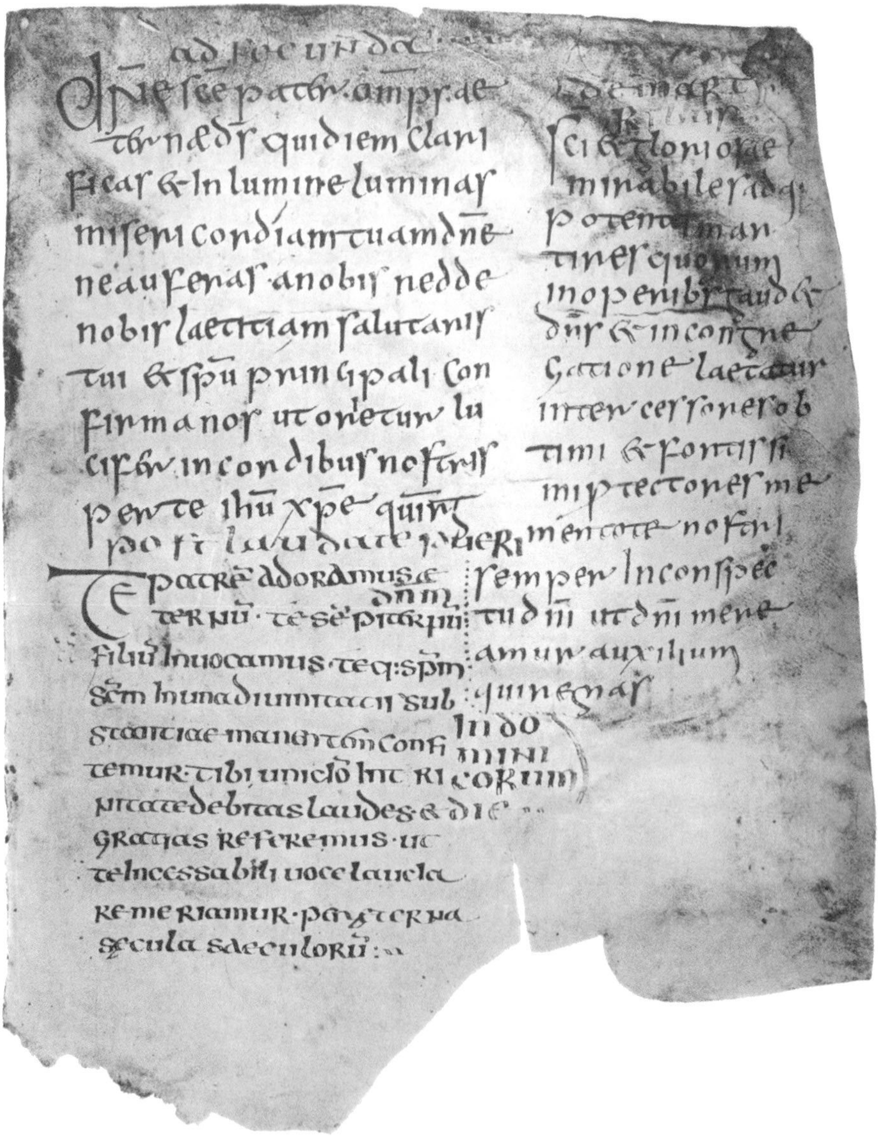

[*Fol. 35 recto.*]

AD SECUNDA.

D*omi*ne s*anct*e pater. om*ni*p*oten*s. ae
ternæ d*eu*s qui diem clari
ficas et in lumine luminas
misericordiam tuam d*omi*ne
ne auferas a nobis redde
nobis laetitiam salutaris
tui et sp*irit*u principali con
firma nos ut oretur[1] lu
cifer in cordibus nostris
per te ih*es*u *christ*e qui re*gnas*

POST LAUDATE PUERI[2]

TE[3] patre*m* adoramus æ
ternu*m* . te se*m*piternu*m*
D*OMI*N*UM*
filiu*m* inuocamus. teq*ue* sp*iritu*m
s*anctu*m in una diuinitatis sub
stantiae manentem confi
temur. tibi uni d*eo* in tri
nitate debitas laudes. et
gratias referemus. ut
te incessabili uoce lauda
re meriamur. per ęterna
sęcula saeculoru*m* :

DE MARTY
RIBUS

S*anct*i et gloriosae
mirabiles adq*ue*
potentes mar
tires quorum
in operibus gaudet
d*omi*n*u*s et in congre
gatione laetatur
intercessores ob
timi et fortissi
mi p*ro*tectores me
mentote nostri
semper in conspec
tu d*omi*ni ut d*omi*ni mere
amur auxilium
qui regnas

IN DO
MINI
CORUM
DIE

---

[1] An 'i' has been written *prima manu* above and between the second and third letters of this word.

[2] A perpendicular line of points bearing afterwards to the right and ending in a semicircular convex loop connects the lower part of this title with the upper.

[3] The handwriting of this collect does not occur elsewhere in the MS.

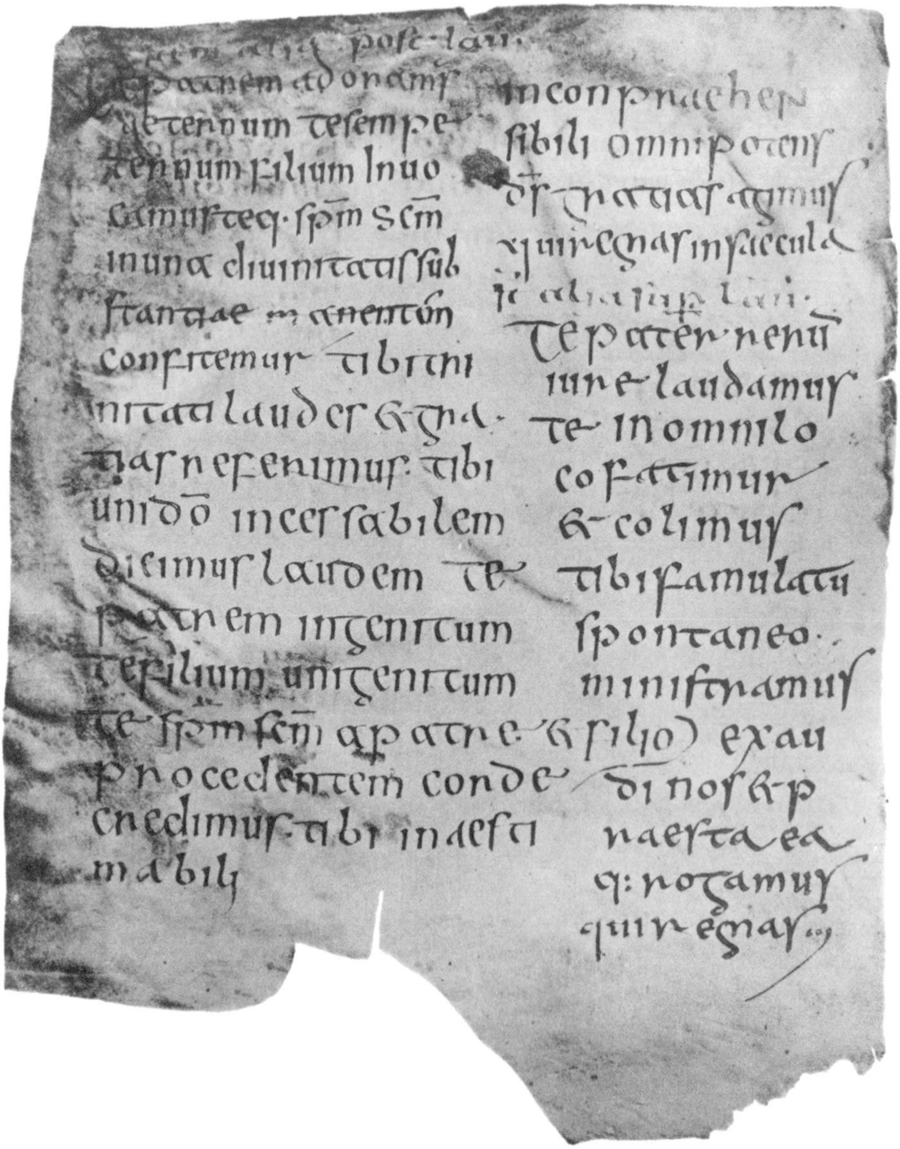

[*Fol. 35 verso.*][1]

ITEM ALIA POST LAU*DATE.*

Te patrem adoramus
aeternum te sempe
ternum filium inuo
camus teq*ue* sp*iritu*m s*anctu*m
in una diuinitatis sub
stantiae manentem
confitemur[2] tibi tri
nitati laudes et gra
tias referimus. tibi
uni d*e*o incessabilem
dicimus laudem te
patrem ingenitum
te filium unigenitum
te sp*iritu*m s*anctu*m a patre et filio[3]
procedentem corde
credimus. tibi inaesti
mabili
inconpraehen
sibili omnipotens
d*eu*s gratias agimus
qui regnas in saecula

I*TEM* ALIA SUP*ER* LAU*DATE.*

Te pater reru*m*
iure laudamus
te in omni lo
co fatimur
et colimus
tibi famulatu
spontaneo.
ministramus
exau
di nos et p
raesta ea
q*uae* rogamus
qui regnas . . ,

---

[1] Independently of the titles, there appear to be three different, but contemporary, handwritings on this page, the first ending with 'confitemur' in the seventh line of the first column; the second with 'saecula' in the fourth line of the second column; the remainder of that column being in a third handwriting.

[2] There is a long thin stroke slanting upwards and thickening from left to right after this word. It seems to be connected with the change of handwriting which occurs here.

[3] It is important to notice that the words 'et filio' were not part of the text in the first column as originally written, but were tacked on subsequently, yet not later than when the text of the second column was written, from which they are separated by an irregular loop.

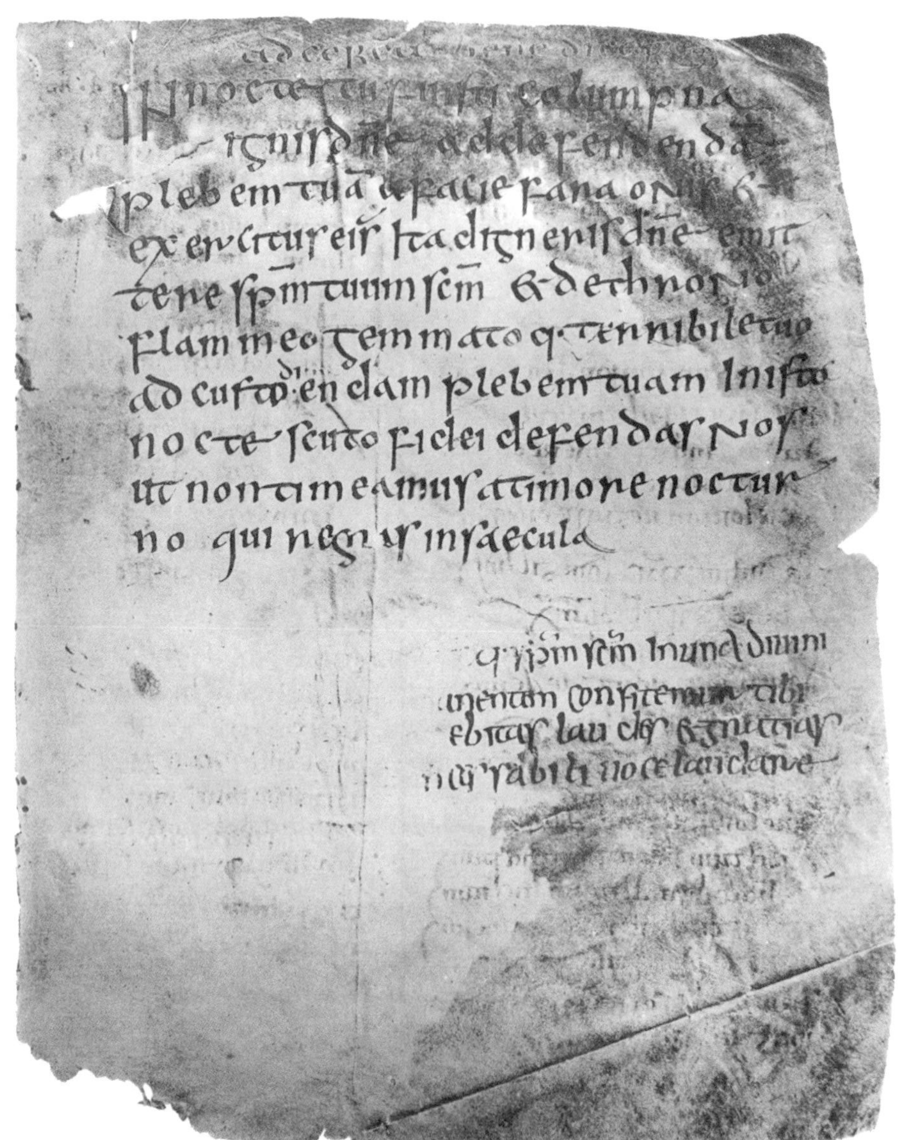

[*Fol. 36 recto.*]

AD CEREA*M* BENEDICE.[1]

IN nocte tu fuisti columpna
ignis d*omi*ne ad defendenda*m*
plebem tua*m* a facie faraonis et
exercitus eius ita digneris d*omi*ne emit
tere sp*iritu*m tuum s*anctu*m et de throno
flammeo gemmatoq*ue* terribile tuo
ad custoendam[2] plebem tuam in ista[3]
nocte scuto fidei defendas nos
ut non timeamus a timore noctur
no qui regnas in saecula

q*ue* sp*iritu*m s*anctu*m in una diuini
anentem confitemur tibi
ebitas laudes et gratias
ncessabili uoce laudare[4]

[1] The rest of this title is illegible. The next letter looks like a 'P' with a horizontal bar through its lower limb. It may be an 'R,' in which case the word might be 'BENEDICERE.'

[2] A point between the 'o' (which itself has been altered from 'i') and the 'e' in this word calls attention to the omission of the syllable 'di' which has been written above it in smaller letters.

[3] The last letter of 'ista' is an altered 'o.'

[4] The remainder of this collect, which has been erased, is illegible. In the case of the four half lines printed above, it will be noticed that the marks of contraction are hooked at each end, and that the letters are rather smaller, and the lines are closer together than in the upper text. The rest of this collect was perhaps erased when it was found that it had already been written on fol. 35 recto, and with variety of text again on fol. 35 verso.

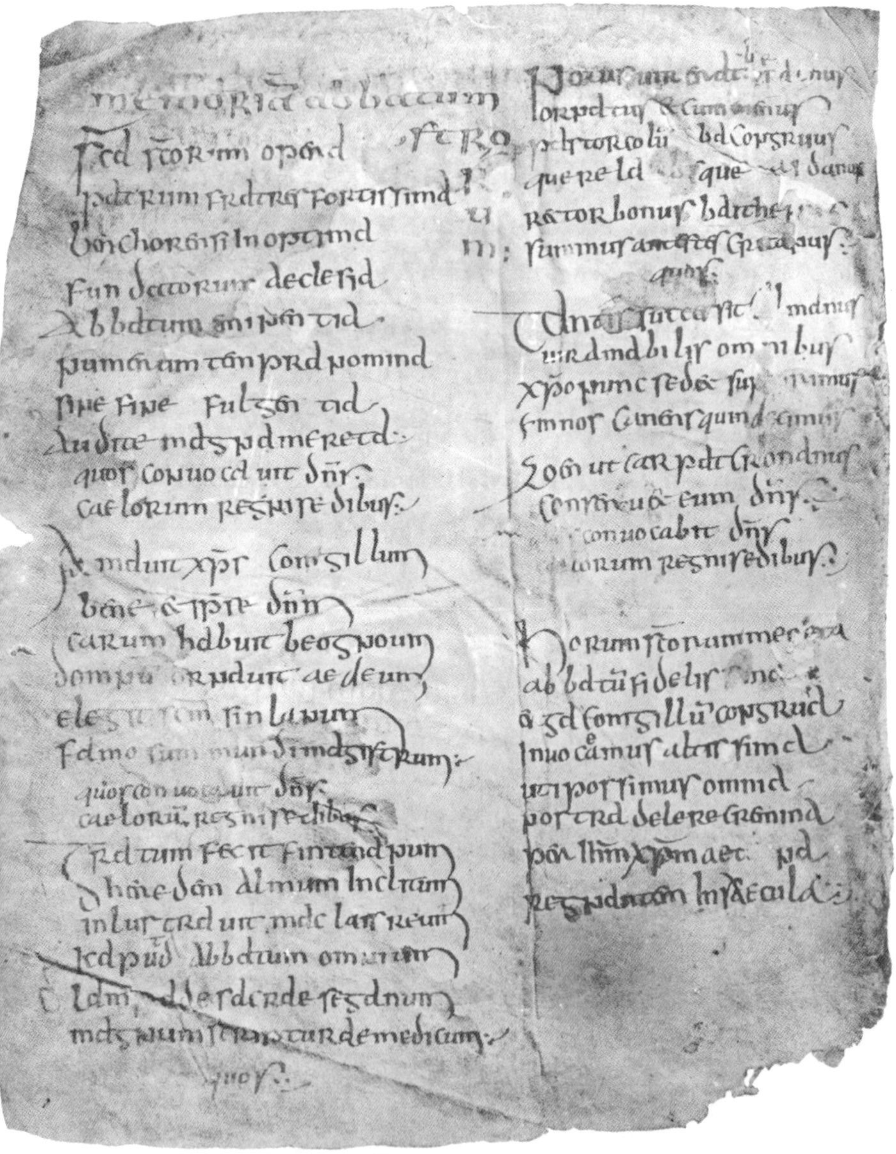

[*Fol. 36 verso.*][1]

MEMORIA*M* ABBATUM

S*anct*a s*anct*orum opera [N]OSTRO
patrum fratres fortissima R
benchorensi in optima U
fundatorum aeclesia M:
abbatum eminentia
numerum tempra nomina
sine fine fulgentia
audite magna mereta :,
quos conuocauit d*omin*u*s*.
caelorum regni sedibus :.,

.Amauit *christu*s comgillum
bene et ipse[2] d*ominu*m
carum habuit beognoum
domnu*m* ornauit aedeum
elegit s*anctu*m sinlanum
famosum mundi magistrum :.,
quos conuocauit d*omin*u*s*.
caeloru*m* regni sedibus :
Gratum fecit fintenanum
heredem almum inclitum
inlustrauit mac laisreum
kapud[3] abbatum omnium
lampade sacrae seganum
magnum scripturae medicum :.,
quos . . ,

be
Notus uir erat[4] rachus
ornatus et cumenenus
pastor colu*m*ba congruus
querela absque aidanus
rector bonus baithenus
summus antestes critanus :.,
quos :
TAntis successit camanus
uir amabilis omnibus
*christ*o nunc sedet supprimus
ymnos canens quindecimus
zoen ut carpat cronanus
conseruet eum d*omin*u*s* .·,
q[uo]s conuocabit d*omin*u*s*
caelorum regni sedibus . . ,

Horum s*anct*orum mere[ta]
abbatu*m* fidelissima
erga comgillu*m* congrua
inuocamus[5] altissima
uti possimus omnia
nostra delere cremina
per ih*esu*m *christu*m aet[er]na
regnantem in saecula · ;

[1] This page being somewhat worn, letters now illegible from wear have been placed in the text within square brackets. The size of the letters, the elevation of the upright stems of the 'a,' and the semicircular prolongation and extension below the line of the last down strokes of the 'm' (though these features are found elsewhere), mark off the hymn as in a different handwriting from the preceding pages.

[2] The mark of contraction over 'ipse' must be a clerical error caused perhaps by the mark over 'xps' in the line above.

[3] A 't' has been written *prima manu* above and rather to the left of the last letter in 'kapud.'

[4] There is a point after 'erat,' and a point before 'be' which has been added above the line *prima manu*.

[5] An 'e' has been added *prima manu* above the 'a' in 'inuocamus.'

Selected Translations from the Bangor Antiphonary

IN THE NAME OF THE ALMIGHTY GOD

(1) THE SONG OF MOSES

1. Let the heavens listen to what I have to say; let the earth hear the words of my mouth.
2. Let my teaching give nurture like the rain; let my eloquence flow like the dew, like the rainfall upon the grass, like the raindrops upon the flowers.
3. Because I will call upon the name of the Lord, grant majesty unto our God.
4. The works of God are perfect and all His ways are just.

   Listen.
5. Those who have sinned are not His children in their evil.

   Listen.

   Your generation is wicked and evil.
6. Is this the way you repay the Lord, O foolish and stupid people? Is He not your Father, to whom you belong and who made you and created you?

   Listen.
7. Remember the days of old, think of former generations one by one; ask your father and he will tell you; ask your ancestors and they will tell you.

   Listen.
8. When the All Highest was dividing the nations of the earth, when He was separating the Sons of Adam, he established the boundaries of nations according to the number of the Sons of Israel. Those belonging to the Lord are His people.
9. Jacob is the rope that binds his inheritance.

   Listen.
10. He found him in a desert land, in a place of dread and of vast solitude; He took him by the hand and taught him and watched over him as if he were the apple of his eye.

    Listen.

11. Just as an eagle calls upon its nestlings to fly and, hovering over them, spreads its wings around them, so He took him up and bore him on his shoulders.

Listen.

12. The Lord was his only guide and for him there was no other God.

13. He placed him high upon the earth, to eat the fruits of the fields and to suck honey from rock and olive oil from the hardest stone.

Listen.

14. And butter from the herd and milk from the sheep and fat from the lambs and rams of the Sons of Basan; and the flesh of the goats and the grain of the wheat, and to drink the pure juice of the grape.

Listen.

15. And the loved one prospered but when he grew fat and well-fed and puffed up, he abandoned and forsook the Lord his Creator and departed from God his Saviour.

16. They enraged Him with their gods and by their detestable deeds they drove Him to anger.

Listen.

17. They sacrificed to demons and false gods whom they did not know, and not to the true God. New and strange gods came whom their fathers had not worshipped.

Listen.

18. You abandoned the God who made you and you forgot God your Creator.

19. The Lord saw this and was moved to anger, because His sons and daughters enraged Him.

20. And He said, "I will hide my face from them and I will see what is going to happen to them in the end."

Listen.

For the people are idolatrous and their sons are without faith.

21. They have infuriated me with their selfishness and I will harass them with those who are not a nation and I will plague them with a foolish people.

Listen.

22. The fire of my anger has been kindled and will burn right to the very depths of Hell; it will devastate the earth together with its crops and the conflagration will uproot the foundations of mountains.

Listen.

23. I will heap evils on them and will pour my arrows upon them.
24. They will be emaciated with famine and the vultures will feed upon them with hateful beaks; and I will send against them the jaws of wild beasts and of serpents who live violent lives upon the earth.

    Listen.

25. The sword will maim their bodies and inwardly they will be ravaged by fear, both the young man and the maiden, the woman with child and the old man.

    Listen.

26. I have said, "Where are they? I will make the memory of them vanish from the minds of men."
27. But I have held my hand because of the hostility of their enemies; in case perhaps their enemies might boast and say. "It was our might, Lord, and not the Lord who did all these things."

    Listen.

28. The people are without intelligence and good sense.
29. Would that they had wisdom and understanding and foresaw the end that faces them.
30. How could one pursue a thousand and how could two put to flight ten thousand?

    Listen.

    Surely it was on account of this that the Lord God sold them into slavery and fettered them.

31. For our God is not as their God and our enemies are senseless in their folly.

    Listen.

32. Their vines are from the vineyard of Sodom and their fruit is from Gomorrha; their grape is the grape of bile and their cluster is the cluster of bitterness.
33. Their wine is the poison of dragons and the incurable venom of asps.

    Listen.

34. Are not these things stored with me and recorded among my treasure?
35. Vengeance is mine; I will repay in due time, so that their foot may stumble.

    Listen.

    The day of destruction is at hand and time races on.

36. The Lord will judge His people and will feel sorry for his servants.

    Listen.

    He will see that their hand is weak and those who were shut up have expired and those who were left have been destroyed.

37. And He will say, "Where are their gods in whom they put their trust?"

    Listen.

38. Let those gods, who eat the fat from your sacrifices and drink the wine from your libations, rise up and help you and protect you in your hour of need.

    Listen.

39. Take notice that I am the only one and that there is no other God but me; I will kill and I will let live; I will strike and I will heal and there is none who can rescue anyone out of my hand.

    Listen.

40. I will lift up my hand to heaven and I will say, "I live for ever."

41. And if I sharpen my sword like a lightning flash and if my hand delivers judgement, I will have my revenge on my enemies and I will pay back those who hate me.

    Listen.

42. I will make my arrows drunk with blood and my sword will devour flesh, from the blood of the slain and from the prisoners and the defenceless head of my enemies.

    Listen.

43. Let the nations praise His people, because He will avenge the blood of His servants; and He will inflict retribution on their enemies and He will be gracious to the land of His people from century to century.

    Listen.

(8) HYMN SUNG DURING COMMUNION OF THE PRIESTS

1. Come forward, you who are holy. Receive the body of Christ and drink the sacred blood by which you will be redeemed.
2. Saved and sustained by the body and blood of Christ, let us sing praises to the Lord.
3. By this sacrament of the flesh and blood all have been rescued from the jaws of Hell.

4. Christ, giver of salvation, Son of God, has saved the world by shedding His blood on the Cross.
5. For all mankind our Lord was sacrificed, himself both priest and victim.
6. It is laid down by law that victims be sacrificed and, because of this, divine mysteries are shadowed forth in expectation.
7. The Giver of Light and Saviour of all has bestowed on His saints a lustrous grace.
8. Let all who believe in Him come forward with pure minds and receive the eternal guardian of salvation.
9. The Lord, protector of saints, the ruler of the world, bestows eternal life on all believers.
10. To the hungry He gives the bread of life and to the thirsty a draught from the fountain of life.
11. Christ Himself, the Lord, Alpha and Omega, has come and will come again to judge mankind.

(13) HYMN TO ST PATRICK, TEACHER OF THE IRISH

1. Listen, all those who love God, to the exemplary deeds of a man blessed in Christ, Bishop Patrick, how on account of his good deeds he is likened to the angels, how on account of his perfect life he is compared with the Apostles.
2. He kept the sacred commandments of Christ in all things. His actions shine forth radiantly among mankind, who follow his illustrious and sublime example and glorify the Lord who is their Father in heaven.
3. He is steadfast in his respect for God and never to be shaken in his faith. On him, like a rock, is built the Church and his mission he received from God. Before his gates the powers of darkness will be repulsed.
4. The Lord chose him to teach the barbarians to cast before them the net of his teaching and to bring all believers from worldliness to a state of Grace, so that they might follow the Lord to His Heavenly Dwelling.
5. In his mission among the tribes of Ireland he sells Christ's elected talents and demands them back with interest. As a reward for this voyage and this work he will be with Christ and will gain the joys of the heavenly kingdom.
6. This faithful minister of God and this illustrious bearer of good news sets

an apostolic example and pattern of life for the righteous. He teaches the people of God as much by word as by deed. The one he does not convert by word he inspires by deed.

7. He has glory and honour with Christ in this world. He is respected by all, like the angel of God. Like Paul, God sent him as a missionary to the nations of the earth to provide a way for mankind to the Kingdom of God.
8. A humble man in body and spirit because of his fear of God, God relies on him because of his good deeds. On his devout flesh he bears the marks of Christ and, enduring these, he glories in the Cross alone.
9. Unresting in his efforts he nourishes believers with the celestial bread of life so that those who are seen with Christ do not falter and weaken on the way. His words of inspiration are like the staff of life and they gain strength like manna in his hands.
10. His flesh he has kept chaste on account of his love of God and he has offered it up as a temple to the Holy Spirit, by which he is constantly possessed with his good deeds. This flesh he presents as a living and pleasing sacrifice to God.
11. A great light illuminating the world has been kindled, raised on a candlestick, shining over the whole earth, a royal city well-fortified and set on a hill, in which there is a great population who belong to God.
12. For he will be called the greatest in the kingdom of the heavenly ones, he who performs by deed what he preaches by devout word; by his example he sets a pattern of life for the faithful and in his pure heart he keeps faith with God.
13. Fearlessly he preaches the name of God to all nations, to whom he gives the eternal grace of salvation and the cleansing of sins. For their sins he prays to God every day and for them he makes worthy sacrifice to God.
14. Because of the Law of God he rejects all worldly glory which he regards as worthless frippery before his table, nor is he alarmed by the rushing thunderbolt of this world, but rejoices in adversity and suffers pain for Christ.
15. A good and faithful shepherd of his flock, God chose him to watch over His people and to nourish His people with inspired teaching. For them he follows the example of Christ and devotes his life to them.
16. For his good deeds our Saviour has appointed him as Pontiff to instruct the clergy in the service of the Heavenly one. To them he gives celestial food and vestments, because he is filled with the sacred words of God.

17. As minister of the King of Kings he invites believers to a marriage ceremony. He dresses and invests himself in marriage garments and drinks heavenly wine in ceremonial goblets and with spiritual libation pledges himself to the people of God.
18. He has found pure treasure in the sacred volume and he perceives the divinity in the flesh of our Saviour. This treasure he has gained by his devout and saintly deeds. And his soul, seeing God, is named Israel.
19. He is a devoted witness to our Lord in the universal law, whose words are expressed in holy places, so that human flesh may not decay and be eaten by worms, but may bound forward in pure exultation in sacrifice to the Lord.
20. He is a true and illustrious cultivator of the missionary field. The seeds, which he sows in inspired utterance into the ears of the wise, whose hearts and minds he nurtures with the Holy Spirit, burst forth to proclaim the gospel of Christ.
21. Christ chose him to be his minister on earth. From a two-fold subjection he rescues mankind. Many he has freed from the bondage of man; countless others he has set at liberty from enslavement to the devil.
22. He chants the hymns of the Revelation and the psalms of God and uses them to regenerate the people of God. He believes in the sacred name of the Trinity and its doctrine and teaches that in three persons there is one substance.
23. Invested with the girdle of Christ, day and night without pause he prays to the Lord God and will gain the reward for this great labour when in purity he will rule with the Apostles over Israel.

    Bishop Patrick, pray for us all, so that the sins which we have committed may forthwith be forgiven.

    Let us always sing the praises of Patrick so that we may live with him for evermore.

HYMN TO ST COMGALL OUR ABBOT

Let us remember the shining justice of our patron, St Comgall, glorious in deed, aided by the spirit of God and, by the holy and radiant light of the sublime Trinity, directing all things under his rule.

God has raised him to a dwelling in the heavens, a dwelling guarded by angels and destined to last for ever.

1. Listen, everyone, to the deeds of this champion of God, who has been introduced to the secrets of the angels. From the first flowering of his youth his uprightness, strengthened by his faith, was nourished on the pages of the Law and was introduced to the joys of God. The virtues which he showed in his great life were abundantly in keeping with his faith.
2. He lived a good life, saw justice done, displayed delightful kindness and a most resolute love devoted to God first and foremost, a love that was unflinching according to God's ordinances, a love that was outstanding in the kingdom, a love often unrequited from his neighbours, a love that was pleasing in a tranquil heart and acknowledged to be fruitful for the future.
3. There was his unyielding contempt for those fleeting desires of this world, for those vices which destroy the weak and for these words and thoughts which turn on evil. This contempt he felt in the innermost part of his watchful flesh.
4. He was schooled in the ordinances of God and in His words. He was strengthened by his resources that were devout and always pleasing to God. He was dedicated in his character and, like Stephen, Saint of God, he taught the others and his words were shaped by his deeds.
5. He chose from the start of his life the One, who was from the beginning of the world the Eternal and True Word, uttered from the Sacred Heart of the Father Almighty and dear to that same Shining One, who was the Pledge constant in the excellence of His Soul and in His work of peace.
6. He shone with splendour in the glory of his faith, like the lofty sun blazing at mid-day in the heights. He was determined in his heart always to trust in God, confident in the mighty bulwark of his piety.
7. In his heart he felt the joy of the Holy Spirit, inhabiting a kingdom for the exalted, worthy of God and in his devout hands he bravely held the sword of the Spirit upraised against the wicked and ready to lay low the proud.
8. Humble, holy, kind, upright in the commandments of God, civilised, just, obliging, praiseworthy in character, cheerful in appearance, temperate, radiant with the blossoms of love, accessible to men of every class.
9. Learned in the Scriptures, divinely inspired, far-seeing in his prayers, a distinguished scholar in the canonical writings of the Old Testament and in the Acts of the New, he was fiery in Spirit, yet gentle, dear to God and most devout.
10. In his unshaken desire for love and chastity he has trampled underfoot the deceitful world, despising every vice, planting a field of flowers and

adorning his radiant breast, a holy dwelling consecrated in the name of the Trinity.

11. He has placed in his heart a lamp of wisdom in a treasury of knowledge built by gift of God. Greatly illumined by the light of true justice he has been raised to the heights by the might of the Law, the Spirit and the Word.

12. He has obtained the great prize, wholly deserving of eternal life, and, after his most steadfast striving, has gained his reward in heaven. We call upon his perfect merit to help us so that we may earn the destruction of all the vices.

13. Renowned in the companies of Saints, in the ranks of Abbots, in the legions of monks, in the lonely thoughts of anchorites and in the devout members of synods, he was indeed a man worthy of the Apostles, distinguished in all his doings and raised on high among the exalted.

14. O, most solid rock set in the foundation, O, despiser of all the wickedness of this world, O, devout leader of soldiers fighting for the Lord, O, most valiant disciple totally dedicated to the Lord.

15. He set himself like a barrier of iron in front of the people to rout, to uproot and to destroy all evil and to build and implant good for the benefit of all, like St Hieremia set on high.

16. Who else despised the decadence of this age? Who else aspired with all his heart to the joys of heaven? Who else wanted to reject the flesh and rise to heaven, gaining such holy rewards as he deserved?

17. He governed the holy catholic church by his ordinance. He kept his faith unshaken against evil and wickedness. He guided his soul according to the pages of Holy Law. May his love, I pray, adorn my soul.

18. In his wisdom lifting up his devout inner eyes in his holy head he used to direct them eagerly to the heavens above. He would show his compassion by giving with his right hand and throughout all his saintly works he bore in mind the good deeds of the centurion.

19. Possessed of a soul dear to God and radiant, he has borne his memorial to the mansion up above, despising the deceitful world, conquering all vain folly and proceeding with Abraham to that other world of excellence.

20. Under a crown of flowers he has gained eternal life and there he will receive rewards destined to last for ever. He will join the illustrious companies of angels, always seeking after what is good and ever vigilant in the service of the Church.

21. He would pray to Christ our Master, carrying out his obligations honourably and performing his duty to Christ by acts of devotion. Now, following in His footsteps, he leads God's army into that blessed and most excellent dwelling of the Three in One.
22. He used to offer to Almighty God a hymn of praise, often praying in exultation both day and night. Now joining with a choir of angels he has sung in harmony a new hymn of praise to God, blessed in a mighty cry of joy.
23. He is girt with the girdle of righteousness and covered in a pure mantle of glorious chastity. Thigh bandages completely cover his loins as a sign of his radiant purity. To him deservedly for his saintly work a worthy reward will be given.

    For the sake of the good works and prayers of St Comgall our Abbot, watch over us all, O Lord, in the paths of Thy peace.

(16) COLLECT FOR THE SECOND HOUR

Be our Protector on this day, O Lord, Holy Father, omnipotent and eternal God. Take pity on us and be merciful towards us. Help us and be our guide and enlighten our hearts. Watch over, O Lord, our thoughts, our words, our deeds, so that we can be pleasing in Your sight, O Lord, and carry out Your wishes and walk in the path of righteousness all the days of our life.

(18) FOR THE THIRD HOUR

At the third hour we pray to Christ to have compassion and to grant us His eternal favour, who rules for ever and ever.

(19) FOR THE SIXTH HOUR

O Christ, spare those who humbly kneel before you and offer prayers at this sixth hour, at the very time You were placed on the Cross for all of us.

(20) FOR THE NINTH HOUR

O Christ, hear the prayers of all of us at this ninth hour, at the very time You visited Cornelius in the form of an angel.

(21) FOR THE EVENING HOUR

At this eventide we call upon You, O Lord. Smile favourably upon our prayers and grant forgiveness to our sins.

(22) COLLECT AT NIGHTFALL

O Christ, we are devoting this time of night to Your praises; take pity on us all who pray to You from the depth of our hearts.

(23) COLLECT AT NIGHT

O Jesus, be merciful and visit us as we offer our prayers in the middle of the night at the time when You with Your divine power loosed the bonds of Peter.

(24) COLLECT IN THE MORNING

O God, help all those who glorify You and acknowledge You to be the Three in One and One in Three, as they raise their voices in sacred hymns of praise.

(25) ANOTHER COLLECT FOR THE MORNING

O Christ, as the crowing of the cocks rings out, I pray to You. Give ear to our prayers, as formerly You did to the cries of Peter.

(26) ANOTHER COLLECT FOR THE MORNING

O God, who has driven away the shades of night and now shines upon us with the radiance of daylight, shed upon Your servants the dawn of the true light.

(42) A PRAYER FOR THE ABBOT

The Lord watch over him and sustain his life and make him happy on earth. The Lord protect you from all evil; the Lord take care of your soul. The Lord watch over your coming in and going out from this day, now and for evermore.

(43) A PRAYER FOR THE BROTHERS

O Lord, watch over us, like the apple of Your eye and guard us under the shadow of Your wings.
Almighty God, deign to protect and bless all of us.

(44) A PRAYER FOR THE FRATERNITY

O Lord, save us and take care of us from this generation and for evermore. Hear our prayers on behalf of our brothers, so that You, O Lord, may be merciful towards them.

(58) A MORNING PRAYER

O God, our God, before You we must be wakeful at daylight. Rouse our souls from our deep sleep and free them from drowsiness, so that in our beds we may be stung by remorse and we may be rightly mindful of You.

(60) A MORNING PRAYER

You, dwelling in high places and in heaven, looking down upon all that lies below You, both on land and sea and in all the lower regions, from the bottom of our hearts we beseech You to strengthen our hands for battle and our fingers for war so that in the morning we can destroy all sinners upon our earth and unfailingly deserve to be Your holy temple, O Christ.

(96) COLLECT FOR A PERSON WHO IS POSSESSED BY THE DEVIL

O Lord, holy Father, eternal and omnipotent God, drive out the devil and his kindred from this man, from his head, from his hair, from his brain, from the crown of his head, from his forehead, his eyes, his ears, his nostrils, his lips, his mouth, his tongue, his epiglottis, his jaws, his throat, his neck, his heart, his whole body, all the joints of all his limbs, both internal and external, his bones, his veins, his sinews, his blood, his perception, his thoughts, his words, all his deeds, his virtue, all his conversation, here now and in the future.

May you be filled with the goodness of Christ, who suffered before us that we might enjoy eternal life, through our Lord and Jesus Christ His Son.

(97) PRAYER FOR MARTYRS

O God, who bestowed your Kingdom upon your martyrs, deign to forgive us sinners. They deserved their crown for their suffering on account of their faith; we seek forgiveness and compassion from You for our sins and transgressions, through Jesus Christ our Lord.

(129) COMMEMORATION OF OUR ABBOTS

1. Brothers, listen to the devout and indomitable deeds of our holy fathers who served in the illustrious church of Bangor. Listen to the outstanding and majestic works of our abbots. Listen to their number, their times and their names which shall shine brightly and never fade. These men God has called to His Kingdom in the heavens.
2. Christ loved Comgall; well, too, did he love the Lord; He held Beogna dear and shed lustre on noble Aedh. He chose the saintly Sinlan, far-famed teacher of the world.
3. He made Finten accepted, a gentle and illustrious heir. He enlightened Maclaisre, foremost amongst all the abbots and with His torch he kindled the fire in Segan, great physician of the Holy Scripture.
4. Berachus was a distinguished man, and Cummian also pre-eminent in glory. Columba was a shepherd who worked for concord, and Aidan was without complaint. Baithene was a virtuous ruler and Cretan was a divine of great authority.
5. These great men were succeeded by Colman, a man beloved by all. Now he sits on high singing hymns of praise to Christ. May the Lord preserve Cronan, fifteenth in line, so that life for him may be a joy.
6. We call upon the good services of these holy abbots, loyal, time-honoured and in accord with Comgall, so that we may wipe out all our transgressions, through Jesus Christ, who reigneth for ever and ever.

POSTSCRIPT

The Last Abbot of Bangor

NOTHING REMAINS OF the original monastery itself, except perhaps a slight depression in the Abbey Church graveyard. This may indicate the circular vallum with which it was once surrounded. Over a century ago James O'Laverty wrote:

> "Along the west of the site of the ancient vallum flows a stream, which, no doubt, in former times turned the abbot's mill, and, as it flows through the centre of the town, it passes an ancient well, overshadowed by a huge old thorn. The waters of this well are said to be medicinal, but the popular belief in its healing powers may be only the last remains of a tradition that St Comgall, or one of his sainted successors, pronounced over it the benediction which is still preserved in the old Irish missal found at Bobbio, which has been published by Mabillon."

The holy well is probably that known to have existed in the vicinity of the present Southwell Road and called 'The Eye Well' by the old inhabitants of Bangor.

The Abbey Church was commenced by Sir James Hamilton about the year 1617, within the old Augustinian Abbey, and was not finished until year 1623. The tower dates from the late fourteenth century, and was the central tower of the former large Augustinian Church; and there remains the structure known as Malachy's Wall. The nave of this church lay to the west of the tower, while the chancel stood on the site of the present nave and chancel. The present Abbey Church was recorded by Edmund McCann in his *Irish Itinerary* of 1643, which also tells of "the monastery of Bangor, once the most celebrated in the whole world, of which even the ruins do not now exist." But no one more than Mary O'Fee, the former Mayor of the area, did more in recent times to keep the history and heritage of that monastery alive.

The Abbey Churchyard is a justly celebrated one and was once more extensive than it is today, as evidenced by the discoveries of remains on the site of the Health Centre to the south, under Church Street, Abbey Street, where my father owned a shop and I ran for a time Pretani Press, and Castle

Park. Among the so-called 'Prophecies' originally translated by Nicholas O'Kearney and attributed to Coireall MacGronan, one reads:

> "Did the Irish only learn the truth as it is –
> All their men, women and young ones –
> (Did they know) the privileges of this smooth cemetery?
> It is in it they would arise to the general judgement.
>
> Were all the Irish that ever lived and shall live
> Interred in the mould of this cemetery?
> Darkest demons should not have power to carry away
> The least among them from Bangor.
>
> Consecrated from this day henceforth for ever
> Is this spot which will prove beneficial to all.
> There is no place similar to it.
> This level spot is the third Rome!"

Yet there is also in that graveyard one of the saddest reminders of Ireland's troubled history. This is the gravestone of one of my family, Archibel (Archibald) Wilson, the Carpenter from Conlig, who was accused of treason following the 1798 Rebellion and hanged with two others at the Far Rocks above our village. Archibel was said to have gone on his knees to the gallows singing psalms to God and died protesting his innocence. The headstone is a split slate one with hammer, axe, trowel and knife between two sets of leaves at the top.

> "Here lieth the body of the Archibel Wilson of Conlig who departed
> this life June the 26 in anno 1798, Eg. 26 yr.
>
> Morn not, dear friends, tho I'm no more
> Tho I was martyred, your eyes before
> I am not dead, but do sleep hear
> And yet once more I will appear.
>
> That is when time will be no more
> When they be judged who falsely sore
> And them that judged will judged be
> Whither just or on just, then they'll see.

Purpere, dear friends, for that grate day
When death dis sumance you away
I will await you all with due care
In heaven with joy to meet you there."

Not so very long after this tragic event there visited the Abbey Church an aged cleric, whose whitened locks and venerable appearance threw around his person an air of strange interest and marked him out as no casual visitor. As he approached the Communion Table, near where the altar had once stood, a gleam of the very sunshine of youth seemed to light up the old man's face. Suddenly his prayers, which had at first been silent ones, were raised to a level of audibility which embarrassed his companion, Dr McDonnell of Belfast, not less than it astonished the sexton. That old man was Lord Abbot McCormick, the last Abbot of Bangor.

O'Laverty asks us to picture the scene:

"That old abbot, bowed down with years – a stranger and unknown – the connecting link between the present age and the remotest past, standing on the same spot whence his predecessors thirteen centuries ago – ere nations that have long since disappeared had yet come into existence – sent out those bands of missionaries who converted the Franks and the Longobards and for ever linked the name of Bangor with the history of the Church."

The Lord Abbot McCormick was born in County Antrim in the year 1726. Like so many priests of his faith in the eighteenth century he was forced to seek on the Continent of Europe that learning which was denied to him by the laws at home. The French Revolution, however, deprived him of that asylum, which the houses of his order afforded and he came back to close his days as Sacristan of Maynooth College. It would appear that Dr Patrick McMullan, Bishop of Down and Connor, expected that the Abbot would claim some of the privileges of his ancient predecessors, for the Bishop's agent in Rome, the Rev Luke Concanen, wrote to him:

"Rome, Minerva 28th May 1796

I pointed out how you were to behave with Rev. W. McCormick, by threatening him with suspension, should he come to cause any trouble or disobedience in your diocese under colour of his empty title of Abbot of Bangor. You may safely refuse him any promotion, if you think him

> not qualified to do good. You need not fear, whilst I have the honour of acting for you, that he will give any trouble from this quarter."

Dr McCormick at no time attempted to exercise any jurisdiction in Down or Connor. He died on 7 May 1807, and his ashes mingle with the sacred dust of a long line of abbots, the successors of St Senan, in Laraghbrine. The inscription on his tomb does not style him Abbot of Bangor. At that time the existence of a member of his religious order was against the law; consequently Maynooth College, a royal institution supported by the State, could not openly admit that it employed clergymen of that outlawed class. But his spirit lived on, for it was the Spirit of Bangor.

Their spirit is no more evident than in the fine painting by Kenneth Webb in the chancel of Bangor Abbey. The mural was commissioned as part of the modern renovation of the church under the guidance of Canon James Hamilton. The use of the triangle, denoting the Holy Trinity, pervades the whole design and leads the eye upwards from the figures of Comgall, Columbanus and Gall in the foreground to the central figure of the Ascending Christ. The features of Christ are those of a black person, emphasising the mystic nature of the Son of Man. He is conceived as giving his last command:

> "Go ye into the entire world and preach the Gospel."

Maps

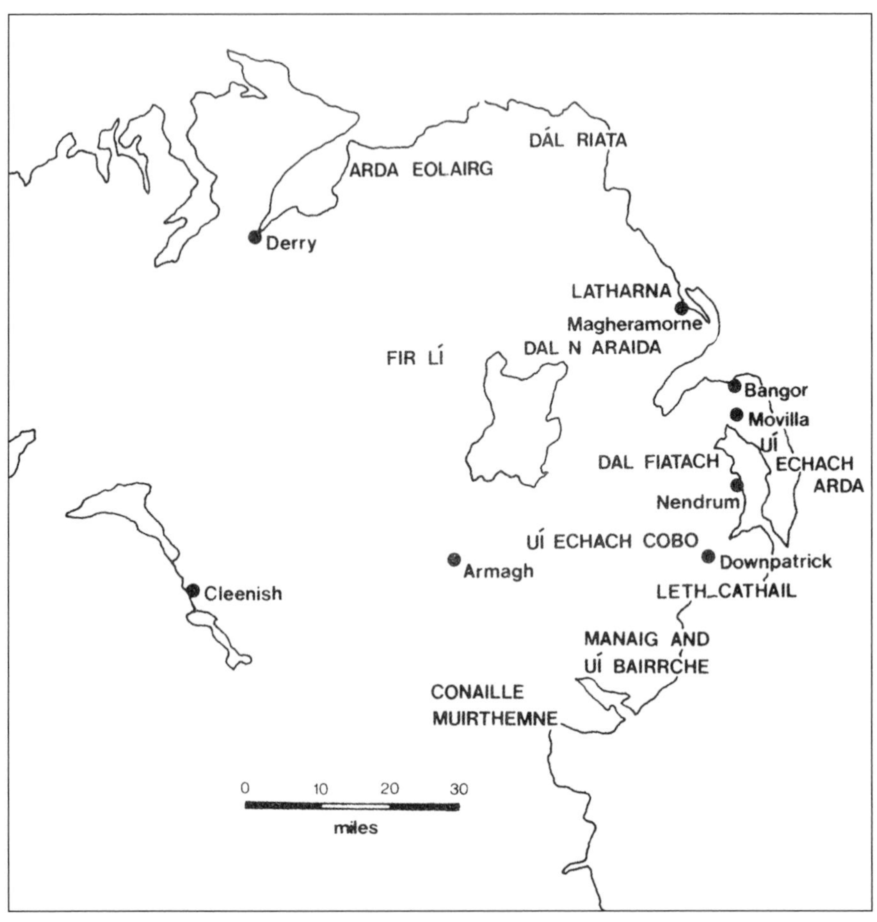

Ulster at the time of Comgall

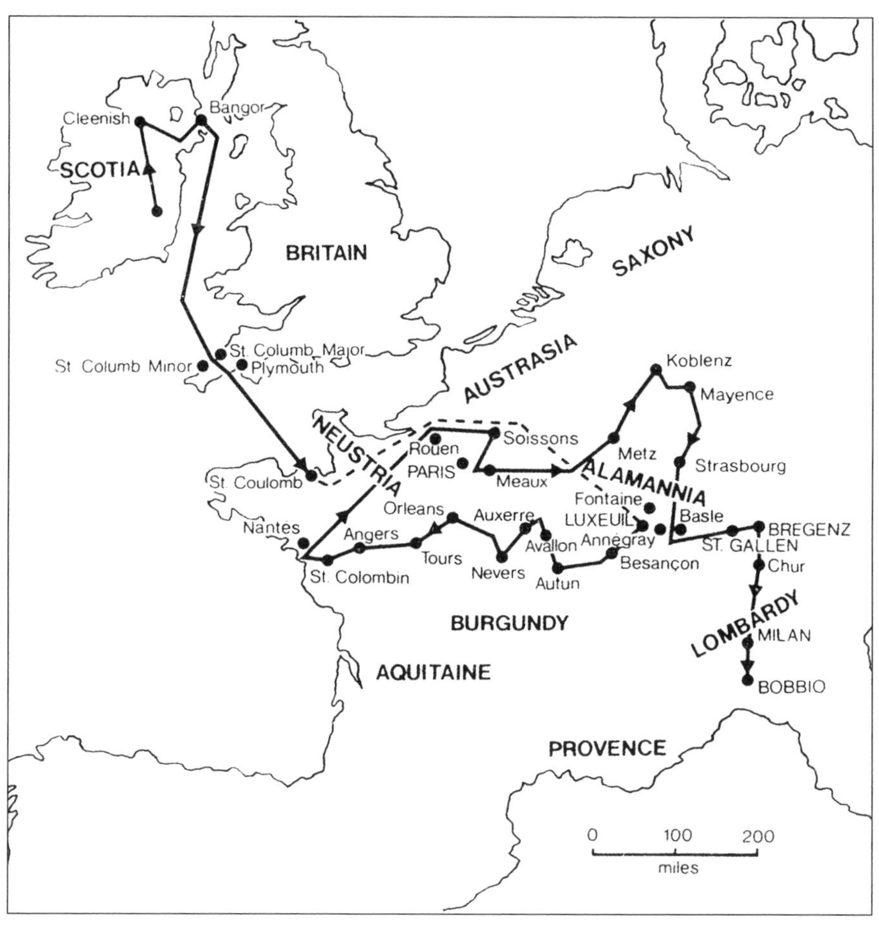

In the steps of Columbanus

Bibliography

Adamnan, *Life of Columba*, edited from Reeve's text by Fowler, JT, Oxford University Press, Oxford, 1894.

An Archaeological Survey of County Down, Her Majesty's Stationery Office, Belfast, 1966.

Aslan, Reza, *The Life and Times of Jesus of Nazareth*, The Westbourne Press, London, 2013.

Atkinson, ED, *Dromore, an Ulster Diocese*, W Tempest, Dundalgan Press, Dundalk, 1925.

Barber, Richard, *The Figure of Arthur*, Longman, London, 1972.

Beckett, JC, *The Making of Modern Ireland 1603–1923*, Faber and Faber, London, 1966.

Bede, *A History of the English Church and People*, Shirley-Price, Leo, trans, Penguin Books, London, 1955.

Bethan, Sir W, *The Gael and Cymbri* or *History of the Irish Scotti, Britons and Gaels*, Dublin, 1834.

Bromwich, R, *The Welsh Triads (Trioedd Ynys Prydain)*, Cardiff, 1961.

Brooke, Daphne, *Wild Men and Holy Places: St Ninian and the Medieval Realm of Galloway*, Canongate Books, Edinburgh, 1995.

Byrne, Francis, J, *Irish Kings and High-Kings*, Batsford Ltd, London, 1973.

Colles, Ramsey, *The History of Ulster*, Gresham Publishing Co Ltd, 1919.

Cruden, Stewart, *The Early Christian and Pictish Monuments of Scotland*, Her Majesty's Stationery Office, Edinburgh, 1964.

D'Arcy, Mary Ryan, *The Saints of Ireland*, Irish-American Cultural Institute, St Paul, Minnesota,1974.

Danielou, Jean, *The Dead Sea Scrolls and Primitive Chistianity*, Helicon Press, Baltimore, Maryland, 1958.

Davies, Oliver, 'A summary of the Archaeology of Ulster', *Ulster Journal of Archaeology*, 3rd Series, Vol XI, 1948.

De Paor, Maire and Liam, *Early Christian Ireland*, Thames and Hudson, 1958.

Dick, Rev CH, *Highways and Byways in Galloway and Carrick*, Macmillan & Co, London, 1927.

Dobbs, Margaret E, 'The Dal Fiatch', *Ulster Journal of Archaeology*, 3rd Series, Vol VIII, 1945.

Ehrman, Bart D, *The Great Courses, The New Testament*, Chantilly, Virginia, USA, 2000.

Flanagan, LNW, *Ulster*, Regional Archaeologies Series, Heinemann Educational Books Ltd, London, 1970.

Flower, Robin, *The Irish Tradition*, Oxford University Press, Oxford, 1947.

Gallico, Paul, *The Steadfast Man, A Life of St Patrick*, Michael Joseph Ltd, London, 1958.

Grant, Michael, *The Jews in the Roman World*, Weidenfield and Nicholson, London, 1973.

Grant, Michael, *St Paul*, Weidenfield and Nicholson, London, 1976.

Grant, Michael, *Jesus*, Weidenfield and Nicholson, London, 1977.

Hamilton, James, *Bangor Abbey through Fourteen Centuries*, Belfast, 1958.

Hayward, Richard, *In Praise of Ulster*, illustrated by Humbert Craig, J, Arthur Barker of London, London, 1938.

Hayward, Richard, *Ulster and the City of Belfast*, illustrated by Piper, Raymond, Arthur Barker, London, 1950.

Hayward, Richard, *Border Foray*, illustrated by Piper, Raymond, Arthur Barker, London, 1957.

Healy, J, *Ireland's Ancient Schools and Scholars*, Sealy, Bryers & Walker, Dublin, 1902.

Henderson, Isabel, *The Picts*, Ancient Peoples and Places Series, Thames and Hudson Ltd, London, 1967.

Hennessy, William M, ed and trans, *The Annals of Ulster*, Vol 1, AD 431–1056, Her Majesty's Stationery Office, Dublin, 1887.

Hill, Peter, *Whithorn and St Ninian*, The Whithorn Trust, Sutton Publishing, Stroud, 1997.

Hughes, Kathleen, *Early Christian Ireland, Introduction to the Sources*, Sources of History in association with Hodder and Stroughton, London, 1972.

Hutchinson, Wesley, *Espaces de l'imaginaire unionist nord-irlandais*, Presses Universitaires de Caen, France, 1999.

Jackson, Kenneth H, trans, *The Gododdin of Aneirin*, Edinburgh University Press, Edinburgh, 1969.

Jones, Gwyn, and Jones, Thomas, trans, *The Mabinogion*, Everyman's Library, London, 1949.

Khalidi, Tarif, *The Muslim Jesus*, Harvard University Press, Cambridge, Massachusetts, USA, 2001.

Lacey, Brian, *Cenél Conaill and the Kingdoms of Donegal AD 500–800*, Four Courts Press, Dublin and Portland Oregon, USA, 2006.

Lawlor, HC, *The Monastery of St Mochaoi of Nendrum*, Belfast Natural History and Philosophical Society, Belfast, 1925.

Lett, Rev HW, 'The Great Wall of Ulidia', in *Ulster Journal of Archaeology*, 2nd Series, Vol III, No I, 1897.

Leyburn, James G, *The Scotch-Irish*, The University of North Carolina Press, Chapel Hill, 1962.

Lieberman Leo and Beringause (eds), *Classics of Jewish Literature*, Castle, Secaucus, New Jersey, USA, 1988.

Lloyd, Laing, *The Archaeology of Late Celtic Britain and Ireland*, Methuen, London, 1975.

Macalister, RAS, ed and trans, *Lebor Gabála Erenn*, Parts I–V Irish Texts Society, Dublin, completed 1956.

Mackenzie, WC, Gardiner, Alexander, *The Races of Ireland and Scotland*, Paisley, Scotland, 1949.

MacLysaght, E, *The Surnames of Ireland*, Irish University Press, Shannon, Ireland, 1969.

MacNeill, Eoin, 'The Pretanic Background in Britain and Ireland', *Journal of the Royal Society of Antiquaries of Ireland*, 1933, Vol LXIII, Part 1.

MacQueen, John, *Welsh and Gaelic in Galloway*, Transactions and Journal of Proceedings, Dumfriesshire and Galloway Natural History and Antiquarian Society, 1955.

Maqsood, Ruqaiyyah Waris, *The Mysteries of Jesus*, Sakina Books, Oxford, 2000.

Meharg, JM, *Bangor from the Sixth Century*, Bangor, 1903.

Menzies, G, ed, *Who are the Scots?* BBC, London, 1971.

Merrick, ACW, *Gravestone Inscriptions, County Down, Vol 17*, Ulster Historical Foundation, Belfast, 1978.

Meyer, Marvin, *The Gnostic Gospels, with an introduction by Marvin Meyer and Elaine H Pagels*, The Folio Society, London, 2008.

Moody, TW, and Martin, FX, eds, *The Course of Irish History*, Mercier Press, Cork, 1967.

Mullin, TH, and Mullan, JE, *The Ulster Clans*, Belfast, 1966.

O'Connor, Tom, *Hand of History, Burden of Pseudo History*, Trafford Publishing, Victoria BC, Canada and Oxford, United Kingdom, 2005.

O Connor, Tom, *Ireland's Queen Maeve*, CreatSpace, Amazon, 2014.

Ó Fiaich, Tomás, *Columbanus*, Veritas Publications, Dublin, 1974.

O'Laverty, James, *Historical Account of the Diocese of Down and Connnor, Vol II*, Dublin, 1880.

O'Rahilly, Cecile, ed, *Táin Bó Cúailnge from the Book of Leinster*, Dublin Institute for Advanced Studies, Dublin, 1970.

O'Rahilly, Thomas, F, *Early Irish History and Mythology*, Dublin Institute for Advanced Studies, Dublin, 1964.

Pender, Seamus, MA, 'The Fir Domnann', *Journal of the Royal Society of Antiquaries of Ireland*, 1933, Vol LXIII, Part 1.

Pickthall, Marmaduke, *The Meaning of the Glorious Qur'an*, Jajarmi Publications, Tehran, Iran.

Pooler, LA, *A Short History of the Church of Ireland*, Olley & Co, Belfast, 1890.

Powell, TGE, 'Barbarian Europe, from the first farmers to the Celts', from *Dawn of Civilisation*, Sunday Times Publications, London, 1961.

Powell, TGE, *The Celts*, Ancient Peoples and Places Series, Thames and Hudson Ltd, London, 1967.

Reeves, William, 'The Bangor Antiphonary', *Ulster Journal of Archaeology*, 1st Series Vol I, 1853.

Robertson, John F, *The Story of Galloway*, Outram and Co Ltd, Castle Douglas, Scotland, 1963.

Scott, Archibald B, *The Pictish Nation, its people and its Church*, TN Foulis, London, September 1918.

Skinner, W Cumming, *Candida Casa - The Apostolic Centre of Scotland*, David Winter, 1931.

Smout, TC, *A History of the Scottish People 1560–1830*, William Collins, Glasgow, 1969.

Stone, Brian, trans, *Sir Gawain and the Green Knight*, Penguin Classics, London, 1959.

Stokes, George, *Ireland and the Celtic Church*, London, 1907.

The Imperial Gazetter of Scotland, Edinburgh.

The Prophet Ezekiel in *The Holy Bible.*

Thomas, Sir Charles, *Britain and Ireland in Early Christian Times AD 400–800*, Thomas & Hudson Ltd, London, 1971.

Vermes, Geza, *The Authentic Gospel of Jesus*, The Folio Society, London, 2009.

Walmsley, Thomas, Mogey, John M, and Gamble, David P, 'The Peoples of Northern Ireland: An Anthropometric Survey', *Ulster Journal of Archaeology*, 3rd Series, Volume IX, 1946.

Warren, FE, ed, *The Bangor Antiphonary*, 2 vols, Henry Bradshaw Society, 1893-95.

Watson, WJ, *The Celts (British and Gael) in Dumfriesshire and Galloway,* Transactions of the Dumfriesshire and Galloway Natural History and Antiquarian Society.

Whiston, William, trans, *The Works of Flavius Josephus*, William P Nimmo, Edinburgh, 1865.

Woodburn, James Barkley, *The Ulster Scot*, London, 1914.

Wright, Thomas, *The Celt, the Roman and the Saxon*, Hall Virtue & Co, 1852.

Index